IF BORROWED AT DUBBO, PLEASE
REFER TO PRINTED RECEIPT FOR
DATE DUE.

DATE DUE			
5 APR			
AUG			

JOURNAL OF THE CENTRAL AUSTRALIAN EXPEDITION 1844–5

and
AN ACCOUNT OF THE SEA COAST AND INTERIOR OF SOUTH AUSTRALIA

(Facsimile of Charles Sturt's
Narrative of an *Expedition
into Central Australia,* Volume 2,
1849, pp 145-286)

In addition to the publication of Sturt's Journal, this edition also includes a facsimile of the Appendix to Sturt's *Narrative Of An Expedition Into Central Australia* (Volume 2, 1849).

JOURNAL OF THE CENTRAL AUSTRALIAN EXPEDITION 1844–5

by

Charles Sturt

Edited with an Introduction and Notes
by
Jill Waterhouse

CALIBAN BOOKS

© Caliban Books 1984

This edition first published 1984
by Caliban Books
25 Nassington Road,
Hampstead, London, N.W.3

51 Washington Street, Dover, New Hampshire 03820, U.S.A.

ISBN 0 904573 31 1

Library of Congress Cataloging in Publication Data

Sturt, Charles, 1795-1869.
  Journal of the central Australian expedition,
1844-1845.

  1. Central Australia – Discovery and exploration.
2. South Australia – Description and travel. 3. Natural
history – Central Australia. 4. Sturt, Charles, 1795-
1869. I. Waterhouse, Jill. II. Title.
DU390.S925 1984   919.4'042   84-12683
ISBN 0-904573-31-1

Printed and bound in Great Britain by
A. Wheaton & Co. Ltd., Exeter, England.

CONTENTS

A Note on the Edition   vi

Acknowledgements   vi

List of Illustrations   vii

Frontispiece. Charles Sturt by Charles Wheeler   viii

Introduction   1

Journal of the Central Australian Expedition   15

Notes to Journal   101

Appendix: Captain Charles Sturt to the
    Right Honourable Lord Stanley, 16 March 1843   107

Index to Journal   112

An Account of the Sea Coast and Interior
    of South Australia   115

A NOTE ON THE EDITION

Sturt wrote the *Journal* in his tent, often after dark when he was exhausted from his travels. Although his handwriting is generally legible, some sentences are little more than jottings with vagaries of spelling and punctuation. Where punctuation has been added or spelling standardised for the sake of clarity, the model has been Charles Sturt, *Narrative of an Expedition into Central Australia*, 2 volumes, T. and W. Boone, London, 1849 (prepared and published while Sturt was in London) in which both the spelling and punctuation more nearly conform to present-day useage. Running heads, similar to those in the *Narrative*, have been added. The holograph of the *Journal* is held in Rhodes House Library, Oxford.

ACKNOWLEDGEMENTS

The staff of Rhodes House Library, Oxford, the State Library of South Australia, (Archives), the Australian National Library, Cambridge University Library, and Mr and Mrs Anthony Sturt of Gloucester, Mr and Mrs David B. Davies of Bristol and Mrs Elaine Butt of Homerton College, Cambridge have all contributed special help to the preparation of this edition.

LIST OF ILLUSTRATIONS

Charles Sturt, by Charles Wheeler
National Library of Australia *Frontispiece*

Map showing the limits of European exploration of Australia
   in 1842 7

Charles Napier Sturt   *Bodleian Library, Oxford* 11
Charlotte Christiana Sturt   *Bodleian Library, Oxford* 11
Charlotte Eyre Sturt   *Bodleian Library, Oxford* 11
Napier George Sturt   *Bodleian Library, Oxford* 11

Map of Sturt's Central Australian Expedition, 1844-45 14

Evelyn Gawler and Charles Sheppey, Sturt's youngest sons
Reproduced by kind permission of Mr and Mrs Berrington Davies 16

Calton's Old Spot, Gawler, 1845   *National Library of Australia* 18

Koonunga in 1845   *Bodleian Library, Oxford* 19

The River Murray above Moorundi, by George Fife Angas
Bodleian Library, Oxford 23

George Gawler   *Bodleian Library, Oxford* 24

George Grey   *Bodleian Library, Oxford* 38

Two birds shot at the Depôt, by Charles Sturt
Reproduced by kind permission of Mr & Mrs Anthony Sturt 48

A Jerboa, by Charles Sturt
Reproduced by kind permission of Mr & Mrs Anthony Sturt 58

The Departure of Captain Sturt, August 1844, by S. T. Gill
Bodleian Library, Oxford 86
Sturt's Reluctant Decision to Return, by Ivor Hale
Commonwealth Historic Memorials Committee 86

Aboriginal huts, by Charles Sturt   *Bodleian Library, Oxford* 92

Charles Sturt in the heroic mould of the text book.
From Hon. Andrew Garran (ed.),
Australasia Illustrated, Volume 1, Sydney, 1892 *opposite* 107

Charles Sturt, by Charles Wheeler
Wheeler's work bears a striking resemblance to the often published Crossland portrait of Sturt.

'. . . . *like diving rods, men's souls*
Bend down to where the unseen river rolls.'
Brunton Stephens, *Dominion of Australia*, 1877

INTRODUCTION

Sitting alone in his Adelaide office in the winter of 1842, Charles Sturt knuckled his strained eyes, feeling absolutely and utterly at the end of his tether. He considered that his present employment as Registrar-General of South Australia was a dreary muddling in the detritus of other people's misfortunes, a calculated insult to his talents from a jealous superior, and a meagre financial answer to the needs of his growing family. 'It is a worthless, idle post', he groaned, 'I would rather enter the Zezein Pass with all its horrors than my office.'[1] And therein lay his answer. He would leave the clutter of deeds and writs and throw himself into strenuous exploration.

The following *Journal* describes his attempt, from August 1844 to January 1846, to overcome accumulated misfortune with a hazardous journey to the centre of Australia. By laying 'bare the bones and blood vessels of bodies terrestrial,'[2] he would also be taking a knife to personal confusion.

The *Journal* was written for his wife, Charlotte Christiana, while the expedition was in progress. The greater part is a summary of the journey, but it adds to the official account by seeking to explain as well as to record. Why would a forty-nine year old man, whose eyesight was said to be so poor that he could see only a few paces in front of him, leave a loving wife and four young children, and deliberately expose himself to peril? In the face of his family's heart-rending anxiety, how could he convince them that it was for their own good?

Charlotte was well aware of the injustices Charles felt he had suffered and, for his sake, was upset that Governor Grey had caused him 'much vexation and annoyance.' But she was still puzzled by the depth of his frustration. As she wrote in great consternation on the day her husband left for the desert, 'I am still as it were stunned by all that has happened, for with all the resolution in the world I could not prepare myself for such a separation. Indeed I had hoped such a one would never again have fallen to my lot.'[3]

Dr Edgar Beale in *Sturt, the Chipped Idol* (1979) comments on the general lack of information about Charlotte's personality and attitudes. He wonders if the Sturt family papers might add anything to Professor Manning Clark's assessment that she had the expression of a 'woman who allowed a husband to go on and on trying to prove something to himself about himself, while she grew sadder, and sadder, and sadder.'[4]

It is worth looking more closely at this explorer's wife, the sad recipient of this *Journal*. Sturt's apology in his opening sentence about the unhappy scenes on the eve of his departure refers to his stubborness in the face of Charlotte's understandable anxiety. He was setting off on a dangerous expedition, leaving her with four children under nine, the youngest of whom had suffered severe teething convulsions, and he spent Saturday 10 August, her forty-third birthday, at a farewell breakfast in Grenville Street at which he was observed to shed tears as he laid his hand on his eldest son's head. The day they finally parted, 15 August, was marked by another 'breakfast' given by Colonel Robert Torrens that lasted until six in the evening, and for Charlotte, who signed the document giving her power of attorney from that day, the departure was painfully drawn out. While Adelaide was rejoicing in breakfasts and a public holiday, she was sick at heart that she might never see her husband again.

He had been busy telling his friends that it would be 'better for me to run the risk of letting my bones blanch in the desert than to remain where I am without any prospect of advancement.'[5] She doubted that it was worth the risk.

The family history, kindly lent by Charles Sturt's great-grandson, Mr Anthony Sturt, and one of Charlotte's letters held by the Public Library of South Australia, show that her love for her 'excellent Charles' was never in doubt. He confirmed that apart from the birth of a still-born daughter in 1835, no sorrow had crossed their private threshold.[6] Charlotte, though, had been apprehensive about their pioneering life. Arriving in Adelaide in 1839, she had found it a 'wilderness... a primitive spot', and was homesick for the society, foodstuffs, and lower prices of New South Wales. She had started her new life with 'no assistance from my good hubby, for as usual he is truant like and gone on a survey expedition...' She had needed time to adjust. 'There are some pleasant families here,' she wrote, 'but *all* living in discomfort, though apparently in contentment, and so I hope to do.'[7] Now, when they were finally settled in their own house, Grange, and she could have the pleasure of relaxing on the verandah playing the harp in a small orchestra of her musical friends, Charles was planning to leave her.

Charlotte had faced similar situations before. While she was in labour with their second child, Sturt had been risking his life in the breakers at the mouth of the Murray. Now her anxiety was heightened by her first-hand experience of the hazards facing exploring parties. In 1840 she had been on a short expedition with her husband, Governor Gawler, and other friends. Some of the men, exploring further afield than the women, were forced to kill a horse, and to drink its blood for want of water. One of the party, Henry Bryan, was lost and never seen again. The ordeal of trying to follow his frantic wanderings haunted his companions for years afterwards. Charlotte knew that her husband was going to pass through the same country again, and worse, that he regarded this as one of the least dangerous sections of the journey.

She loved Charles for his kindness and affection, so typical of all the Sturt family, she wrote, but felt powerless in the face of his wanderlust. In any case he was the breadwinner, she the help-meet. The final decisions about his work rested with him. There was no choice but to be philosophical: '...how true it is "our ways are not God's ways" and although the present moments are looked upon with gloomy foreboding, it may be the means in God's hands to bring about that which is good for us.' She was comforted by a letter from Charles' brother, Evelyn, written at Mt Gambier, approving of the situation: 'I can hardly express my satisfaction at his determination to follow out his proposal, and equally your firmness & affection in assenting to such a sacrifice. It was imperative on him to undertake the expedition.'[8]

Was it imperative? The reader of the *Journal* may need to put Sturt's cryptic comments into a wider context before judging.

Up to 1839, Sturt had enjoyed a fair measure of good fortune and well-deserved success, but the various phases, encompassing military duties, extensive exploration of Australia's eastern river system, and an administrative post as Commandant of Norfolk Island, had not been welded into a satisfying or a particularly remunerative career. There had never been any suggestion that Sturt would be given the freedom and resources to embark on government-sponsored exploration as a permanent occupation. But one opening seemed particularly attractive. In 1839, he was offered the challenging post of Surveyor-General in the infant colony of South Australia, succeeding William Light.

Sturt staked everything on this move, which was to take his family from drought-stricken New South Wales to a new colony that owed its origin, at least in part, to his earlier exploration of the Murray river. He left his property, Varroville, and paid £270 for the sea-passage, a trip for which he was reimbursed only £20. He did not begrudge the sacrifice because he believed he was going to a permanent and stimulating post, to a seat in the Council, and to a comfortable salary of £600 per annum.

His first task on arriving was to set up a strong framework for the Survey Department. His employees in the field worked under conditions similar to those later experienced by the Central Australian expedition, and scurvy was a persistent problem. Some of those who later went on the expedition, including David Morgan, John McDouall Stuart, James Poole, and Louis Piesse were well known to Sturt from these days. He soon gained a good reputation for his interest in the men's welfare. In view of Daniel Brock's statement that during the expedition Sturt desecrated Sunday by working,[9] it is worth noting that Sturt did so only in the most trying circumstances. As Surveyor-General, he insisted on conventional religious observance on Sundays, even in the field. Sturt belonged to the generation who changed the name of 'Mount Damnable' to the less blasphemous 'Mount Terrible': whatever the depth of religious belief, outward form was observed where possible.

Even though Sturt worked hard, there were major problems barring his advancement. From the beginning he was criticised for his lack of formal surveying qualifications, but more important, there were serious doubts about Governor Gawler's power to make a permanent appointment. Authority in the two-year old colony was juggled by various hands, and Sturt's appointment slipped between those of the Governor and those of the Commissioners in England. Barely six months after Sturt had taken up his position, Lieutenant Edward Charles Frome arrived in South Australia, having been appointed to exactly the same post by the Commissioners without reference to either Gawler or Sturt. In answer to Sturt's indignant protest, they replied that Gawler was entitled to make only a provisional appointment, and that Sturt should have known better than to expect any other arrangement. In private, Frome assured Sturt that he never would have come had he known the situation in advance.[10] There was no antagonism between the two appointees, but it was clearly too late to have Frome's appointment reconsidered.

Embarrassed, Gawler helped to secure Sturt the post of Assistant Commissioner of Lands, with responsibilities in the Public Works, Emigration, Land, and Store Departments, and Sturt retained his seat in the Council. He might have gone on to a prominent public career from here, had it not been for another blow: Colonel George Gawler was recalled to England and was replaced by Captain George Grey.

Sturt was shocked by Gawler's recall. Though admitting the Governor had spent heavily, he knew this had been prompted by despatches from the Commissioners urging him to avoid pauperism at all costs. Sturt believed that Gawler had acted from the best motives, 'that every new Colony requires assistance at the hands of the Government is a position which even Jeremy Bentham admits.'[11] Gawler's recall was also a personal loss for the Sturts who had marked the friendship by choosing 'Gawler' as their third son's middle name.

On first impression, the new Governor who had exploring experience in Western Australia might have seemed a potential ally of Sturt. But Sturt was critical of the way Grey had conducted harrowing journeys and, dismayed by the thought of this headstrong twenty-nine year old coming to administer the colony, he offered his own services as Governor when Grey was already on his way. On arrival, the new appointee was naturally suspicious of his would-be rival. In addition, Grey had been ordered to reduce the colony's debts, and Sturt's tenuous post was an obvious target for administrative cuts.

Sturt was blind to the impending danger. Indeed, he still cherished the idea of rapid promotion. He claims in his letters that he had been offered the position of Colonial Secretary when Mr Gouger was ill, and had taken over much of the work, only refusing the formal position out of consideration for the convalescent.[12] Sturt later refused an offer to head the South Australian Agricultural Company, perhaps in the hope that the Colonial Secretaryship would eventually fall to his lot.

But when Grey summoned Sturt into his office, it was to tell him that the Colonial Secretaryship was unsuitable because it might further injure Sturt's weak sight, and, even worse, that his existing position of Assistant Commissioner was abolished. Sturt explains, 'All [my duties] Captain Grey on his arrival at once swept away, and having left me nothing to do, he recommended the abolition of my appointment.' He continues scornfully, 'he then offered me the post of Sheriff!!! A pretty sheriff I should have made.'[13]

Accordingly, Grey appointed him Registrar-General, leaving Sturt complaining that he was the oldest man at the head of a Department, the oldest member of Council, and the oldest magistrate, all of which amounted to being a senior man in a junior job.

The insult to his honour was painful enough but the drop in salary was even more serious. He had come to South Australia with a promise of £600 a year as Surveyor-General; as Assistant Commissioner he had earned £500 a year, and other emoluments had made it up to £600, but before he had time to enjoy more than a year on this scale, he dropped to £400 as Registrar-General. As he felt he could not live in a manner befitting one with a say in the colony's government, he resigned his seat in the Council. He had already borrowed money from his youngest brother, Evelyn, and from his friend Charles Campbell, and now that he had passed the mid-point in his working life, he wondered how he would ever be able to earn enough money to make his family comfortable, and to give his sons a good education.

The demotion certainly undermined Sturt's sense of security, but Grey's concern for Sturt's sight was not entirely the tame excuse it seemed. Sturt suffered blindness after earlier explorations, and confessed that he could not even see across the desk to where Grey was correcting his proposals. Colleagues commented on Sturt's manner of walking with his arms outstretched. He often had to work back in the office late at night because his reading was so slow, he was unable to read any public paper before the Council, and was forced to commit much of the paper work to memory.[14] Grey may well have believed that a job involving more mechanical paper work would be better suited to Sturt's physical impediment. But Sturt thought differently, and apart from delegating the use of his sextant to others, he did not think his work in the field was seriously handicapped. In the *Journal* he never mentions that his poor sight is a problem, and in his original expedition proposal to Lord Stanley in 1843 refers only briefly to 'the tardy progress I made towards the recovery of my sight...'[15]

Concerning Grey's motives, Sturt wrote to Sir Ralph Darling, 'I believe that Grey is jealous of my success and greater claims, and instead of acting with generosity would lower me in the estimation of the community. However, you know, my good friend, that I am not of a revengeful or jealous disposition, and I pass these events as nothing. They do not disturb a moment of my tranquillity.'[16] In fact, nothing was further from the truth. The rebuff tortured him, and he confessed at one time that his mind was in a state of abstraction amounting almost to oblivion.[17]

The final straw came on the eve of Sturt's departure when Grey and the Council censured him for having written an indiscreet letter to the firm of Borrow and Goddiar over a contract to build a new gaol. Sturt felt the censure was far too harsh, and though some efforts were made to placate him, the incident confirmed his belief that Grey was his enemy.

Although Sturt never sought revenge, the Governor clearly frustrated him beyond endurance. Sturt was not the only one to react in this way. Grey, though he could be pleasant and companionable at times, soon gained a reputation for unpredictability. Uncharitable comments about him are not unnaturally preserved in the Sturt family papers, but they are also found in so many other sources that they probably had some basis. His youth and the responsibility for making drastic and unpopular cuts in the colony's expenditure undoubtedly accounted in part for his manner, but, even years later when he was in New Zealand, the Maories said of him, 'Guv'ner, when him want something, him no go straight like a bird, him always go crooked like a snake.'[18] Lady Fox Young claimed that Grey had once told her, 'Not only do I never forgive an opponent, but I never forgive a difference of opinion.'[19] Perhaps, then, Sturt can be excused for thinking that nothing less than a dramatic and heroic action would win him favour in the Governor's eyes and make him 'square with the world.'[20] Although Sturt saw the expedition as a vital last chance, his guilt at leaving his family is clearly apparent in the *Journal's* long passages of self-justification and in his fear that Charlotte and the children have been snatched away from him. This dread had some foundation because he did not expect their little 'Rose of Australia' to live, and once before he had returned from an exploration to learn that their son Napier had almost drowned.

It would be a mistake, though, to interpret his melancholy as a newly-developed facet of his character. The sentiments written during earlier absences, when his responsibilities were lighter, are almost interchangeable with those written during his South Australian expedition: 'Could I have foreseen the tedious length of this journey, I had never left my home. Time is flying on his iron swing, cruel, unrelenting time, and oh, I would not be from home much longer...Does she give her husband credit for affection, or hopes that he thinks of her, as I live she is never absent from me waking and sleeping, I have seen her as palpable to my touch as if she had been present, but where was my boy? Almighty Father thou hast not in thine anger bereft me of him...?' (1838)[21]

Sturt, though he often claimed otherwise, was fully aware of the probable length and dangers of the journey, and what tormented him was he knew in his heart of hearts that he would have embarked on it whatever the dangers. Had he been single, he certainly would have gone;[22] now that he was married, he had to rationalise his desire so that it became a duty.[23] But the more he rationalised it in terms of duty, the more entangled he became.

A duty to whom? To his family? To himself? To the nation? Certainly he needed money for his sons' education, but he also knew that his wife's expected inheritance of about £5,000 would help meet these expenses.[24] Moreover, there was no suggestion that he was permanently barred from promotion. Grey, though obstinate, was not vindictive, and had even tried, albeit ineffectively, to

Map showing the limits of European exploration of Australia in 1842
'Let any man lay the map of Australia before him, and regard the blank upon its surface, and then let me ask him if it would not be an honourable achievement to be the first to place a foot in its centre'.
Charles Sturt

retain Sturt's £600 salary. Mrs Grey visited Mrs Sturt after the expedition's departure, a gesture which was probably kindly meant even though Sturt saw it as typical snake-in-the-grass behaviour.

Certainly the veil over Australia's heart intrigued everyone, but the initiative for lifting it at this particular time came from Sturt himself. Inland exploration was low on the government's list of priorities; Sturt had to beg Stanley to let him go; Grey probably tampered with Sturt's letter so that it was delayed in reaching England;[25] the government did not promise Sturt either increased salary or position if he were successful, and indeed Sturt set out on half pay, much to Charlotte's relief because she thought that lack of funds might force him to hurry home.[26] Grey knew that one of the men Sturt most admired, Edward John Eyre, had failed to find an inland sea, and also that, even if Sturt were more successful, the government had few resources at hand for developing new areas. It is not surprising, then, that Stanley modified Sturt's proposals, and limited the main object of the expedition to discovering the existence or otherwise of a watershed at the twenty-eighth parallel to help solve the mystery of the river systems. Sturt was forbidden to trace any streams towards the far north, and was required back within a year.

Being the initiator of the venture, then, Sturt indulged in rather obsessive talk about predestination. 'I have a kind of presentiment that I shall unfold the Interior to the world', he wrote. And again, 'So strong has this feeling been upon my mind that I did not expect Mr Eyre wd succeed in gaining the Centre when he undertook his last fearful journey.'[27] The idea of destiny is commonplace among the justifications for human endeavour, and there were prestigious parallels to be drawn. 'Like Columbus', wrote Governor Darling, 'he appears urged on by fate.'[28] Sturt also knew that an expedition to the interior would eventually take place, perhaps led by Frome, and so there was little room for hesitation. Sturt stressed his special qualifications for the mission, claiming that he had more mental stamina than men who were apparently physically stronger, and that he had the capacity to 'cheer those with me where without hope, all would be confusion.'[29] Though he would grant Eyre 'the palm of daring', he did not think he had the patience to traverse the desert slowly and painstakingly. Moreover, Sturt, unlike Eyre, still believed that an inland sea existed.[30]

The details of the seventeen month journey are recorded in a number of contemporary documents, including Sturt's *Narrative of an Expedition into Central Australia*, published in 1849, and accounts by Daniel Brock and John Harris Browne,[31] and so only a few observations are needed as a backdrop to the *Journal*.

For an expedition that had been planned for so long in Sturt's mind, the last minute plans were rather hurried. In spite of Grey's claim that it was well equipped, Sturt was scornful of the 'trumpery instruments' supplied by the government, 'as if a man is to find his way across a desert with as much care as across an English common.'[32] For his part, Sturt had never met John Harris Browne, who was to be the party's doctor and one of Sturt's gentleman companions. This highlights one of the features of both Sturt's and E.J. Eyre's exploring parties: there was only one leader, and so it was not necessary to discuss all the plans with even the senior men. It was fortunate that Eyre's warm recommendation of Browne was well founded, and Browne, in turn, acknowledged that Sturt 'had such a happy knack of imparting knowlege that to have lived with him so long and so intimately as I did was a liberal education.'[33] Browne's main regret about the expedition was that camels had not been available, as they were later, to help open up the interior.

The trials the explorers faced, and their vivid accounts of the terrible heat, when even the crows sat still with their beaks open, panting hard like dogs, are well known. Even so, no description or pictorial illustration can do justice to the desert's impact on the men: 'There was a peculiar hue over the scene from the colour of the sand; and it almost appeared as if we were the last of the human race left to witness the destruction of our Planet. Fancy never coloured such a place; imagination could form no idea of its chilling and repulsive aspect.'[34]

As Beale has demonstrated by comparing the previously published reports of the expedition, Sturt's records of dates and distances are not always accurate.[35] Although the *Journal* does not resolve all the contradictions, it often gives a clearer point of reference. It seems certain, for example, that on Sunday 27 July 1845, the drays rested while Sturt inspected the site of the second Depôt. He wrote the entry the same evening and it contains the homely touch that he returned in time for prayers.

Sturt, like Eyre, was a compulsive writer, yet his record has many omissions. Although he was constantly worried about the well-being of his own son, Napier, he never mentions that Daniel Brock had left behind a sick boy, William, who died during the party's absence. Nor does he comment on personalities and frictions within the group in the way that Brock and Browne do. We know from these two that the men 'agreed together about as well as so many Cats and Terriers generally do.'[36] His main concern was that the men should carry out their duties for which they were being paid (Poole £200, Browne £150, and the men £1 per week) and he was not curious about their private lives except in so far as these related to their duties. He would not tolerate insubordination. As a result of an argument over who was in charge of the bullocks after the relief party arrived, Brock reports that Sturt dismissed Mack. Piesse forced others to carry all their goods for the last hundred miles.[37]

Sturt did not allow any member of the expedition to send letters home without his seeing them first, and his own account would not have revealed many secrets even if it had fallen into the wrong hands. Although the native runners carried most of the mail with remarkable speed, Charlotte reported that some despatches were lost, and Sturt did not want to take any chances.[38] He is, though, more frank about Grey, Poole, and Thomas Mitchell in his record for Charlotte than he is in his official account. He also reveals his emotional problems, a subject which he may have found easier to write about than to talk about because, as Charlotte observed, he was always afraid of saying more than he intended.[39]

In the *Journal*, Sturt makes no attempt to jolly his Beloved with amusing or intimate stories. She was to be his confessional, the recipient of his heart's sorrows. He speaks so often of impending death, and with such resignation, almost as if he were willing it to come, that Charlotte suffered the agony of imagined bereavement for weeks at a time. Her companion at Grange, Mrs Nichols, who, as Miss Conway, had helped sew the flag to be planted in the centre of Australia, confirms that the arrival of the *Journal* and other mail did little to dispel anxiety. Charlotte learned that even Bawley, the friendly, shiny-coated horse Sturt intended to bring home to her as a present, had died of thirst. Her reaction on receiving her husband's letters is predictable. She sat up all night, crying.

The reader who has accompanied the men through their gruelling adventures, and has sorrowed with Sturt about leaving his family will want to know what happened to them in the years that followed. A sample must suffice.

Louis Piesse, who had set off through the bush in his flaming red shirt and conical hat, was not, according to at least one of his contemporaries, a very good bushman. He went to Calcutta and became a seal engraver. When he died about 1879, his widow returned to Adelaide. Many of the rocks he had collected on the expedition were apparently thrown away, no one yet quite realising the extent and importance of the wilderness's mineral resources. Similarly, contemporaries were only slowly drawing the conclusion from the healthy condition of the sheep that salt-bush vegetation was suitable for grazing.

Sturt's great admirer, Robert Flood, accompanied A.C. Gregory on a later expedition. Flood was also employed by John Harris Browne for a year or two, but being a cattleman, did not like life on a sheep station, and left without notice to become a stableman at a country inn. Browne reported that this 'dissipated old scamp' eventually died in an asylum. Joseph Cowley visited Browne to tell him he was about to be married, and came away with a saddle and a cow as wedding presents. Browne went to England but returned to Australia in 1853.[40] Davenport invested in Adelaide property. Lewis became a prosperous farmer, and like Morgan and many of the others, lived to a ripe age. Daniel Brock became a shipping agent. John McDouall Stuart subsequently conducted distinguished explorations, achieving, in 1860, the long-held dream of reaching the centre of the continent. As legend has it, his remarkable endurance included the vast consumption of alcohol. Richard MacDonell's exaggeration about Stuart's drinking had an element of truth: 'I doubt if it would be safe to leave him with a spirit level.'[41]

And what of Sturt himself? What difference had his seventeen month long trial made to him? In the *Journal*, Sturt tells his wife that the iron sea has mocked him and that the journey has been a failure. But by the time he came to write the official account, he was able to take a more dispassionate view and to conclude that he had fulfilled his orders. He had established the absence of any substantial mountain chain at the twenty-eighth parallel; he had shown good leadership in turning back when he did; he was proud of the good impression he had made on the Aborigines and hoped that this would assist future travellers. And, though he had not found an inland sea, he was convinced that such a sea had once existed.

The specific moral he draws in the *Journal* is that God, by punishing him with a long and an inconclusive journey, was trying to teach him moderation: that from now on, he should stay with his family and be content with his humble place in the colony.

As it turned out, the future was brighter than he expected. The Royal Geographical Society awarded him a gold medal, and Grey was suitably impressed. Better still, by the time the expedition returned, Grey had been replaced by Major Holt Robe. Sturt's application, made shortly before his departure, for the position of Colonial Treasurer to be held jointly with that of Registrar-General, was accepted, and on 17 February 1846 he was appointed on a permanent basis. Although the combined salary totalled only £500 per annum, honour was restored. In 1849 he was appointed to the long wished for position of Colonial Secretary, a post he held until 1851 when he retired on the grounds of weak eyesight.

Charles Napier Sturt

Charlotte Christiana Sturt

Charlotte Eyre Sturt

Napier George Sturt

Whatever the cause and seriousness of his poor vision,[42] the reader can only be grateful that he accomplished so much in spite of this recurrent disability which prevented him from seeing even Queen Victoria's entry at a reception to receive a souvenir of his expedition.

As for Sturt's children, their education was secure, though he never ceased to worry about the expense. Although he had reservations about army life, Napier and Charles both had distinguished military careers. The third son, Evelyn, described by his father as 'the wild Australian boy', worried his parents by his thoughtlessness. Evelyn gradually came to realise this, and wrote an apologetic letter to his mother.[43] This letter was doubly treasured because, after joining the army, he died suddenly of cholera in India at the age of twenty-three. Missey stayed at home, a sweet-natured girl occupied with a little music, a little sewing, a little dancing, but she never married. She continued to be delicate, flying to the sofa at the first sign of illness and stress. Her father thought it would be better if they stopped calling her by the childhood name of 'Missey', and both parents encouraged her to mix with young people, but she clearly preferred their company.[44]

Charlotte outlived her husband by sixteen years. She was given permission to bear the title 'Lady Sturt', even though her husband did not live long enough to have the promised knighthood bestowed. Sturt, who had run so many risks in the bush and the desert, died on 16 June 1869, a short time after breaking a leg crossing the road.

Sturt would hardly have believed it if he had been told during the Central Australian expedition that, with the painful exception of Evy's death, he would lead a relatively peaceful life to the age of seventy-four. The *Journal* is the work of one who believed he was 'a blighted and blasted man over whose head the darkest destiny had settled.'

Homerton College
Cambridge

1   Mrs Napier George Sturt, *The Life of Charles Sturt*, London, 1899, p.214.
2   Sir J. Barrow, quoted in Charles Sturt, *Narrative of an Expedition into Central Australia, performed under the Authority of Her Majesty's Government during the years 1844, 5, and 6*, London, 1849, Vol. 1, p. 56.
3   Quoted in Revd Napier Evelyn Sturt, Sturt Family History (typed manuscript), XIV, 2, 32, lent by kind permission of Mr and Mrs Anthony Sturt.
4   Edgar Beale, *Sturt, The Chipped Idol*, Sydney, 1979, p. 127; Manning Clark, *Occasional Writings and Speeches*, Melbourne, 1980, pp. 63–4.
5   Charles Sturt to Sir Ralph Darling, 5 March 1844, Mrs Napier G. Sturt, Notes Received after the publication of the book, *Sturt Papers*, Mss Austral. S7, p. 39, Rhodes House Library, Oxford.
6   Mrs Napier G. Sturt, Notes … p. 53.
7   Charlotte Sturt to Mrs Hely, 20 April (?) 1839, State Library of South Australia, Archives, A713 (B2).
8   Sturt Family History, XIV, 2, 32–3.
9   Daniel George Brock (ed. Kenneth Peake-Jones), *To the Desert With Sturt*, Adelaide, 1975, pp. 29–30.

10 Mrs Napier G. Sturt, Notes ... p.21.

11 *Ibid.*, p. 24.

12 *Ibid.*, p. 28.

13 *Ibid.*

14 Charles Sturt to George (Macleay), 19 May 1852, *Sturt Papers*, Vol. 2, Mss Austral. S4.

15 Charles Sturt to Lord Stanley, 16 March 1843, State Library of South Australia, Archives, GRG 2/12 Tsf. 391, Governor's Office.

16 Charles Sturt to Sir Ralph Darling, n.d., in Mrs Napier G. Sturt, Notes ... p. 29.

17 Charles Sturt, extract from letter complaining about Grey, n.d., *Sturt Papers*, Vol. 2, Mss Austral. S4.

18 (Mrs Napier G. Sturt), Notebook (with last entry 24 November 1899), *Sturt Papers*, Mss Austral. S. 5b.

19 *Ibid.*, Lady Fox Young, 13 October 1897.

20 Charles Sturt, *Sturt Papers*, Vol. 1, Mss Austral. S4.

21 *Ibid.*

22 Mrs Napier G. Sturt, Notes ... p. 30.

23 Charles Sturt to Miss Cooper, 7 May 1847, *Sturt Papers*, Mss Austral. S4, Vol. 2.

24 Charles Sturt to Sir Ralph Darling, 5 March 1844, in Mrs Napier G. Sturt, Notes ... p. 39.

25 Mrs Napier G. Sturt, Notes ... p. 20.

26 Mrs Sturt to Lady Darling, 30 January 1845, *Sturt Papers*, 1844–69, Mss Austral. c5c(3).

27 Charles Sturt to Sir Ralph Darling, 5 March 1844, in Mrs Napier G. Sturt, Notes ... p. 39 and p. 48.

28 Quoted in Mrs Napier G. Sturt, *Life of Charles Sturt*, London, 1899, p. 228.

29 Mrs Napier G. Sturt, Notes ... p. 42.

30 For the basis of Sturt's belief in the existence of an inland sea, consult his *Narrative of an Expedition...* Vol. 1, pp. 32–5.

31 Daniel Brock, *To the Desert with Sturt,* and H.J. Finnis, 'Dr John Harris Browne's Journal of the Sturt Expedition, 1844-5', in *South Australiana*, Vol. V, No. 1, March 1966.

32 Mrs Napier G. Sturt, Notes ... p. 59.

33 John Harris Browne to Colonel Napier Sturt, 1 December 1895, *Sturt Papers*, Box 5.

34 Charles Sturt to Charles Campbell, 18 June 1845, from Long. 141.31.00E, Lat. 29.40.7 *Sturt Papers*, Vol. 1. Mss Austral. S4.

35 Beale, *Sturt...*, pp. 181–4.

36 H.J. Finnis, 'Dr Harris Browne's Journal ...', p. 48.

37 Daniel Brock, *To the Desert ...* p. 222.

38 Charles Sturt to George Macleay, 27 April 1844, *Sturt Papers*, Vol. 2, Mss Austral. S4; Mrs Sturt to Lady Darling, 26 May 1865, in Mrs Napier G. Sturt, Notes ..., p. 64.

39 Charlotte Sturt, 'Memories from the past', Old Family letters from Lady Sturt's writing table, *Sturt Papers*, Mss Austral S 5d. (1).

40 John Harris Browne to Colonel Napier Sturt, 1 December 1895 and John Harris Browne to Mrs Sturt, 1 May and 1 June 1897, Mss Austral. Box 5.

41 Richard MacDonell, 16 January 18(?), *Sturt Papers*, Mss Austral. S 5c(3).

42 For a discussion of this problem see Beale, *Sturt...*, Chapter 13.

43 Evelyn Sturt to Charlotte Sturt, 3 June 1860, Mss Austral. S 5d (2).

44 Charlotte Sturt to Napier Sturt, Letters 1861-3, Old Family Letters from Lady Sturt's writing table...

14

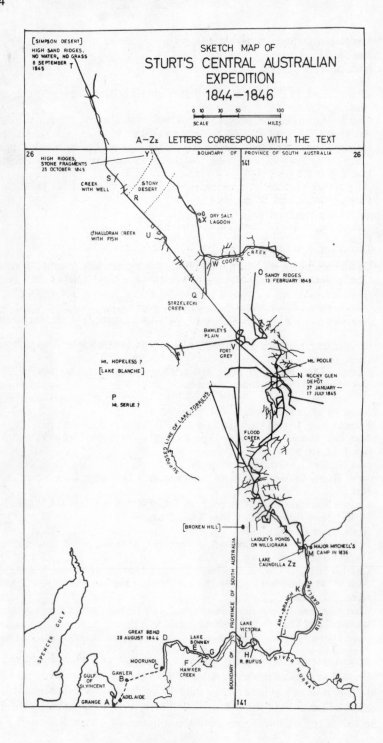

SKETCH MAP OF
STURT'S CENTRAL AUSTRALIAN
EXPEDITION
1844–1846

SCALE
0 10   30   50   100
MILES

A–Zz LETTERS CORRESPOND WITH THE TEXT

[SIMPSON DESERT]
HIGH SAND RIDGES,
NO WATER, NO GRASS
8 SEPTEMBER 1845   T

26   HIGH RIDGES,   Y   BOUNDARY OF   PROVINCE OF SOUTH AUSTRALIA   26
STONE FRAGMENTS   141
25 OCTOBER 1845

CREEK   S
WITH WELL   STONY
                R   DESERT

                                    X   DRY SALT
                                        LAGOON
O'HALLORAN CREEK
WITH FISH   U

                        W COOPER CREEK

                                O SANDY RIDGES
                                   13 FEBRUARY 1845
                Q
STRZELECKI
CREEK

                BAWLEY'S
                PLAIN
                                        Mt. POOLE
                FORT V
                GREY   N   ROCKY GLEN
Mt. HOPELESS ?   DEPOT
[LAKE BLANCHE]   27 JANUARY —
                                           17 JULY 1845

P
Mt. SERLE ?

                                    FLOOD
                                    CREEK

[BROKEN HILL]   I

                                LAIDLEY'S PONDS
                                OR WILLIORARA
                                        L
                                        M   MAJOR MITCHELL'S
                                LAKE   CAMP IN 1836
                                CAUNDILLA Zz

                                    K

                            LAKE
                            VICTORIA
GREAT BEND   D   I
23 AUGUST 1844   LAKE
                        E   BONNEY
MOORUNDI   C   F   G
                        HAWKER H   R. RUFUS
GAWLER   CREEK
B
GULF
OF
St. VINCENT
GRANGE A
        ADELAIDE

                                141

SPENCER GULF

SUPPOSED LINE OF LAKE TORRENS

ANA-BRANCH OF

DARLING RIVER

RIVER MURRAY

BOUNDARY OF PROVINCE OF SOUTH AUSTRALIA

(The capital letters from A-Zz in the text correspond with the letters on the map – Ed.)

I shall not, my Dearest Charlotte, allude in the course of this narrative to any of the events that occurred prior to the day on which I left Grange,[41] beyond what may be necessary to render it clearer to you. I shall commence it therefore from the day on which we parted. A day that will never I believe be forgotten by either of us, for it was a day of trial to us both. To me, however, the remembrance of the close of that day is another cause of regret, not that I blame Mr Torrens for any pangs the recollection of its close occasions me.[2] I blame my own weakness and indecision alone, for I was not in a fit state of mind to participate in its scenes and should therefore have avoided them. However, Dearest, let it pass. Those scenes are as a dream to me now, painful though they be.

I intend the writing of the journal to be my Sundays' occupation, and in whatever circumstances I may be placed I have determined to add something to you every succeeding Sabbath.[3] You will then know that I have ever thought of you on that day, and it may be that our united prayers will yet be heard. Prosperity, Dearest, was the blessing of the Old Testament, Adversity is the blessing of the New, and the knowledge of this should be a useful lesson to us, and if it please GOD to permit my return to you, it may be that this long and fearful separation will be another proof of what both religion and reason point out to us that, "whatever is, is right".

It may be however, that my days are numbered and that the Book of my Destinies is all but closed. That, my fate is sealed and that we shall meet no more on this, perhaps never on the other side of the grave, if so, it will here soothe you to know that at those times when I have sought relief from intensity of thought and feeling I have ever flown to you, and that it has been a consolation to me to know that I fall either by the hand of the savage against whom I have never lifted my own, or by sickness.

I shall leave my beloved children with so prudent and excellent a mother. In such case a heavy task will fall on you, and I would ere it is too late, give you such advice as to their future advancement as may perhaps assist you in any difficulty. Of my boys, the one about whom I am most anxious is Napier.[4] He is a boy of early promise and will if he attains manhood under God's blessing make a good and a great man, but he is too gentle and docile to struggle against the world. I have long thought of giving him an education to suit him for diplomatic employments, to teach him the living languages, and to ground him in those studies, which would qualify him for any civil appointment. Amongst my papers you will find a letter I have addressed to Lord Stanley,[5] in which I have asked his interest to secure Napier an appointment in Downing Street, as if I survive the service on which I am engaged I should ask that favour at Lord Stanley's hands. In that letter I have fully explained my views and wishes to the Secretary of State and I think it more than likely that he would attend to my request. His reply to my letter would at all events enable you to decide on

Napier's future career. I would leave it to your own judgement and to his inclination into what profession to put him in the event of my letter to Lord Stanley failing in its object, but if he should hold out reasonable hopes to you, it would be necessary as far as your means went to give him a corresponding education. To have him well grounded in mathematics which expands the mind. To let him be familiar in his more advanced years with Locke, Stewart and Bacon, whose writings would give him a reasoning intellect, and to teach him during his youth every useful modern language, French, Italian, German, and the language of such countries as the presages of the times would lead to the conclusion that they will sooner or later be the theatre of great political events. It is to those who have been previously fitted for such events, that prosperity throws open her doors.

With regard to Charley[6] and Evy[7] I have thought of putting the one into the navy under some experienced officer to whom I am known and the other into the legal profession. I do not like the army[8], but, with regard to them, Dearest, I should leave it to your discretion and to circumstances.

'Fine boys but fickle.' Charles Sturt
Evelyn Gawler (left) and Charles Sheppey, Sturt's youngest sons. Artist unknown.

As regards the general treatment of the boys it is a consolation for me to know that it is unnecessary for me to suggest any improvement. I would early habituate them to the use of money, and would even now give Napier a purse. The good effects of this would I am sure be felt hereafter. I would leave the expenditure of his money discretionary with him, but make him account to me for it, and I would encourage him in acts of benevolence and generosity, and so far from withholding any valuable instruments or other thing in the house from him, I would allow him the free handling of them all. They would not then be novelties to or desired by him at a time when the purchase of them might embarrass.

I need not, my Beloved Charlotte, ask you to be strict with the boys in their attention to their religious duties, and in obedience to yourself.[9] On these two last points depend their future characters and happiness. I will not now however continue this subject; I shall have frequent occasion to recur to it as fresh thoughts occur to me, for next to yourself the future welfare of my children is always on my mind.

You will remember that on the day on which we parted, you to return to your peace-broken dwelling and I to pass into the desert,[10] it was late before I left St Clare with my two companions[11] for Gawler Town[B]. We reached Calton's[12] at midnight and I there found Mr Newland,[13] Francis Dutton,[14] James Hawker,[15] [illegible], and Captain Hall,[16] as I dare say Newland will have informed you.

He and Mr Dutton were on their way to the north and James Hawker was on his return to Moorundi, so that they proposed to accompany me to Captain Bagot's[17] in the Murray. I here learnt that the drays had reached Angus Park[18] in safety, but that one of the bullocks having been taken ill, my storekeeper Mr Piesse had purchased another from Captain Hall. I was also told that Mr Calton had given my men a magnificent breakfast in passing at which there was a profusion of hams, fowls, pies and cold meats, and that the party was cheered on its departure. The townspeople assembled to shew me the same kindly feeling, but they would have spared themselves the trouble if they had known mine at that moment. Nevertheless it was not thrown away upon me.

On Friday morning according to arrangements Newland, Dutton, and Hawker accompanied me and Mr Poole to Captain Bagot's, Mr Browne branching off to Lyndoch Valley to take leave of his sister.[19] We reached *Castle Bagot* at 3 p.m. and were most kindly received by Mrs Bagot[20] in the absence of her husband. She had dinner prepared for us, and what I believe is unusual in their house put wine on the table. I was really glad that I paid this visit more especially during the absence of Captain Bagot, whose boisterous volubility would have been insupportable, whereas it soothed my worn down spirit to converse with Mrs Bagot who is really very quiet and ladylike. She expressed much regret that she had not seen more of you, and a desire to be more intimately acquainted, and as I really think she is a person who would grow on your esteem, I hope you will have met during my absence. Miss Bagot was at

Calton's Old Spot, Gawler, 1845
'Mr Calton had given my men a magnificent breakfast in passing, at which there was a profusion of hams, fowls, pies, and cold meats. . . .'

home and the amiable Mrs Jacob[21] with her son was on a visit to her mother.

On the morning of Saturday we took leave of the ladies after breakfast, and then separated. Newland and Mr Dutton continued onwards to the north, whilst Mr Poole and James Hawker turned to the eastward for the Murray.

I cannot say much for Captain Bagot's property. The land is good and he has an abundance of water, but it is brackish. His house is low, but the interior is more comfortable than its exterior would indicate, and there [is] in the sitting room a fire place large enough to keep the whole house warm during the winter where I am sure it must be bitter cold in that part of the Province. Just before we got to the White Hut Mr Browne enjoined us, and a little beyond it we overtook the drays, in their slow but sure progress; Mr Piesse the storekeeper walking in front with a flaming red shirt on and a thick stick in his hand. At the Dust Hole[22] I understood that Flood who I had sent to Mr Frederick Dutton's[23] station for 200 sheep, was on the hills feeding them, having got them so far in safety. But I neither saw him or them but pursued my journey and at three entered the Murray belt through which we rode until sunset, when we arrived at Moorundi[c].

Mr Eyre[24] had been long and anxiously expecting us, and told me that he had great difficulty in detaining two natives[25] whom he had engaged to accompany us up the Darling. They were now however quite satisfied on seeing me make my appearance, and said they would wait for the drays.

The day after our arrival at Moorundi being Sunday I went with Eyre to the settlement to attend divine worship. In the afternoon the party arrived and drew up in the avenue at a little distance from the house.[26] About an hour after Davenport made his appearance with the light cart, and another which he had been obliged to hire from Chambers.[27]

Koonunga in 1845, the station Sturt refers to as Castle Bagot.
'I cannot say much for Captain Bagot's property . . . His house is low, but the interior is more comfortable than the exterior would indicate. . . .'

On Monday morning the 19th August the avenue at Moorundi presented a busy scene. The Expedition had left Adelaide in such haste and confusion that it became necessary to rearrange the loads. Most of the men were therefore engaged at that heavy task. Brock, who is an armourer by trade, was employed cleaning and preparing the firearms, and Morgan, who had managed to snap one of the shafts of the horse drays, was hard at work with Sullivan putting in a new one. This was the first accident that occurred, and it is somewhat remarkable that ill luck has pursued Morgan ever since. I have been obliged to take the horses away from him, and he is always sullen and dissatisfied. The truth I believe is that he expected to have cooked for the tents and was therefore disappointed.

The whole party was now for the first time assembled, and independently of myself, Mr Poole, who was to be my Assistant, and Mr Browne the Medical Officer, consisted of fourteen individuals distributed as follows:[28]

Mr J. M. Stuart	Draftsman
Mr Louis Piesse	Storekeeper
D.G. Brock	Collector and Armourer
Robert Flood	Overseer of Stock
George Davenport	Servant
Joseph Colley	Servant
David Morgan	Sailor in charge of Horses
James Lewis	Sailor
John Mack	
John Jones	
Hugh Faulkes	Bullock Drivers
Adam Turpin	
John Kirby	
John Sullivan	

There were attached to the Expedition
11 Eleven Horses
32 Thirty two Bullocks
5 Five Drays
1 One Horse Dray
1 One Light Cart
1 One Boat[29]

The weight of the stores was somewhat more than seven tons. Each dray had 2900 weight upon it, independent of the horse teams. In the afternoon I sent Chambers' men back by whom I returned (20) blankets to Mr Stuckey[30] and 480 yards of sheep netting to Mr Bentham Neales,[31] who had tried to impress too much upon me.

On Tuesday the men were equally engaged, but by sunset Morgan's shaft was replaced by a new one, the arms were brushed up, the drays loaded, the tarpaulins lashed down, and the party ready to move up the river. I therefore gave them but little respite but gave orders for the whole to be in readiness to proceed on their journey at 8 o'clock on the following morning, Wednesday.

Feeling that my own stay at Moorundi would only be for a few days, feeling also that I should not leave it satisfied if I did not get tidings of you up to the last moment, I had in the morning sent Flood to Grange with positive orders to return to me with all speed as soon as you should dispatch him, and in order to ensure regularity on his part I prohibited his going into town as I informed you.

I now arranged therefore that Mr Poole and Mr Browne should take the party on and that I would overtake them with Mr Eyre as soon as Flood returned. At 8 o'clock then on Wednesday morning the calvacade was ready to leave Moorundi, and Mr Poole only awaited my orders to move on, but I thought it was a fitting moment to address the men and to explain some of their duties to them. I consequently desired that they might be called together, and said to them, that as they were now about to leave the most distant outpost of the Province, and as I should remain behind for a day or two, I considered it necessary to acquaint them with some of the arrangements I had made for the discipline and security of the camp: that I had directed Mr Poole to mount a guard of three men at sunset who were to continue on duty until sunrise and that I expected this guard would always be on the alert with their firearms in their hands, that one of the guard as sentry was to patrol the camp, and that each sentry was to remain two hours on watch. As I said the whole safety of the party depended on the vigilance of the guard I would severely punish any neglect.

I then positively forbad all intercourse between the men and the natives, whether men or women. I told them that to this all the scenes of violence and murder that had taken place on the river might be attributed, and I assured them that if any one of them (I did not care who it might be) disobeyed my orders in this respect I would strike his name out of the List and he should cease to receive pay from that hour.

I then called Mr Piesse forward and confirmed him in his office as storekeeper, I intimated my intention of giving Flood the charge of the stock. To Morgan I gave the immediate charge of the horses, and to each bullock driver the charge of his own immediate team. I placed the sheep in charge of Brock and Kirby. I gave Davenport the charge of the tents, with Joseph as his assistant, and I directed Sullivan to carry my gun. Lastly I observed that as the men might now consider that they were about to commence a journey from which no one knew who would be permitted to return, I thought it was a duty they owed to themselves, to ask the guidance and support of that Power which could alone conduct them in safety through it, and having read to them a short prayer which I had prepared for the occasion to which I added the Lord's Prayer, [32] I intimated to Mr Poole that he was at liberty to proceed on his way as soon as he pleased.

The teams issued from the avenue in regular succession, and the long line of drays and animals reached from the one end of the Moorundi Flat to the other. I could not but behold such a scene with deep and painful interest. I watched the party cross the flat, saw it ascend the opposite hill, and ultimately lost sight of the whole train as it turned to the north and entered the scrub. Yet I stood gazing on the spot, unconscious that I stood there alone, that Eyre and those who had witnessed the departure of the party had retired and left me to myself and to my reflections, and thick and fast Dearest did they crowd upon me. The certainty of the past – the probability, I had almost said the certainty of the future, rushed upon my mind with the force of a whirlwind. The bare recollection of scenes through which I had so lately passed unmoved now completely unmanned me.

How many of those who had just passed me in such exuberant spirits and with such high expectations would be permitted to return to their homes?

Should I, the leader of this doubtful enterprise, be more successful than the daring and altruistic officer whose guest I was in penetrating the deserts from which he had been forced back and the bare remembrance of which made him shudder, or was it decreed that I should return baffled and disappointed from those gloomy and inhospitable regions?

My thoughts then, Dearest, settled upon you, and upon my children. Had I indeed parted from you forever and were the steps I had taken at such a sacrifice of happiness, to ensure future comfort, only to plunge those I most loved into deeper distress? My mind had for some time been afflicted by the most gloomy forebodings and it now appeared to me that my very nature had been changed under the effects of a morbid melancholy. I known not how long I should have stood upon that spot, if the intensity of my own feelings had not roused me. I was then unwilling immediately to join Mr Eyre, so I turned to walk down the avenue, to compose myself but that, Dearest, was not the place to withdraw my thoughts from those on whom they were fixed. The broad expanse of the Murray was before me, and I saw you on its waters almost as distinctly as if you had really been there. I recurred to the time when our peace and our happiness were alike unbroken and when I could look on the clear blue sky without a feeling of regret. I gave you a willing credit for your affection and anxiety, and bitterly reproached myself for every angry word I had spoken to you, whose only endeavour it had been to call me to myself, and whose only aim had been the welfare of your husband and of your children. However, Dearest, I will not pain you by dwelling on these matters. I have sufficient to atone for without thus reviving your sorrows, and yet, GOD knows that you and my children are never out of my thoughts.

When I returned to Mr Eyre I found him busy writing, and without saying a word I sat down to the same silent occupation. At length Eyre put a letter into my hand which he had been penning to Lord Stanley volunteering his services to conduct an expedition overland from Moreton Bay to Port Essington. Poor fellow, his heart and soul were set on this service and it really grieved me that circumstances had obliged me to step in between him and his ambition.[33] In this letter to Lord Stanley, however, he had expressed an opinion of the Interior directly contradicting mine, and he had expressed it with the utmost confidence.[34] "Have you", he asked me when he saw that I had read the letter, "any objection to what I have written?" "None whatever," I replied. "All men," I added, "are free to think what their experience dictates to them. I can only say, as regards the opinions you have expressed that I would not have expressed them so confidently." Nevertheless he closed and sent his letter as it was. Eyre then adverted to a letter I had brought him from Captn Grey in reply to his application to be allowed to go some distance up the Darling with me. This letter was one of the Governor's jesuitical productions, apparently granting the request that had been made to him, but clogging it with such conditions and restrictions as to render it all but mystery. Eyre said that he was puzzled what to do, that he had intended going up the Darling to distribute some blankets, and therefore that at all events he would accompany me to a certain distance, but he said that Grey had shewn him a portion of a letter he had received from Lord Stanley and that it was his, Captain Grey's, opinion that the Secretary of State had sent orders to Sir George Gipps to organise an expedition to proceed to Moreton Bay of which he, Mr Eyre, might expect to have the command. Now, I saw that letter, and feel assured that Captn Grey had no grounds to form such an opinion. Lord Stanley merely said that he had intimated to the Lords of the Treasury that he might have further occasion to draw on their Lordships, evidently on account of the present Expedition. However, poor Eyre grasped at a shadow of hope, to find in the end that he had been deceived, and that Grey's only object had been to prevent his accompanying me.[35]

As I have mentioned in a former part of this journal, Mr Eyre had secured for me the services of two natives, who I sent on with the party on Wednesday. As I shall have frequent occasion to mention these men I may as well introduce them to you altho' it is probable you will have seen them ere this reaches you. The one was Nadbuck, a native of Lake Victoria. The other [Camboli] or as he was called Jackey, a native of the river beyond Lake Victoria. The one was a crafty intriguer, the other a bold energetic and open-hearted savage, both were superior to their fellows in intellect, and were men of undoubted influence on the river. Nor do I mean by what I have said of Nadbuck to detract from his merits. I only give his character to make the contrast between him and his companion the stronger. Besides these two, I determined on taking Tampawang[36] with me, whose services I thought would be useful to me in the event of our losing any of the animals.

The River Murray above Moorundi, by G. F. Angas
'*We kept on the cliffs for some time (and) at 1 a.m. descended into one of the river flats. . . .*'

The morning following the day of Mr Poole's departure, five of the horses came back to the settlement having broken loose but Mr. Browne was close at their heels and drove them back. In the evening of the same day Kusick[37] arrived with despatches from the Governor, and with your letter of the 16th of August. Captn Grey's letter to me was in reply to the application I made for the Treasury, and he said as much as under existing circumstances perhaps he could have said. I also received a letter from the Judge[38] and another from Captn Frome[39] – the one from the former, full of benevolent feeling, and intrinsic worth. My heart truly warms towards Mr Cooper. I would gladly take upon me his failings and infirmities to possess his virtues. Frome's letter was such as you would have expected him to have written. Your letter, Dearest, did not contain the information about which I was most anxious, but it was a relief to me to hear from you at all.

Saturday morning broke clear and cold over the valley of the Murray, and the sun was fast descending to the west before Flood made his appearance. It was after five indeed when he rode up, having been detained at Gawler Town in consequence of the late rains. We had however anticipated his arrival some time during the day, and had sent Kenny the police constable at Moorundi with Tampawang forward in the morning to join the party. As soon therefore as I had read and replied to your letter, we left Flood to rest, and mounting our horses at 7 p.m. left the settlement attended by Tenbury a native who always accompanies Eyre into the bush.[40] We kept on the cliffs for some time and as the moon was nearly at the full saw her light at times beautifully reflected in the river. At 1 a.m. we descended into one of the river flats, and there made a fire, as the night was bitter cold and frosty, and having warmed ourselves, rolled ourselves in our cloaks and laid down for a few hours.

George Gawler

On the following morning we mounted our horses early, and about 8 o'clock neared the Great Bend[D]. As we approached it I recognised the ground over which I had wandered in search for that ill-fated boy.[41] I questioned Tenbury long and anxiously on the subject, who told me that neither had he or any of the natives seen or heard any thing of him. I think poor Bryant's fate therefore is beyond all doubt, that in truth he must have perished from exhaustion and thirst, and it is more than probable that his remains lie undisturbed to this day on the ground on which he breathed his last. Poor boy! We pity and lament his fate. His was indeed an early doom, but it had been better for many who have lived to maturer years, if they had sunk unto as premature a grave.

As we rounded the angle of the river I turned, Dearest, to look upon the last spot I should see under any circumstances for many a month that we had trodden together. It was now as still as death and I thought looked gloomy. Again my recollections flew back to that time, and I rode silently by Eyre whilst Tenbury was communicating something of moment to him. We kept on the upper part of the flat close to the base of some little hills that you may remember backed our tents. Tenbury, it appeared, was recounting to Eyre the occurrence of a flood which took place when he was a young man (it might be twenty years ago) that laid the whole valley of the Murray under water, and reached up to the hills near which we were riding. He said that the natives caught crayfish and ducks on the flat, and that the waters continued for a long time. To a question I put to him he said that the weather at the time was remarkably fine, and that the natives did not know whence the flood came but that it came from a great distance.

Here then was another proof of the sudden and heavy rains to which this continent was at one time exposed, but which now appear to have ceased, for the Murray has shewn no disposition to such freaks since its discovery. It now rises gradually and slowly at the rate of one inch per day, beginning to rise in December and attaining it full height sixteen feet above its winter level in July. But this rise is caused by known and natural causes, and is looked for by the natives, with as much anxiety as did ever the Egyptians to the overflowing of the Nile. If the one rewarded the husbandman by enriching his lands and giving him an abundant harvest, the other replenishes the Murray with fish, converts all the dried up lagoons into sheets of water, to which thousands of wild fowl resort, and overflowing the flats, resuscitates the crayfish that have laid dormant underground for months, and softening the ground, sends them forth in myriads as food for the Children of the Desert. There can be no doubt but that both are the provisions of the Almighty for the support of His creatures and it proves that civilized and uncivilized man fall equally under His protection.

Yet the occurrence of such a flood as that of which Tenbury spoke happening now would sweep away the whole settlement of Moorundi. It appeared clear to me indeed that Eyre became suddenly aware of the precarious nature of his property there, and I am sure it will influence him to dispose of it as soon as he can. The floods of last year did him an infinity of mischief and destroyed his harvest, and I fear the floods will have forced his embankments this year also for water is too powerful an element for anyone to control with limited means.

We overtook the party about eight miles beyond the bend. Mr Poole was again detained in consequence of some of the bullocks having strayed away. They were recovered, however, shortly after we rode up, and as it was only just past noon, we yoked up and proceeded on our journey. We travelled on the cliffs above the river flats, but the ground was sandy and heavy. At 4 p.m. I descended to the river and encamped upon its banks.

The cattle had an abundance to eat of fresh green grass, and the appearance of the vegetation led me to hope that we were still in time to profit by the grasses before they should be parched up by the summer heat. The Murray was on the rise and had a much greater body of water in it than when you was on it. On Tuesday, we again ascended to the higher ground, and endeavoured to shorten the road by cutting across the river angles, but I do not know how much we gained this for the surface of the country was undulating and sandy, and it was studded with clumps of cypress and fusani. At noon we entered a dense and intricate wood of cypress and eucalyptus, growing on pure sand. Through this the bullocks toiled for six miles when we cleared it, and found ourselves on more open ground. I then turned towards the river and descending to it encamped between it and a long narrow lagoon.

On the following morning we went along a flat for about three miles, when we were obliged to ascend as the cliffs left us no room to pass. We had to yoke two teams to each dray to master the hill which was tolerably high and afforded an extensive view to the south, altho' it was confined to the north. From the east, however, southwards to west the eye wandered over a dark and gloomy brush of uniform hue and appearance. In truth I never gazed over a more dismal scene. At this particular place there is a long succession of hills, and broken stony ravines leading down to the river so to make the approach to it almost impracticable. Foreseeing, therefore, that if we attempted to descend to it, we should have some difficulty in getting up again, I encamped on the heights, and had the cattle driven down to the flats. I expected that thus elevated above the valley of the Murray we should have suffered less from the intensity of cold and frost, but the night was equally severe in both situations. In the morning we had thick ice in our pails and the thermometer a little before sunrise stood at 27°. When the cattle were yoked up in the morning we pursued our journey along the cliffs or hills and at noon reached an angle of the river from which Lake Bonney was visible bearing east by south distant about nine or ten miles. From this point we descended to the river, and encamped. The afternoon turned out to be very rainy. In the midst of it, however, James Hawker, who I should have told you left Moorundi in a boat with my quondam friend [Mr Hodden?], came up to us and took shelter in our tents.

On the following morning we left the Murray for Lake Bonney,[E] and as I wished to lay down its position, I directed Mr Poole to chain from the river to it a distance of 4¾ miles.[42] Lake Bonney, Dearest, is an insignificant sheet of water of about twelve miles in circumference. It is filled by the backwaters of the river, as the Murray rises, and consequently falls as it falls, so that during a part of the year it is dry. It lies in the centre of barrenness and is altogether an unimportant feature which I should have passed, but Mr Poole, all anxiety to make the map of everything, asked me to let him survey it which detained us two days. I assisted him in the survey by laying down the creek by which it is filled. I made Hawker assist me in this and for his services I called the creek Hawker's Creek[F], and it was the first feature I named on this journey. On the 3rd of September we resumed our journey, keeping along the lake side for about five miles, to avoid some sand hills when we left it to proceed on our journey. We found very few natives at the lake and had not seen one on our way up. Here, however, there are about a dozen who have only just arrived from the hills.

On the 4th September, we cut through the scrub, and gained the angle of the river corresponding with the one to the westward of Lake Bonney[G] a little before sunset. It is a remarkably pretty spot, and had before attracted my notice, in so much that I took a sketch of it. (It is the last of Mr Montefiore's[43] pencil sketches next to the sea mouth of the Murray. The one before is a different view.) [There is an unfinished pencil sketch in the manuscript.]

It now looked beautiful, and the grass was so green and fresh that it was quite a treat to the animals. The decomposition of the rocks had formed a better soil than that on the banks of the Murray, and the spot being sheltered from the SW winds, all kinds of vegetation grew luxuriantly there.

On the following morning we left this cheerful scene and traversed a long polygonum[44] flat, over which it was with difficulty that the bullocks pulled the heavy loads. Arrived so high up the river, we found all the creeks full of water, and we were consequently cut off from all communication with it for a time. This day we encamped on the banks of a creek, in the neighbourhood of which the feed was as bad as it had been good at the place we had left in the morning. Nothing of moment occurred until the 7th when we stopped at the point at which the native path from Lake Bonney strikes the Murray River, to take a meridian altitude. Whilst the horses were quietly grazing one of the pistols in Mr Poole's holsters went off with a loud report, but fortunately no accident happened. The poor horse was a little alarmed but was soon pacified. We were all sitting on the bank of the river at the time, so that some sudden pressure must have caused the discharge.

At about two miles from this ground we had to cross a creek at which we found a small tribe of natives, and at two and half miles more, another creek and another tribe. We there had a broad and beautiful flat before us, as green as a meadow in England. The line of the creek bounded it to the right, and some small but distant sand hills to the left. In front of us to the north we could not see its termination. As we crossed this we found ourselves walking in water, the floods being in amongst the grass. We also observed innumerable cattle tracks all over the flat and were told by the natives that there were very many wild cattle in the neighbourhood. I therefore sent Mr Poole and Mr Browne with Flood and Mack to try and shoot one, and as the cattle had fared so badly the previous night, I led the party down to the creek and encamped upon it, to give both the bullocks and horses the benefit of the rich feed so close to them.

We had scarcely pitched the tents when Mr Browne returned to inform us that they had killed a magnificent beast and that on his way back to us he had also killed an enormous kangaroo. Here then was a feast for the blacks and all. I accordingly sent Morgan out with the horse dray to bring in the spoils, and I certainly never saw such splendid meat in my life. The animal had well chosen his pasture and his condition shewed how truly nature had pointed out to him the haunt best suited to him. He could not have weighed less than a thousand weight. Morgan only brought the fore and hind quarters, which averaged 750 lb, yet this enormous quantity of meat was wholly consumed in nine days by the men, who were allowed to take what they liked of it as it would otherwise have gone to waste. Yet, it is a proof that these men are little better than savages when left to the uncontrolled influence of their appetites and passions. Mr Browne told me they had greatly enjoyed the hunt, and that they had selected this animal from amongst forty, that they had had a long gallop, and that the wild cattle raised a cloud of dust as they tore along under the sand hills.

We now proceeded steadily up the river and on the [c. 7 September] reached the Rufus.[H] On the [c. 10 September] however we had encamped opposite to Fort O'Halloran and in the centre of the Hornets' Nest as he called the neighbourhood. It was here that O'Halloran[45] came up with the natives, when he headed the police and a party of volunteers for the recovery of Inman's sheep, or rather for the protection of Mr Langhorne's party or both.[46] Captain Grey gave him sealed instructions which he was not to open until he should come in the presence of the blacks. When he did, the natives drew up in a long line to await the attack, whilst the volunteers and the police also drew up in order of battle. O'Halloran then opened his instructions which positively forbad all fighting unless the party was attacked and holding O'Halloran answerable for any lives that might be lost.

Thus were they obliged to draw back and [rubbed out] that they refused to proceed any further, and consequently returned to Adelaide having done more harm than good.

The Hornets' Nest is also celebrated as being the spot on which Miller[47] shot the old man of whom you have heard me speak. It may be that the natives were troublesome and this old fellow might have deserved punishment, but nothing could justify the cold blooded murder of which Miller was guilty. But the man had a thirst for blood, and I never saw him, but that I wished I had a pistol to guard against his treachery.

On this occasion it would appear the old man was talking to an emigrant of the name of Cameron on the bank of the river when Miller walked up, and going behind Cameron put a pistol under his arm and shot the old fellow dead upon the spot, to the horror and alarm of the poor emigrant. On another occasion on the same journey Miller gave a black fellow a blanket to shew him the way across a marsh. This the native did and having guided Miller and the cattle safely through it he turned back, when Miller fired at and shot him dead, and on a third occasion when he met a native woman and child, he knocked the brains of both out with a tomahawk. Retribution however soon followed. He was himself speared by the blacks, and altho' he did not die of his wounds, they were the direct cause of his death. He had aneurism of the heart and was told never to use any violent exertion. Regardless of this, however, he was once visiting a friend in gaol where he ought to have been himself, and in leaping the ditch before it, he fell dead on the other side, without having had time given to him either for repentance or reflection. He received £200 for his last trip!

Mr Eyre whose heart and soul seemed to be centred in the service on which he was thus only temporarily engaged, never had the sextant out of his hands. Anticipating that his services would soon be required he was constantly taking lunars, and so engrossed the books that I could never use them. I was not however anxious as to our position then and therefore did not check him, besides which he assisted me greatly in taking altitudes from latitude as neither Mr Poole [n]or Mr Browne had as yet acquired the proper use of the sextant. Both those gentlemen, however, practised daily and did every thing they could to assist me also.

Mr Eyre preceeded us to the Rufus with the police constable and Tenbury, as we expected to find a large assemblage of the natives. On our reaching the Rufus, however, we found only sixty-five men, in the midst of whom Eyre was seated. Few of them had their spears and they had evidently assembled rather from fear than from animosity. I gave one of them a tomahawk for a canoe to assist in our operations on Lake Victoria which was now about four miles to the north of us.

Some few weeks before this period Mr Eyre had been up the Darling, and in crossing the country had struck upon its ancient channel, as he said about 30 miles on this side of the present one. He traced this up for many miles, but found no water in it. As however the Murray was now flooded I thought it probable the Darling might also be full and that consequently this Ana-branch, as such features are called, would afford us the means of moving up to Laidley's Ponds by a much nearer line than by going up the Darling, and I was also anxious to avoid the chance of collision with the tribes at the [junction]. Mr Eyre therefore secured the services of one of the natives to accompany Mr Browne and Mr Flood to the Ana-branch to examine it, while we were detained at the Lake.

This native Pulcanta[48] by name was the man who was captured at the affair on the Rufus when the police and Mr Robinson[49] who had been fighting with the natives for three days, got the poor devils between them and shot from forty to eighty in that low and swampy channel. This man Pulcanta was wounded in the action, but in order to secure him his hands were put in irons behind him. On reaching the Great Bend of the Murray, however, this bold savage threw himself off the cliffs into the river and endeavoured to make his escape, but the police fired at and wounded him in three other places so that he was retaken. I should have respected his courage and allowed him to escape. In appearance Pulcanta was the worst-looking savage I ever saw. He had deep set sparkling eyes, a broad nose, thick lips, a forehead rapidly falling back, and the greater part of the brain – technically speaking the cranium or skull behind the ear, the seat as phrenologists say of all the worst passions. He was sullen and morose in disposition and his scowl was like a thunder cloud. Yet I had no hesitation in sending him with Mr Browne, and accordingly the morning after our arrival at the Rufus the three started with a week's provisions – this being the first excursion from the camp.

On the evening of the same day I walked out with Mr Eyre to visit the different tribes scattered along the banks of the Rufus from which he wished to select some old men to whom to distribute blankets, and would you believe that before we returned to the camp we walked eighteen miles? In all, men, women and children, we saw about 230 natives. Nadbuck's tribe was amongst the rest, and he had temporarily left us to visit them. We returned to the camp with about two dozen men who walked before us and cleared the way, holding such branches as would have checked us on one side until we passed. Suddenly the leading native stopped at a large mound of earth, and explained to us that that was one of the places in which they had buried their dead after the affair on the Rufus. They spoke of it without any apparent feeling of revenge but with marked emotion.

It was on this occasion, too, that Eyre availed himself of the opportunity of our being alone to tell me that he should be obliged on the morrow to return to Moorundi. He said that he expected letters from Sydney, and that he was sure he should be employed on the Northern Expedition for that Grey had led him fully to expect it. Poor fellow! How well I knew his hopes would end in disappointment. However he is exceedingly obstinate, Charlotte, and therefore I avoided argument. Most willingly would I have resigned my command to him, but I felt that I could not do so. I was going into the depth of the interior, a reluctant emissary, whereas he would have been an enthusiastic one, but I felt that I could not recede. I felt too that whatever sacrifices I had made, I should if I succeeded make up for them, that if I fell I should leave [diaries] behind me that could not well be refuted. I was however extremely sorry at the thoughts of losing Mr Eyre, who had been as a companion to me, and who had been of real service. I only hoped that if he went to England as he said he would do in the event of his being disappointed, he would be employed by Lord Stanley.

I know no one who had greater claims on Her Majesty's Government for the good he has done on the Murray. He has done more to soften the natives on its banks than all the missionaries and protectors would effect in a thousand years, and he has so managed that he is both beloved and feared by them. He goes by the name of Heyomatten, strictly meaning the master of the vessel, but why they should have given him that name it is difficult to say. Be that as it may, he had intimated to me his intention of returning and accordingly, on our arrival at the camp, he set about his preparations after he had distributed the blankets. Mr Eyre told me that he intended returning to Moorundi by the hills, but I advised him not to do so, as I was quite aware of their distance from the river, and knew that if he attempted to gain them he would be two or three days without water. Nevertheless he started in the morning to make the attempt, and we all parted with him with regret.

On Mr Eyre's departure I moved the camp to Lake Victoria' and encamped on a beautiful piece of ground, which had a gentle slope to it and was as green as a young wheatfield. There were some magnificent trees scattered about and we had a dense mass of gums close behind us that completely sheltered us from the cold southerly winds. There was an abundance of feed for the cattle, and the fusanus, of the fruit of which Davenport made some excellent jam, grew around us in great abundance, absolutely loaded with berries. They are insipid when eaten raw and appear to be neglected by the natives, but when boiled down they have a pleasant acid taste. The same tree grows on the sandhills near Grange but it seldom bears fruit I believe.

I directed Mr Poole to chain around the Lake, and to take angles of its margin to lay it down, and continued to move round it with the party as he advanced. On the 14th Mr Browne returned, having found water in the Ana-branch to a considerable distance up it. My mind, therefore, was for the time set at rest on that point, but we were detained in the neighbourhood of the Lake until the 18th by heavy rains, during which it was bitter cold. We had left all the rich and park-like ground near the Rufus behind us and had got into a barren and swampy hollow. The change indeed from good to bad soil had been surprising and instantaneous.

It was at this place that we first heard of the massacre of the white people on the lagoon of the Darling. Jackey had left us at Fort O'Halloran, so that Nadbuck only remained with the party as guide. He came to my tent one morning with a young native who had only just arrived from the Darling, and who he said had something to tell me. This was that only a week before the natives of Williorara Laidley's Ponds had killed fifteen white men and a woman, that they had a number of bullocks and ten drays, from which the natives got plenty of blankets and shirts. He said that the white men were all asleep when the natives crept on them and killed them, no native having been hurt. The young rascal told this story so circumstancially and so minutely that it was impossible not to attach some degree of credit to it, more especially when I took into consideration that the men who were said to have executed this butchery were those with whom Major Mitchell had been twice engaged, and whom he called Fire Eaters.

The boy was going down to Moorundi and as I felt assured that he would spread the report I thought it better to anticipate him by writing to you and to the Governor. Under an impression that some of the party might have escaped, I was anxious to press on, and it so happened that just at this time a native of the Darling came up from Adelaide where he had been to satisfy his curiosity. This man I enlisted into my service. He questioned the boy whom he knew and he persisted in the same story, so that we all felt assured that some fatal tragedy had been enacted. My new guide 'Toonda' was a very remarkable man, rather advanced in years, but as erect as a post, he was stern silent and haughty evidently a man of peculiar temperament and more than ordinary intellect. He was accompanied by his nephew, a fine boy of about fifteen, to whom he seemed particularly attached, and I was not sorry to have him with me to study his character, for one could see in a moment that he was a remarkable man. When we reached that part of the Murray to which Jackey belonged he had introduced us to his wife and family, and had treated us with a corrobory, but whether it was that the natives were alarmed at our appearance or that they were too few in number, the dance was not carried on with any spirit. At the Lake Nadbuck introduced us to his family, having no fewer that three wives, and he would also have exhibited the proficiency of his tribe in the corrobory but for the rain, and as we had here about one hundred and fifty natives I have no doubt it would have been something worth seeing.

On the 18th the weather cleared up so that we left Lake Victoria at 7 o'clock and proceeded to the eastward over barren sandy plains. Lake Victoria, like Lake Bonney, is surrounded to the north and north west by sand hills, and if I except the precincts of the Rufus, lies in the midst of a desert.

It is, however, a much finer sheet of water than Lake Bonney, being 25 miles in circumference, besides which the scenery on some parts of it is really beautiful and it is of undoubted value as being a permanent sheet of water. At 3 in the afternoon we struck a creek which prevented our approaching the river and on it we encamped at 4 o'clock.

On the 19th this creek in like manner prevented us from going as much to the south as I wished, but at length it turned to that point. I then struck across the plains to where I knew I should again find the river, and we struck it at one of the most lovely spots you ever saw. It is in the dry season one of the river flats, but had numerous little grassy mounds, and the floods having filled the hollows it was now a small but beautiful lake studded with islands.

The evening shadows had a most softening effect upon it. Its parting brightness seemed to linger on so fair a scene. We encamped between this pretty spot and the river on a spot of ground on which the grass was most luxuriant, and as it was at the place very narrow, altho' it again expanded, it was as a stock yard from which our cattle could not make their escape. We had as we crossed the plains observed numerous and recent cattle tracks, and at night our camp was infested by lowing herds. Some of our bullocks had very sore necks so that I thought it would be a good plan to avail ourselves of so favourable an opportunity to run some of the wild cattle in towards the river and to secure some workers. I accordingly again sent Mr Poole and Mr

Browne, with Flood and Mack, to drive them down, whilst I kept our bullocks on the plain to attract them towards us. In about two hours Mr Browne returned with Flood, and I immediately saw that some accident had happened. On alighting Mr Browne told me that Flood had had his carbine go off by accident whilst he was reloading, and that it had carried away three of his fingers. On further examination we found that the forefinger was uninjured and that the top joint only of the other three had been shattered. Flood bore the dressing very well and said he should not have cared so much about the accident if it had occurred after we has passed Laidley's Ponds, for there he said he should now be useless. About 2 Mr Poole and Mack returned, without having succeeded in driving the wild cattle out of the brush, but they had shot a fine heifer, for which I reluctantly sent.

At this place we were not more than six miles from the junction of the Ana-branch to which I had sent Mr Browne, but as Flood was feverish the day after his accident I did not move, and heavy rain detained me here for another day. On the [c. 22 September] we moved on and reached the Ana-Branch' at half past eleven. I had not seen the Murray for some days for altho' we encamped close to it, there were high reeds on its banks through which we could not see the water. It was now however rolling along its muddy waters at a tremendous rate, and throwing them into the Ana-branch as the flood swept past it. The scene was not a pretty one, but from appearances, I was led to hope that I should find water high up the old channel of the Darling. Having taken a meridian altitude to fix the latitude of the spot, I followed the drays to the north, and in so doing turned my back upon the Murray. We soon found a loss in this, in the change the country underwent for the worse. We had no more rich flats and lofty trees, but traversed barren sandy places, and at ten miles encamped to secure a small corner in which there was grass for the cattle, as we had seen so little that we did not know where we should find any more if we passed it.

On the following day we again pushed up the Ana-branch, and it promised well as far as the water was concerned, but the country was barren in the extreme. At 3 o'clock Nadbuck came to tell me that we should have to encamp immediately, for there was no water higher up. I was astonished at this information but on galloping to the front I found he was correct. There was a kind of bank or dam across the channel which prevented the floods from going beyond this point. I encamped therefore from necessity, but the feed was so bad that I was obliged to have the bullocks in yoke all night. At this place there was a small tribe of natives, who confirmed the reports we had heard at Lake Victoria, so that I determined as soon as we should reach the Darling to which I foresaw we must now cross, to take double precautions for the security of the camp.

One course, or that I desired to pursue, was a north one but both Toonda and the natives insisted on it that in the morning we should have to go to the eastward, and they said that we should have to start early or that we should not reach the river by sunset. I was rather suspicious of this information as I could not get Toonda or Nadbuck to tell me why there was a necessity for our going so far out of our way; however, after mature consideration I determined on letting them have their own way.

In the morning therefore after crossing the Ana-branch we pursued a due east course over an immense barren plain. At about 7 miles we passed so as just to clear it, but entering into its outskirts in dense and dreary brush that stretched away to the north, and this which we could not have penetrated. As it was, the crash of timber as the drays tore down the rotten trees in their way was awful, and it was to avoid this brush that the natives wished us to go to the eastward. At 5 miles we got on firmer and more open ground on entering a plain across which we could see to a distance of ten miles.

I gave the bullocks half an hour's rest at the edge of the brush, and on dismounting had well nigh trodden on an enormous snake, that was coiled up and asleep. The men called out to me to draw back, and their noise I fancy woke the animal for he unfolded himself and raised his head to a level with my knee. I could not retreat from [it] for I knew that if I stirred he would spring at me, but I had borrowed a sabre from Mr Eyre, which I had not intended to wear, but had put on that morning as we were going over to the Darling. I drew it therefore with the rapidity of lightning and making a cut at the poor snake, I swept his head from his body to the great delight of poor Toonda, who expected that I should have been killed. After this little adventure we pushed on, and the sun was low when we began to descend in to the valley of the Darling, a dreaded stream in the annals of Australian discovery.*

It was late however before we reached its banks, but you cannot fancy any thing more beautiful than the scene was. We entered ground like the park land near the Botanical Gardens, studded with beautiful trees, and with a sward of grass upon it of the most vivid green. The Darling itself, however, was all but dry, and could only be called a muddy ditch. Yet I recognised it in a moment, the same sloping and grassy banks the same weeping and umbrageous trees, and the same death-like silence pervaded this spot, as with the other parts of the river on which I had been. Mr Browne stood with his arms folded looking at the scene and declared he had never seen anything as lovely, and our first night on this singular river was tranquil and undisturbed. I thought it necessary however to double the guard and assigned a tent to it, wherein the men were ready for immediate action if required. I also drew up the drays in a square, and put the sheep in the centre so that they could not be molested.

In rooting about amongst the trees Mr Browne had found a beautiful new net secreted in a hollow tree. This net I would not allow to be removed. In the morning a solitary native came to the opposite bank of the river, and was with some little trouble induced to swim across. He it was who owned the net, and on our pointing to the tree in which it was hid, shewed great satisfaction in finding that we had not taken it. This man knew me the moment he saw me, a most remarkable instance of the acuteness of his vision and the retentiveness of his memory – fourteen and half years having elapsed since he saw me, and then only for a moment.

We commenced our journey up the Darling with the fairest prospects. A lovely morning broke over us and we passed flat after flat of the same fresh herbage, and the same park-like scenery with which we had at first been so much taken, and again encamped on as verdant a lawn, and as beautiful a spot, as ever was seen. The next day the river trended to the eastward and for two days held the same course thus taking us out of our way. On the third day however it gradually came up to the north-east, and at last to the north. It would not interest you to hear a sameness of detail, for our progress over heavy ground was slow and we had no incident to break the monotony of our journey. Both Mr Poole and Mr Browne practised with the sextant, with indefatigable zeal and perseverance to relieve me from the trouble of taking observations, and were getting fast with the use of the instrument. Every care was taken of the cattle and horses, nor did any of them stray. I was obliged to have the bullocks yoked up all night in our then uncertain state as to the disposition of the natives, and had consequently to halt early to enable them to feed during the afternoon. I pushed them so hard however that their necks were in a horrid state, and the rotten hollow nature of the ground shook them to pieces.

The fifth day we were on the Darling, I was measuring its banks to form a section of the channel, when both Mr Browne and I thought we observed a stronger current than before in it, with hay and small pieces of bark floating on the surface of the water but we took no more notice of it. The next day however the same indications of approaching flood were visible. The waters of the river seemed as if they were being pushed on by something behind them, and there was a great quantity of rubbish floating about. Such was the state of the Darling when we went to bed, and you may judge of our surprise when in the morning we found it converted from a shallow insignificant stream into a broad and beautiful river, dashing and foaming along, and carrying everything away before it. Its waters had risen four feet during the 12 hours, and in three days they were overflowing the banks and invading the flats. Whence these waters came, whether from the sources of the Kerawla and the Nammoy, or from nearer mountains it was impossible to say. From their suddenness I was led to hope that they were thrown into Laidley's chain of Ponds from the ranges as Major Mitchell has laid down, and that it would facilitate our progress, but I was wholly deceived in the character of that branch of the Darling which, on our arriving at it, was found to be nothing more than a channel connecting the Lake of Cawndilla with the river.

During our progress up the Darling we saw but few natives, and only one numerous tribe, the whole of the men of which were remarkably handsome. As we neared the scene of the reported massacre I became suspicious that there was something brewing from the fact of our not seeing any natives, but we reached Williorara[L] in safety on the 10th of October, it having taken the drays just two months to perform the journey, being just the time Eyre had given us. I was sadly disappointed at finding Laidley's Ponds, or as the natives call it Williorara, perfectly dry. The waters of the Darling had only just entered it, and I saw at once that it was not a mountain stream but a paltry creek. Neither could I see any ranges. From some sand hills near us we could see some inconsiderable hills to the north of us, and whilst I remained with the party to prevent if possible any rupture with the natives none of whom we had as yet seen, I sent Mr Poole to the hills to overlook the country from them. He came back in ecstasy told me that there was nothing but water, water, water to be seen, with numerous islands and rocky promontories. I had great doubts as to all this and asked him if it might not have been the effect of refraction and mirage. Oh! no, he was quite sure it was water and that I might prepare to launch my boat as soon as I pleased.

During Mr Poole's absence we had been visited by the very tribe with whom Major Mitchell had fought, and we had pitched our tents nearly opposite to his last encampment which, however, was not so near the river as ours. The natives were very quiet and kept at a respectable distance, so that I was rather pleased than otherwise and with them there was an old man with white hair who particularly attracted my attention. He was under the middle size, but he was the remains of former strength and activity, and the fire of his eye was as bright as ever. He put one in mind of Sir Richard Bourke,[50] from a sharpness of countenance, and a marked intelligence about him. To this old man I gave a blanket and it was evident that he was a man of authority from the satisfaction evinced by the rest of the natives at the selection I had made.

Two days after our arrival at Williorara it came on to rain heavily and it continued to do so for six days. In the midst of it all Jackey,[51] our first guide, arrived from Moorundi with your replies to my letters from Lake Victoria, and with a letter from Eyre. The poor fellow had travelled for ten days at the rate of 35 miles a day, and he reached us in a state of both excitement and exhaustion. He complained of great pain in his limbs, yet would not rest a moment. His calves were all swollen and he kept talking incessantly. "Papung" *Papers*, "Papung Boocolo" meaning me, "Papung Sacoback" Doctor Browne, "Papung Hugomattin", Mr Eyre.

I never saw a poor creature as excited, and so restless. There happened to be some six or seven natives of the Lake tribe at our fire who said something at us, evidently displaying no friendly feeling, on which he seized a gun, and threw himself into an attitude of defiance, pointing to us and then shaking the gun at them in the most resolute manner, and in truth he soon tamed them. I of course fed him well and made him a soft bed to rest, but he was up and down, up and down, and would not be quiet, and at last he went off to assist Mr Browne in cutting a canoe with which to cross the river to examine Major Mitchell's camp.

Jackey, Dearest, brought me your letters of the 27th and 28th of September conveying to me various tidings that have increased my anxiety regarding you, and I have foolishly allowed some trifling circumstances that have occurred to weigh upon my mind so that I turn my thoughts towards my home with the most gloomy apprehensions. I have taken it into my head that both you and Napier have been snatched from me, and if such should be the case I am sure I do not know what I should do. I can forsee that this undertaking will keep me for a fearful length of time from my home, and what may not already have occurred, what may not occur in the interim. I did not intend, Dearest, to reproach you in the letter to which you allude. What I said I cannot call to mind, but I am sure of my own feelings towards you and it would have been doing violence to them if I had done so. I am quite aware that I have many failings, Charlotte, very many, but amidst them my feelings towards you have never changed, or my affection diminished. So far from that I have ever seen reason to be grateful to you for your care and anxiety – and you must lay to the account of a distempered mind any of those feelings which I evince either of petulance or unkindness. I am sure I was too unhappy myself to consider the unhappiness I was inflicting on others, and a very little more would I sincerely believe have made me put an end to it all.

I trust, however that God will yet permit my return, and that this severe trial will issue in our final good. Such at all events is my prayer, my daily prayer to the fountain of All Mercy, and my only consolation is (if you should indeed have been taken from me) that you will most assuredly see into your husband's heart and feelings better than you could do on earth, when no suspicion will cause a doubt, no worldly feeling a pang.

I cannot condemn myself for having sought this service. Much more should I have done so if I had allowed ruin to overtake me, without having made any effort to secure and reestablish your welfare and that of my children. I saw more than you did, and I only feared that I should be deprived of the appointment I held before I had taken measures to bear up against such a reverse – Captn Grey had gradually and cautiously lowered my income and swept my appointments from under my feet. He placed me where I could do no good, and in a position to which I had no claim, and in one that [might] have been reduced in a day, and I had nothing to look for from Captn Grey's feelings towards me. He may be civil to you, Charlotte, and I will repay his civilities, and moreover I will be grateful for them for your sake, but there is a breach between me and Captn Grey that will never be made up. From the moment I rose from the Council Table to pay the last mark of respect I owed to Col. Gawler,[52] when I rose from the Council which he had assembled purposely to prevent such a demonstration of feeling, I made him my bitter foe, and I soon saw that and whatever he may have said to you or whatever Mrs Grey[53] may have said to you, believe me Charlotte they hate us both the more because we deserve it not at their hands, and fancy not that those feelings which Mrs Grey has displayed towards you will be easily removed. Ask Mr Eyre his opinion of either or both of them – ask any one – look to Captain Grey's character and conduct from his treatment of Lushington[54] to his treatment of Jackson[55] then do not fancy that I who have stood between him and his resentment have any reservation from enmity in my favour.

If I could have earned my bread in any other way I would have thrown my appointments in Captn Grey's face long ago, and there is nothing I more earnestly desire than to have my time my own that I may devote it to my children – but my Dearest Charlotte, I scarcely know what I am writing, and am perhaps wrong in exciting you against those from whom you may have received attention and alas! this will reach you too late to caution.

On Mr Poole's return from the hills I directed him to measure a base line on which to commence our future operations, and I determined on proceeding myself to the north-west to ascertain the nature and extent of the waters Mr Poole reported that he had seen, before I moved the party. On the 14th I sent Mr Browne across the river with a young native called 'Topar', recommended to me by Mr Eyre, to visit Major Mitchell's camp, which he found at about ¾ of a mile from the river on a small sand hill.[M] The remains of the fires and other signs of his occupation were still visible.

It is somewhat singular that this lad Topar was a boy of about 11 (being now about 20) when Major Mitchell was there and he was present at the affair between the natives and Major Mitchell's men. The story as he relates it was as follows.

George Grey
'From the moment I rose from the Council Chamber to pay the last mark of respect I owed to Col. Gawler . . . I made Grey my bitter foe. . . .'

Major Mitchell had sent a party of his men, without any responsible person to check them, down to the river to water the cattle and, on going down, they saw in the bed of a small gully on their side of the river a native with his wife and an infant. One of the men went down to her. At this time Topar was on the opposite side of the river with another native, a man. When this man of Major Mitchell's got down into the creek he threatened the black, who threw himself into the river leaving his wife and child. The man then endeavoured to throw the woman down, and on her resisting, he drew a pistol from his belt, and shot her in the thigh, and then effected his purpose. After which he took out his tomahawk, and with it killed both the woman and the child. On hearing the shot fired one of the other men ran to the bank and seeing a native swimming across the river fired at but missed him. The native had just got to the other side and crouched behind a tree when the men Major Mitchell sent to *assist* his men arrived, and they twice fired at the poor native, hitting the tree each time.

Topar had hid himself with the other native behind a polygonum bush, and did not come out until the affair was over. He shewed Mr Browne the little creek in which the woman and child were killed, the tree in which the balls still remain and the bush behind which he hid, and I have given you a sketch of the poor woman's grave, which is close to my tent, at the mouth of the Williorara.

Such was the fearful story related by Topar which was subsequently confirmed by Toonda, and it is somewhat remarkable that the story we heard at Lake Victoria bears on this event. Major Mitchell had a number of drays, and the boy who told us of the massacre said that a woman had been killed but that no black man had been hurt, which so far corresponds with Topar's account of the brutal affair. The character Major Mitchell gave of the natives of the place led me to believe that I should surely have a combat with them, but we passed in perfect quietness.

On 17th I moved my camp to Cawndilla, then a large dry bed of a lake of great size, but the waters were just entering it so much that we crossed the current. I turned to the north after crossing the basin, and we camped on a sandbank close to the Williorara having the basin of Cawndilla on the one side, and that of Minandichi on the other.

On this bank I found the old man to whom I had given the blanket with his tribe, and he politely moved lower down with his people giving me to understand that I might sleep there and that he would sleep elsewhere. He thenceforth came daily to my tent and remained in it during the heat of the day. It appeared that it was his custom to go to sleep in the middle of the day, but he never did so in the tent without asking permission, nor did he altho' present when we were at dinner ever ask for anything, altho' you may be sure he was not ultimately forgotten. He was exceedingly clean in his person, unobtrusive tho' so much with us, and always respectful. I took a great fancy to this old man, and treated him with much attention, and when I left the camp to go to the northwest, he came up to me as I was mounting my horse and embraced me by putting his arms over my shoulders and bowing down his head to my breast.

On this my first excursion I took Mr Browne, Flood, Morgan and Topar, but before I detail the results, I must inform you that Nadbuck left us with Jackey when he returned to Lake Victoria. He had been a faithful attaché, altho' a most finished politician, and was always in his post when wanted, so that we felt his loss exceedingly. Toonda now alone remained with us and he had reached his haunts.

The day before I commenced my journeys we were surprised at seeing Nadbuck reappear and it turned out that he had met with another messenger with letters and had good-naturedly returned. I forget, Dearest, whether this second mail brought your letter of the 27th or 28th, but one or the other did. I learnt that the Governor was at Moorundi intending to stay *for a day or two* in expectation that he should hear from me. Poor Eyre was exceedingly anxious about us and wrote me to send a confidential messenger to him if I wanted assistance. However assistance would have been unavailing then if the natives had been found by me to be what Major Mitchell represented them to be – the Fire Eaters of the Darling.

On leaving the camp I crossed a plain of about thirty miles in breadth guided by Topar who went with us to shew us water. We proceeded straight for a bluff hill in the range of hills Mr Poole had seen, and at sunset arrived on a dry creek with a deep sandy bed. Here we first saw a new and beautiful hawk with black shoulders to his wings, but otherwise almost white in colour. These birds we afterwards noticed in immense flights.[56]

After riding up the creek for about five miles Topar stopped at a native well, which we were obliged to dig afresh before we could get some stinking water. He told us there was a better well higher up, so that we determined on going to breakfast – thus we accordingly started early. This well was certainly better than the first but we had the same trouble of digging, and with difficulty procured sufficient water for our horses. After breakfast we pursued our journey and at fifteen miles came to a third well at which we stopped.

Topar wanted us in the morning to cut across to the north-east but as I began to entertain some suspicion of him I would not follow his advice but made for the bluff, which I was anxious to ascend. All Mr Poole's water had evaporated, and nothing but bleak, empty,and immense plains were before and around us. We had noticed some smoke in the creek and had expected to have found some other natives, but they had gone up the creek. In crossing to the bluff, however, we again saw smoke in its bed, and as I had determined on leaving Topar with the first natives I met, I turned towards the creek again, but the natives having again left their fire I rode up the bed of the creek and at length came on a beautiful serpentine sheet of water from which our vagabond guide had attempted to lead us away. We now stopped at it, and in the morning pursued our way to the bluff.

On reaching its summit we saw nothing but ranges of the most barren description to the north the north-west and the north-east. There were extensive plains between them apparently forming an elevated table land but we saw no creek or any appearance of water. I returned, therefore, to the water we had left in the morning, and determined, against Topar's strong assurance that I should not find any water, to go up the creek and to cross the ranges at the head of it. This we accordingly did in the morning, and notwithstanding all Mr Topar had said found several pools of water.

The ascent to the plains was easy and at noon we found ourselves on the northern and western side of the first range. Here Topar insisted on our going to the north where he said there was water that we could swim in, and as I wanted to pursue that course and did not really know where to turn for water, I thought it better to follow his advice. At 15 miles we arrived at a gorge or pass in the hills through which a creek broke into the plains we had crossed in coming to them. Topar led us into this glen, and at length stopped at a small green hole of stagnant and stinking water, which even the horses would not touch, and I subsequently found that at the point at which he was so vehement in urging us to come to this place, there was a pond of beautiful water within an hundred yards of us. I had luckily filled two casks with water in the morning so that we were not obliged to drink the water to which Topar had brought us, but I made him drink it, and a heavy punishment it was to him.

This being my first absence from the camp I was anxious about the party, as there were a good many natives about. So that having ascertained that there was sufficient water to enable me to push the teams on fifty miles farther I determined on returning to Cawndilla in the morning, and on bringing the whole party up to the ranges without loss of time. I was the more anxious to do this because as I think I have already observed, I was anxious to get the party out of a numerous neighbourhood to which the natives were crowding in all directions for the fishing season. Accordingly in the morning I again crossed the plains, and I do not recollect that in the severest of a Canadian winter I ever had so cold a ride. We were nearly blown off our horses, so violently did the wind sweep over that exposed plain and yet the day before the thermometer had been up to 100 in the shade. The wind fairly blew through us, and we could feel it against our bodies. The consequence was that we were quite benumbed when we reached the camp. The next day, however, we left Cawndilla, but the bullocks being unable to reach the creek, I halted for the night on the plains. The next day we had to dig wells to water the cattle, but the following day I got them safe to a fine pond. The next day I again left the camp for the N.W. and clearing the hills at about 15 miles descended to a boundless plain.

The first day we left we were without water; the next day late in the afternoon we traced a creek on which we had struck into a rocky glen. This creek had a bed of pure sand and I feared we should not find any water in it. We examined every corner until at last I went to a bold, basaltic rock, and under it found a small clear pool not larger than your round table. However we got a spade and enlarged it, and got an abundant supply of the most delicious water we have tasted on the journey. The next day we pursued our way down the glen but we were at length stopped by immense rocks across the glen over which we could not get. A great many natives had however lately been in the neighbourhood altho' we saw none. Forced to abandon our course I returned to the basaltic rock and determined that it would be better for me and Morgan to stay in the glen the next day, whilst Mr Browne and Flood went to discover a pass across the hills.

Accordingly in the morning they left us and in the evening returned having succeeded in finding a good road by which as I have said we descended on to an apparently boundless plain. The ranges tended to the north, and I saw at once from their character and appearance that they would not continue long. I wanted however to go to the north-west and therefore left them. We rode over an open plain for about fifteen miles on which you would have supposed all the stones that had ever been broken for the roads in England had been thrown, but it was remarkable that the different kinds of rocks were not mixed, it appeared as if huge fragments of each had been brought to a particular spot and there shivered to atoms so that the plain was chequered over like a chess board with different colours. From this plain we continued in low scrub and then found ourselves in a country in which long narrow flats alternated with ridges of sand like those near the lea behind us. The ridges were crowned with pine trees, and had an abundance of grass upon them. I had brought the light cart with water and penetrated into this kind of desert as far as I could, the course I had taken up being direct for Lake Torrens. However when our supply of water failed I was obliged to turn back, but I had scarcely reached the hills when it came on to rain violently and continued so to do for five days. On reaching the camp therefore I determined on sending Mr Poole and Mr Browne to the north-west to pass the point to which I had gone and if possible to make Lake Torrens.

They left me on the 18th of November and were absent nineteen days during which they travelled three hundred miles. They got to latitude 29..44..00, and made Lake Torrens opposite to three remarkable peaks laid down by Mr Eyre. They found the Lake to consist at this part of a chain of lakes, none of them very large, but they could not see very far to the north where in all probability it was broader. Mr Poole says the country was very peculiar as you approached the Lake and that any one looking at it from high ground would take it for the bed of an immense sheet of water. Whilst Mr Poole was absent I moved the camp across the ranges, and advanced on to the plains about 80 miles, and encamped on a creek I had myself discovered. Mr Poole and Mr Browne returned a good deal fagged out from so long a journey, but as soon as they had recovered I again sent them out. I wished in truth that as I should have the credit so they might have the gratification of making any discovery.

I told Mr Poole on this occasion to keep nearer the hills that he might have the better chance of crossing any creeks issuing from them. He got as far as latitude 29..14..00, and found considerable supplies of water in several creeks which he intersected. I consequently moved on to latitude 29..46..00, and encamped on a creek of some size, over a long sheet of water, on the 11th

January. On our way, however, we had to pass through a part of the pine ridges, and the weather there was so hot that I preferred travelling by night.

Poor Poole who was leading on the last day but one of the year, unintentionally got us into a hobble, by mistaking one hill for another in the dusk of the morning, and so led us out of the way, and in truth got confused, so that at day light I found myself in the midst of pine-ridges and the bullock drays sinking axle deep into the sand. It was in vain that the bullocks pulled their heavy loads over one hill – another rose immediately before them. The men did all they could but to no purpose, so that by 3 o'clock the whole were knocked up. I now took the teams out of three of the drays and put them to the others so that there were sixteen bullocks in each dray, but still they hung back.

Seeing that we should not get out of this hobble before night, I sent Mr Poole on to water with the horses and sheep and remained myself with the teams with Mr Browne. At sunset, finding that we could not get on with the drays, I unyoked the bullocks, and Mr Browne and I and Mack started to drive them by a shortcut but still a distance of twenty miles to water, for the day had been so intolerably hot that the animals would have died on the following day. Knowing that we should have to go a long way without water I had ordered all the casks to be filled so that there was enough for the men for two days. We found the sheep at a stand shortly after we started with the cattle, and I told Mack to bring them on when the moon should rise, directing Tampawang to go with him to follow our tracks. We then hurried on and reached the creek at 3 in the morning, but not where there was any water however. Two of the bullocks dropped on the way and ultimately died, the others all got safe to the place where Mr Poole was.

The next day I sent Morgan on horseback for two water casks and some provisions as it was impossible that we could send the bullocks so soon for the drays. Morgan ought to have been back by the afternoon but night closed and no Morgan came. Morning broke and no Morgan made his appearance. However, about 11 o'clock I was on the far side of the water hole near which we were encamped smoking out some rats when I saw Morgan come riding slowly along. I observed that he had no casks or provisions, when he came up, I asked what had kept him so long. "For God's sake, Sir," said he, "Don't speak to me just now. I will tell you all presently." And throwing himself off his horse he ran to the water and drank like a fish. When he eased, I again asked what was the matter. I thought some terrible accident had happened when he told me that he went to the drays as I ordered him and got the casks and provisions, but that on his return he stopped to let the horse feed for half an hour when unfortunately he fell fast asleep and when he woke the horse was gone and he only overtook him at the creek. I was very provoked at this conduct of Morgan's, but all I had to do was to remedy the evil.

I sent Flood on horseback to the place to which Morgan directed him for the casks, and determined on his return to collect the cattle and to go for the drays myself. Accordingly on Flood's return at 4 o'clock we collected the strongest of the cattle and got to the drays about 9 when I found the men in terrible alarm for want of water. However I got three of the drays to the creek, but it was so tremendously hot that the poor animals could hardly bear up against it, and when they stopped to rest pawed the ground to find a cooler surface for their feet. My stirrups were so hot that I could not keep my feet in them yet twice on the first of the New Year did I ride through that molten desert. The sheep got safe to water, and the next day I got the other drays out of the pine forest but this accident cost us two bullocks and a week's delay. Thus, Dearest, you see how soon the least error entails misfortune on a party travelling in such regions as these. I took good care in future to know where I was going before I moved my cattle.

On the 11th as I have told you we arrived on the banks of one of the creeks Mr Poole had crossed, and pitched our tents over a fine long water hole in it. At this time, Dearest, our consumption of water was at the rate of from 1000 to 1100 gallons a day and I was obliged to provide as well for our retreat as for our advance, for we had not yet found sufficient water to relieve my mind of anxiety on this all important point. During Mr Poole's last absence I had gone from 90 to 100 miles to the eastward in hopes that I should have found a better country in that direction, but if anything it was worse and I was 48 hours without any water. On the 14th I left the camp to go to the north-west with Mr Browne. Mr Poole went with me the first day, but he was to return the next, and in the event of our finding water was to have moved the party during my absence. As we did not, however, he returned by a line to the westward of where we went to examine a creek the head of which he had crossed on his last journey, and he providentially found a supply of water sufficient for our consumption for twelve months in a rocky glen there. In the meantime I went with Mr Browne over some remarkable ranges in our way, and from there again descended into the plains. From these ranges which were the last of the line of hills to the north we saw two isolated hills at the distance of 40 miles to the W.N.W. and in hopes that they would afford us a good view of the interior we made for them, passing through a most awful desert all the way.

From the highest point of these hills which were low stony elevations we could see nothing but á dense scrub from S.W. to N.E. The line of the horizon was as level as the sea, and the darkness of the scenery was unbroken by a single plain. You cannot imagine so dreary a region or one of such hopeless character. We had not found any water at a greater distance than seven miles from the hills, and as I saw it would be fruitless to try and penetrate farther at that time I turned back and reached the camp on the 26th, where to my astonishment I found all the water dried up, and Mr Poole drawing his supplies from a well. I did not at this time know of the fortunate discovery he had made, but the next day we removed to this place, from which the drays have not since stirred. Sturt's Depôt[N] was near the modern township of Milparinka .

Here, Dearest, we have been locked up as fast as if we had wintered at the Poles, nor have we had a drop of rain for seven long and weary months.

However, so far from repining at this we have cause only to be thankful to the Almighty in that it pleased Him to guide us to the only spot as we now know in which our wants could have been supplied or where we could have existed. My mind was now relieved of one great cause for anxiety, and I was glad that there would neither be a necessity for our retreat or for our [success?] up the Darling, for altho' I did not care about the natives, I was extremely adverse to that course. I was, however, dissatisfied with my last trip to the north and determined on making another effort in that direction. About this time, Dearest, both Mr Poole, Mr Browne and myself began to feel the effects of scurvy. It is not a dangerous disease as much as an annoying one. We had swelled gums, taste as of copper in the mouth, and violent headaches, and I had what perhaps did me good, constant but not profuse bleeding at the nose.

We attributed this attack to our having been obliged to use a good deal of salt meat, your good hams amongst the rest, one of which we had on Christmas Day, and to our being weakened by exposure to tremendous heat. We took every precaution however and hoped the disease would be checked if that which gave rise to it was discontinued. Mr Poole and Mr Browne being too unwell for active duties, I took Mr Stuart my draftsman with me, together with Flood and Joseph who is a remarkably fine boy and by far the most useful and most intelligent lad in the party. I took him because I knew his moral courage would support him in case we fell into any difficulty. My plan was to go to the most distant water to the north there to fill the light cart with water, and leaving Mr Stuart to sketch in the ranges and Flood to take care of my horse, to try how far I could go beyond the hills on which I had been with Mr Browne. Accordingly our arriving at the water on the 11th February we filled our casks and leaving Mr Stuart and Flood as proposed, Joseph and I commenced our journey. With an allowance of six gallons a day for the horse and two quarts apiece for ourselves I should be enabled to gain the 27th meridian.

We soon got into a country alternating with long narrow flats as before, and sandy ridges but they were now destitute of pine trees and had only a few hakea bushes on them. As we advanced the flats narrowed, and the sand ridges became closer, succeeding each other like the waves of a tempestuous sea. There was at first a little grass on the flats but it all disappeared and was succeeded by spinifex, a thick wiry grass generally found on the sea shore, the sharp points of which stuck into us at every step. The flats now became sandy. It appeared as if the ridges had been levelled by successive gales of wind and that the sand from these had been drifted into the hollows beside them. All trees disappeared and only a few hakea bushes were to be seen. The spinifex became so matted that we could hardly walk or the horse drag the cart through it.

At noon my observations (on the 13th) placed me in latitude 28..10..00 and here my horse Punch, the black horse you have seen Mr Frew ride, failed me, and would not go a yard farther. I took him out of the cart therefore, and being anxious to pass the meridian of 28°, Joseph and I took a quart of water and a piece of damper and started off to walk. When we got from 12 to 13 miles I stopped and being certain that I had passed that meridian, I got on a sand hill to look around me.

There we stood, Dearest, Joseph and I on a sand hill, being more than 200 miles to the westward of the Darling, nearly abreast of Moreton Bay in point of latitude, and in longitude 141..22..00, but there was no change in the terrible, for it was terrible, desert we had entered.⁰ It appeared as if we were the last of creation amid the desolation and destruction of the world. There was a solemn stillness around, not a living thing to be seen, not an ant, not a cricket, or a grasshopper. The horizon was unbroken from north all round to north again, nor was there a shadow of hope in that dreary and monotonous wilderness. I could not however neglect the horse on which our own safety depended, so I turned back, after having gone about 67 miles. Just as we turned to go back a parrot flew over our heads with loud cries of alarm, it went thro' the air with a zig-zag flight, and appeared to be just as much at a loss as a bird that has been driven out to sea by a gale. It passed us and went to the north. "That bird, Sir," said Joseph, "does not seem to know where to go to." "No", said I, "He does not indeed, and if he cannot see a place on which to rest, how shall we find one?" "Oh Sir," said the poor boy, "I was never in such a place as this before. It is a dreadful place indeed."

It was with great difficulty that we got Punch back to the waterhole on the 16th where we found Flood and Mr Stuart. Flood had caught three pigeons which I send to dear little Missey.⁵⁷

I had, on coming out this second time, passed to the left of the line I first took over the ranges, and I observed that a creek which had appeared to me to spread over the plains to the east, turned to the west and continued with some promise. I told Flood to examine this creek during my absence and on my return he told me that he had done so and that he thought if I followed it down it would lead to something. I left Joseph therefore with the cart, and taking Mr Stuart and Flood, went down the creek the first day 30 miles, when we arrived at two large water holes at which a number of natives had been but a day or two before and here we slept. But I forgot to tell you that the first time we went out to the little hills we found a small creek close under the ranges in which there was a little water, and at this waterhole a native and his family must have been building a hut when we were crossing the plain for they had evidently only just bolted. However we could not find them – the next morning at about 6 miles we came on another waterhole, the last we saw, and here again we scared away the native from another hut he had almost finished, and he went off this time in such a hurry that he left all his household Gods behind him. I was sorry for this, and knowing that he would return, I stuck his spear into the ground, and fasten[ed] my knife open to it. On our return we found that the native had been to his hut, but was or must have been so alarmed at the sight of the knife that he had again bolted, and had evidently extracted a bag full of curiosities from the far side of the hut to which the spear and knife were, nor did we ever see this unlucky fellow.

The second day we traced the creek for about a mile when it spread over an immense plain, but with some trouble we picked up its channel again at the distance of four miles from where we lost it, and then traced it for eight miles at which distance it suddenly terminated against a bank of clay and sand, but there was a hollow on the top of the bank, through which its superfluous water escapes. On ascending this bank we saw beneath us a most beautiful park, studded with trees and covered with grass. The embankment came all round it and in it the creek terminated.

Having satisfied myself on these heads I rode away to the N.W. but almost immediately got into the same dreadful kind of country from which I had just retreated, besides which it was so intensely hot, that neither could my men or horses stand it. Flood complained that the top of his head was burning, and the horses drooped theirs as if overcome by drowsiness. I therefore stopped under the shade of an unhappy hakea bush until the cool of the evening, and then went back to the water-holes and the next morning joined Joseph, and you may in some measure judge of the tremendous heat to which we had been exposed when I assure you that behind a large tree four feet from the ground the thermometer stood at 132° and that in the direct rays of the sun it rose to 157°, and on our way back to the camp feeling it exceedingly hot and wishing to ascertain the temperature, I desired Joseph to give me the thermometer which was laid in the folds of a clean shirt in a box and in that situation was up to 110°. You cannot indeed conceive the dreadful heat in this exposed and stony region. Every article we have went to ruin before it, the teeth of our combs fell off, the handles of our razors split, every box warped, and every nail was loosened. Our tires fell off the wheels, and the drays rattled all over. The soles of the men's shoes were fairly burnt off, and citric acid melted in the bottle in which it was kept. The dogs would not stir from the water but remained on the bank, after having gone into it up to their necks, repeating their bathing as soon as they were dry.

One day as we were crossing a plain on a most sultry day, when the wind was blowing in our faces as if from a furnace, a flight of large hawks came down upon us from the upper sky in hundreds. I suppose they did not know what we were and fancied they were to have a fine feast. At first we saw two or three dark specks in the sky coming towards, which as they came nearer turned out to be a kind of large hawk. Behind them were other specks to an immeasurable distance, until at length every part of the sky was alive with them. They approached so near that I went at them several times with a whip, and if they really had made an attack upon us, I do believe their numbers would have prevailed against our strength. They flew right into our faces in such rapid succession as to perplex one, but at length having satisfied their curiosity I suppose, they soared up aloft again and disappeared. What they were doing in the upper air it is difficult to say, and in such immense numbers. All I know is that they were enough to frighten a timid man.

After my return hence we had a succession of tremendous weather. Early in

Two birds shot at the Depôt, water-colour sketches by Charles Sturt

March I went to the eastward to a distance of one hundred miles, but could find no water; at the close of the month I went an equal distance to the westward. In April I went away to the N.E. but was obliged to return. I had looked for rain in vain. It appeared as if the sky was never again to be traversed by a cloud. In the state of uncertainty in which we were, I reduced the rations for the third time, that by early measures of precaution I might prevent after distress, but I had no idea that we were destined to remain here for four weary months, as we have done.

About three weeks ago the clouds appeared to hang heavy on the Mount* Serle Range and in hopes that I should have found water, I pushed towards it, but after being three days without water and my horses four, we were obliged to return.

Luckily for us, Dearest, we have seen very few natives, but I have been anxious to get one to the camp, and I had hoped that we should by our good nature have conquered their timidity. However, none ventured to approach the camp. Last week a single native was seen on a neighbouring hill, who called to us, and was immediately rushed upon by the dogs. He defended himself however with his boomerang, until Mr Piesse went to his assistance and brought him to my tent. He was all alone and a stranger, speaking a totally different language from the natives hereabouts. He immediately guessed the use of the boat when he saw it, and pointing to the N.W. made the signs of waves, and of their going over his head. He examined the sheep netting and intimated to us that the fish in the N.W. were too large to get through them. He recognised the codfish of the Murray but none of the other fish of that river, and when shewn some of Cuvier's[58] plates, he gave names to the turtle, the sea-horse and several marine fish, but those he did not recognise he passed his finger over, calling them all by one name. This old man appeared as if sent to cheer us in our lonely confinement, and certainly his information confirms all my own observations and views.

We have witnessed migration after migration of all kinds of birds to the N.W. They have rested for a time over our water, and then at a signal from one of them have simultaneously taken wing, and flown away in the direction I mention. There can therefore be little doubt but that there is either a desert or a sea between us and a better country, and I trust Providence will yet prosper our undertaking.

I am however almost heartbroken, Dearest, at the delay which has taken place in our movements and the weather continues so fine that I see no likelihood of change. I have gradually reduced the men's rations to 5 lb of flour, 1 of sugar, and 2oz of tea a week, but below this I fear I cannot go, but these reductions not enabling me to remain out long enough to examine the country I have determined on sending Mr Poole back with a third of the men. If the party remained entire we should only have 25 weeks supply of provisions, but by this plan I shall ensure 2 months additional supply for those who remain. If I did not adopt some such plan I should justly lay myself open to Lord Stanley's censure and dashing all my hopes, but it will sadly prolong my absence since I shall hardly reach Adelaide before the middle of February, and I shall have all that time of anxiety still to endure. It appears to me that we are within one hundred and fifty miles of an inland sea. That it is some very large feature I am certain from the sameness of the country at different points, and if it should be a sea it will enable us to make up for past delays.

All I am anxious about is to do something that shall entitle me to reward. I should certainly wish to examine the northern parts of the Province, to repay the people for the kindness they evinced towards me, but it will certainly depend on circumstances whether I shall be able to do so or not. Certainly nothing shall stop my progress when once I turn my horse's head homewards.

Part 2
Sunday[?] July 17th 1845 [Thursday July 17th was the date of Poole's burial.]

The receipt my Dearest and Beloved Charlotte of the little journal I sent you last week, and of the several letters that accompanied it, will have put you in the knowledge of the several events that had taken place with us up to that period. Some of those events were, however, detailed to you in letters. I shall therefore briefly restate them here before I enter on my new subject in order to make this little manuscript as complete as possible.

I have further determined, Dearest, to write up the events of the past week every Sunday because I think our movements will then be clearer to you, and that you will better understand the principle upon which I regulated them.

None but those who were my companions in that dreary solitude can form any idea of the severity of the trial that our detention at the Depôt was to us. In truth it was almost insupportable. By the end of February all hope of breaking it had ceased. It had been to no purpose that I had run every creek down to its termination, and had crossed and recrossed the plains; no water any longer remained on the surface of the country, except in the solitary glen on which our depôt was established. My only hope rested in the occurrence of some casual shower or of a passing thunder storm to put us once more in motion. I had no idea that the whole summer would pass without our being favoured with a single drop of rain, but so it was that burning and terrific season progressed with unabated severity. Day after day and week after week the sun rose and set in [inexhausted] splendour, and every cloud that rose on the horizon was beat back by a moon as bright and I had almost said as hot as the sun itself. We had nothing new either to engage the attention or to attract the eye. Nothing could exceed the desolation of the scene around us. Not a herb or flower was to be seen but the land was perfectly bare and scorched. The water we were drinking became putrid and diseased itself, and we had every day to witness its rapid and fearful diminution. Already had it sunk five feet from its first level and half the time it had taken to effect that exhaustion would have left the channel as dry as the plains around it. But we were not to see matters carried to such an extremity.

As I think I told you, Dearest, in February both Mr Poole, Mr Browne and myself were attacked with scurvy, one of the most appalling diseases by which man can be afflicted. The symptoms of which tho' they did not abate, did not increase either on me or on Mr Browne, but Mr Poole gradually became worse and worse. Early in March he walked lame but I apprehended nothing. It was my wont to watch the clouds to the westward in the direction of Mount Serle, and to calculate on the probability of the rain that occasionally fell on that lofty chain reaching us. On the 16th of March dense banks of clouds hung over the mountains for two days tho' above us all was clear and bright. Distant thunder caught my ear, and a strong westerly wind blew. In hopes therefore that rain might have fallen within a tangible distance of us I proposed to Mr Browne, who was himself suffering in a less degree, to take a ride towards Lake Torrens. Mr Poole walked rather lame at this time, but was sufficiently well to take charge of the camp. On the 18th therefore Mr Browne and I started with Flood and Joseph, but after a journey of fifty-five miles we were obliged to turn back, having found only one small puddle of water so muddy that the horses' noses were coated over with it as they drew them out of the water after drinking. I could not stomach it, but Mr Browne managed to swallow a little.

On our return to the camp I was sorry to see Mr Poole on crutches. The next day that being the 26th of March he took to his bed, and never rose from it again. Whether it was from his habits of body, or that he had indulged in the use of salt meat during my constant absence I know not, but the scurvy seized him with the grip of a tiger. He lost the use of his lower extremities, the skin of his legs turned black, large pieces of flesh hung down from the roof of his mouth, and he was at once reduced to perfect helplessness.

Whatever cause I might have had for being displeased with Mr Poole, whose violence of temper, love of interference and uncontrollable jealousy, rendered him unfit for the service on which he was employed, as well as his total ignorance of the duties he had to perform beyond the bare taking of angles from one hill to another, I was really distressed to see him reduced to such a state.

It became both my own but more particularly Mr Browne's care to alleviate his sufferings as much as possible, and throughout the whole of his illness this amiable and kind-hearted young man attended him with the most cheerful sacrifice of his own time.

Days and weeks now flew over our heads, and altho' the temperature cooled gradually down from the burning heat of the summer as the winter advanced, yet no change took place in the weather, nor was there the slightest indication or appearance of rain. The cattle had consumed all the feed round us, and the view from the camp was one of the most gloomy description. Rapidly the water decreased in our water hole and altho' there was no danger, as there was still an abundant supply up the creek, yet I could not see it so diminish without feelings of alarm.

What gave me the most anxiety was that we should be thus locked up in idleness. I saw the weekly consumption of our provisions and could not hide from myself that if rain did not soon fall we should only have provisions enough to carry us home. I had already reduced the rations as low as I could, and in contemplating our situation, I foresaw that nothing but a decimation of my party would enable me to remain out in the field. Having considered the matter well over, after a careful examination of the provisions remaining in store, I spoke to Mr Browne on the subject. This was about the middle of June. Mr Poole was if anything worse, and Mr Browne gave me his candid opinion that so long as he remained with us there would be no chance of his recovery. He had no medicines applicable to his case, and it was a total change of diet, rather than medicine, that he wanted. At this time however, Dearest, I did not, or had not, contemplated sending Mr Poole home. However I now plainly saw that I should either have to do that or drag him after me for seven weary months in hopeless imbecility. Still, seeing that there was no immediate necessity for me to determine on what I should do, I quietly prepared my letters for Adelaide and let matters run on as heretofore. About this time, however, Mr Poole had several relapses and at last an attack of inflammation of the brain that had well nigh carried him off. I again spoke to Mr Browne therefore and asked him if he apprehended any immediate danger. "Not immediate," he said, "but it is evident that the longer he is kept from a change of diet the longer he will be and the less will his chance be of recovery." I made up my mind at once then to send him to Adelaide as soon as rain fell, and I therefore went over to his tent and told Mr Poole to hold himself in readiness to go home at the first break up of the weather. He was, as I expected he would be, adverse to this arrangement, but on my arguing the matter with him seemed to be reconciled. Indeed he admitted himself that he felt he should not be well enough for active duties again. It was, however, natural for him to shew a reluctance in leaving us, altho' if he had been in rude health I should have felt no hesitation in sending him home as the proper person to take charge of a party on its return to headquarters.

Mr Poole told me that Mr Browne was suffering both in his health and in his interests by this ruinous detention at the Depôt. I therefore turned the matter over in my mind and one day spoke to him on the subject, giving him his option to return or not with Mr Poole, but he said that he preferred remaining, and as I was aware that one object he had in view was to find a run for his sheep in some part of the province we should have to cross, I did not press the point. Mr Poole was now tolerably well, and had apparently shaken off his original disease, but the weather appeared as if it was never to break up. We were kept in the most anxious suspense, that was destined to be prolonged for some weeks. In the interim Mr Poole again collapsed and became fanciful, nothing pleased him. He fancied he should be better in a little underground room we had made than in his tent, so I had it arranged for him in a most comfortable manner with a fire place. But poor man he did not occupy it long.

There was an evident change in the weather about to take place, the sky had been for some time overcast, and the wind shifting to the N.E., a steady rain set in. In anticipation of this I had made every preparatory arrangement for Mr Poole's departure. I had had a stretcher made to swing in the centre of the dray, with an apparatus by which he could raise himself if he wished to sit up. I gave him his selection of the men and bullocks, put aside all our little remaining comforts for his use, and did everything I could to contribute to his comfort on his return to Adelaide, and I sincerely hoped that the idea of returning to the haunts of civilized man from such a desert as this, the daily change of scene, and the use of vegetables eaten by the natives of the Darling would go far to restore him to health. He was now indeed apparently so much better that I proposed to Mr Browne to ride down to the termination of the Red Hill Creek, now Mount Poole, as I had some idea of sending the cattle down to the grassy plains there, in the event of our finding water, and I further expected to find a large assemblage of natives in the neighbourhood. It was in the evening of the day before we were to start on this little excursion of three days only, that the old man, of whom I told you in my last, came to us. About 3 o'clock the attention of the men was roused by a coohey from a solitary black who stood on some rising ground on the other side of the creek from that on which the tents were pitched. The dogs rushed out upon him and would have cut off his retreat if he had then repented of his temerity and endeavoured to make his escape, but this evidently was not the feeling of that bold savage. He defended himself against his assailants until some of the men brought him down to the tents where he soon recovered his composure. As I knew it would be no use putting any questions to him at such a moment of excitement and as he intimated his intention of remaining with us for a few days, I forebore trying to elicit anything from him until I should return. On the following morning therefore, after sitting a short time with Mr Poole, Mr Browne and I mounted our horses and started off for the grassy plains at the lower end of the creek. It was a long and a hot ride however of 32 miles, so that we did not reach our destination until sunset. We found a fair supply of water in the creek, but were disappointed as to any number of natives being assembled at it.

There were indeed only two families there, the one consisting of a native, to whom on a former visit I had give a knife, with his two wives, one of whom was our former loquacious friend, with the native who had run away from us when we were going to the eastward, who had his daughter with him, a pretty little girl about 9 years old. We had a partial thunderstorm at sunset, but little or no rain fell. There was however a great commotion in the natives' camp, and the women bundled themselves off to a more substantial hut at some little distance from us, so timorous are they of wet. We returned to the camp in the morning and there heard all the wondrous things the old man had told of there being great water and great fish to the N.W. The old fellow's story indeed to Mr Browne and myself is so clear that there must be something in it, and my hopes of doing something have revived.

On the other hand I was vexed to find Mr Poole worse. He had put himself into a furious passion and said that he was neglected and the consequence was a relapse, so that I found it necessary to speak to him very seriously on the subject. This was about the end of June, and for a few days he seemed to rally, but about the 3rd of July he became whimsical, wanted all kind of things made for him, and was dissatisfied. He thought he should be better in the underground room we had made than in his tent, so I had a chimney and fireplace made to it, and got him removed into it on the 12th, the day it commenced to rain so that poor man he did not long enjoy it. On the 13th and 14th it rained heavily, or rather a mild steady rain, and sufficient having fallen to justify me in breaking up the Depôt, I directed the home-returning party to prepare for their departure on the morrow that is on the [15th][59] and had the dray prepared for Mr Poole's reception. In the morning therefore the men mustered, and Mr Poole was carried up from the underground room and lifted into the dray. Poor man! It went to my heart to see him leave me in such a state but I fully anticipated his speedy improvement as he neared Adelaide. He was much affected when I took leave of him, and assured me that his first visit should be to you. I requested Mr Browne to accompany him the first day, and I told him that I would only go a few miles to enable him the easier to rejoin me. I was in truth anxious to know how he would bear the movement of the dray, and to have Mr Browne's opinion of his prospects to the last moment.

Our separation, Dearest, in such a wilderness as this was sufficiently painful without being aggravated by circumstances, and it was believe me with a beating and a bursting heart that I saw the cavalcade move off.

As is generally the case where one has been for a long time stationary at a place, there were a thousand things to delay us. The horses could not be found, the bullocks so long out of yoke could not be managed and I was at last obliged to give up the idea of leaving the Depôt that day. On the 16th, however, I had the teams up at an early hour, and at 7 we turned our backs on a spot, our sojourn upon which carried not one pleasing recollection with it. It was like a reprieve to me to get away from it and to breathe another air.

The rain, however, had made the ground very soft and our still heavily loaded teams sank deep into it, and one of them fairly stuck in a small gully about a quarter of a mile from the Depôt, and we were labouring to disengage it when Mr Browne rejoined me, and I was glad to learn from him that he had left Mr Poole much calmer, and that he had every hope of his reaching Adelaide in safety and in some measure restored to health. I saw, however, that something unusual had occurred, and on telling Mr Browne so he said that Mr Poole had had one of those violent bursts of passion to which he so often gave way, and that he had had occasion to speak to him in rather angry language and to represent to him that he could not expect the men who have heard him go on in so unbecoming a manner, to respect him who had no respect for himself. I was in truth glad that Mr Poole was gone for he was a mischief-maker in every sense of the word, and had really caused ceaseless disturbances in the camp. Yet he had some good points, and he had a claim to my strongest sympathy, and therefore it was that I did every thing to soothe his mind on his return, and to write in his favour. However let that pass I have forgiven and forgotten any annoyance he ever gave me and only to you, Dearest Charlotte, do I thus open my mind.

This first day of our removal from the Depôt we did not get more than four miles but it satisfied me to get away from it.

Intending to go to Lake Torrens as soon as I had established the Depôt on the western creek, I had employed the men whilst idle in measuring the distance to it, and they had some weeks before we broke up completed thirty miles. In the morning I sent on Mr Stuart with Mr Piesse and a party of chainers to continue the measurement whilst I brought the party up, and they had got on to some distance. It was about 8 o'clock and quite dark when we heard the tramp of a horse, and immediately after it Joseph's voice, with whom I had reluctantly parted to wait on Mr Poole. I called to him and on his coming to the tent asked him what brought him back, for I really thought his temporary master had changed his mind and had determined not to proceed on his journey. But judge of my astonishment when he told me that Mr Poole was dead. Mr B. had left him in the morning about 7 and he had expired at 3 almost without a struggle. Joseph informed me that he was leaning on his side and in the act of taking a dose of your favourite medicine, when he exclaimed, "My God, Joseph, I fear I am dying," and falling on his back he heaved two or three deep sighs, and was no more. This melancholy event gave me sincere pain, in the thought that a companion should thus have fallen and I blamed myself for having sent him away, but God knows it was an event that I had not foreseen. It put a stop however to all my arrangements, and obliged me to remain stationary for a few days.

On considering the matter over I determined on having Mr Poole's remains interred at the Depôt. It struck me that his funeral obsequies would be a fitting close to our residence at that dreary spot. On the morning of the [17th] I rode with Mr Browne to the place at which the home-returning party had encamped, having previously sent Flood to recall Mr Stuart and the chainers, and a party of men to prepare a grave at the foot of an old banksia tree that stood in the middle of the camp.

On examining Mr Poole's remains, Mr Browne was clearly of opinion that his sudden death was caused by internal haemorrhage, that is by the rupture of some blood vessel internally, most probably in the region of the abdomen. The singular fairness of his countenance indeed indicated that such had been the case. Be that as it may, he had breathed his last in as gloomy a desert as man ever entered.

After directing Joseph to bring the body down to the Depôt with all the men excepting one, to remain as a guard with Tampawang, I rode back, and taking the Depôt in my way to see how the men had got on with their work, I reached the tents about 5 in the afternoon. Early on the following morning Joseph came to tell me that he had executed my orders, and about 9 Mr Stuart came up so that the party being once more assembled we proceeded to the Depôt, and after I had read the Funeral Service over them we lowered Mr Poole's remains, rolled up in a blanket and laid upon his mattress into their last bed. We had not the wood to make a coffin, so I desired that a kind of chamber should be made at the bottom of the grave, which we planked over so that no dirt should fall upon the body and so left him to sleep until that great day when we shall all be summoned before that Judge with whom human craft will have no avail, no quibble of law have any weight.

Mr Poole's death, Dearest, had a powerful effect upon me. The immediate consequences were that it obliged me to put another responsible person in charge of the home-returning party, and I accordingly determined on sending Mr Piesse on whose prudence and punctuality I could rely. But, I felt at the same time that I could ill spare him, not that I cared for the reduction of the party, but because he would be of great service to me.

Having closed the short despatches I had to write and given Mr Piesse his instructions, I directed him to proceed with all haste to Adelaide. I must do the poor man the justice to say that he expressed great regret at leaving me and assured me that he should consider it a great honour his having been employed by me, with whom he would go to the world's end.

I now got our teams yoked up, the home returning party pursued a course to the south, and I pushed forward to the N.W. in the earnest hope that I should soon come upon some inland sea or navigable river. The recent rains however had made the ground very soft, so that we have got on but slowly. We are not yet amongst the sand ridges but close to them and have lost sight of the hills, the valleys from them having opened into extensive and level plains.

There is plenty of surface water still remaining, so that I hope to do better the ensuing week.
Sunday July 20th 1845

I have determined, Dearest, on numbering this weekly journal of events instead of a continuous narrative as before since it appears to me that it will be clearer to you. I shall therefore write up the occurrences of the past week every Sunday night when Mr Browne goes to bed.

On Sunday last, Dearest, we had halted just outside the scrub and the sand hills. On Monday, therefore, we entered them, and have been toiling over such a country as I believe bullocks never travelled before. Ever since yesterday afternoon we had chained 62 miles, but the nature of the country is so desperate, and its state after the late rains is so wet, that we could seldom push more than eight miles a day. The wheels of the drays were never more than six inches out of the ground and the poor animals had to strain incessantly over loose sandy ridges like those on the coast or through flats soft with mud. Having run so much to the westward I could not but think that on the bearing on which I had been running I had overshot the point I wanted to make. I have therefore given the bullocks a day of rest, and this morning rode away to the eastward to satisfy my mind on the above point. The grassy plain on which I propose establishing our second Depôt lies in a hollow and is surrounded on every side by sand hills so that you cannot see it until you are close upon it. Accordingly I rode some five or six miles without seeing any change of country, but all at once on ascending a sand bank I observed the plain and creek immediately beneath me, so that the drays passed within a mile and a half of it. After examining the creek and fixing upon a place for the Depôt I returned to the drays and reached them about the usual time for prayers.

Tomorrow I shall take the drays to the creek and establish them there, and as we have run somewhat to the north of Mount Hopeless, I shall direct Mr Stuart to change his line of bearing for it and to continue chaining towards Lake Torrens until I overtake him, and Mr Browne is good enough to volunteer his services to accompany him as I am now short-handed. There is nothing, indeed, that Mr Browne thinks would relieve me of trouble and anxiety that he does not immediately suggest, sparing himself no trouble when he thinks he can be of service to me.

We have captured one of those little animals called the Jerboa about which Major Mitchell makes such a fuss in his book and I have it alive and well. It is a beautiful little animal, something between the mouse and the kangaroo in shape with a very long tail having a bush at the end of it. It is very elegant in its movements, and Major Mitchell's plate is as like it as it is like the Hotentot Venus, a most absurd resemblance of the little animal altogether.

My journal of this week, Dearest, is short, but there is little of novelty here; perhaps next week will open out something fresh. At this present therefore I must lay down my pen commending you to the care of the Almighty.
Sunday July 27th 1845

A Jerboa. A pencil sketch by Charles Sturt
*'We have captured one of those little animals called the Jerboa about which Major Mitchell
makes such a fuss in his book.'*

Sunday August 3rd 1845

Last Monday, Dearest, as I had arranged the evening I returned from the creek, I turned back to establish the drays upon it. Mr Browne went with Mr Stuart and the party of chainers, to continue the chaining on a fresh bearing of 75° to the west of south so as to strike Mount Hopeless.

I reached the creek about noon, and formed the drays in a square on a little elevated piece of ground on which there were seven native huts. There were a sufficient number of trees for shelter and a fine broad tho' not deep sheet of water lined by gum trees in front, whilst the grassy plain lay behind us. As I was about to leave the camp for some days my first care was to have a stockyard erected, and I gave strict orders that the cattle should be tailed and confined every night. I directed that a garden should be dug and sown with a variety of seeds, and I once more cautioned the men as to any intercourse with the natives during my absence. I had an idea of marking out a stockade for them to erect, but I thought that work might be left until my return.

Having done every thing I could do therefore at the new Depôt, I left in the morning of the 30th to overtake Mr Browne, expecting that he would have reached Lake Torrens before I came up with him, but the nature of the country had impeded the chainers, and I overtook them about seven on the 1st of August early in the morning as I had ridden at the rate of forty miles a day. They had then chained 43 miles on the new bearing but we could see nothing either of Mount Hopeless or Lake Torrens. The country I had passed through was of alternate sand ridge and flat, the ridges were very high and of a fiery red colour, their summits were bare but their sides were covered with spinifex. Nevertheless there was no want of grass in the flats.

Where I overtook Mr Browne the country was very open and completely denuded of all trees and bushes, in so much that we were obliged to boil our pots with twigs. About noon Mr Browne and I were riding in front when we heard a black fellow coohey to us, and on looking towards the ridge a little to our right saw a solitary native standing there, on which I desired Mr Browne to dismount and to go to him. The poor fellow was in a terrible plight and danced and capered about at a great rate but seeing that this had no effect, he burst into tears and sobbed violently. Mr Browne then good-naturedly sat down, and by degrees the poor native recovered his composure and came to him, and after a short time giving a low call two others crept from behind a rhagodia bush and came forward, and all three followed us to our camp. The first was a terribly ugly fellow but the other two were good-looking. They had their bags full of those little Jerboa, of which I told you we had caught one. We had the curiosity to count the number they had killed which was no less than 288, so you may fancy what prodigious numbers of this *scarce* animal are here. They burrow like mice and have many runs to their apartments with a perpendicular hole in the centre for air. The natives sit on the top of the burrow and put a long crooked twig down this hole with which to start the little animal, and invariably kill him as he bolts. We have now five alive.

These people are disgusting in their mode of eating anything. They roast these little animals in hot sand, eating hair, entrails and all, only breaking off the lower jaw and throwing it away. These three natives devoured the whole they had and then took their departure. On the 2nd, Dearest, we passed over a very open and barren country, and saw some more natives, 14 in number, standing on a hill, but when Mr Browne and I rode towards them they pointed their spears at us and then ran away to another hill. We followed them over two or three ridges when they formed a circle on the top of the one to which they had retired and began to dance round an old man. I therefore saw that it would take more time than I had to spare to bring them to parley so we left them. About an hour afterwards Mr Browne was in front with the flag and I was in the rear with the chainers, when I heard a native coohey and on looking round saw seven advancing, but they were unarmed. I therefore dismounted and went to them and gave one of them a knife. We halted after having chained $11\frac{3}{4}$ miles. I, from the summit of a ridge close to us, could see some high and broken ranges to the S.S.W., but they are very distant from us, I say 'are' because we can see them from where I am now writing. We also observed from the same ridge a deep hollow in the country in front of us, which at the time I thought was the bed of Lake Torrens and I have still every reason to think that we will find it so. We passed during the day through another miserable country, and one indeed that could only exist near a sea coast. All its productions were salsolaceous, all its waters salt. About three miles from where we slept we crossed a creek of considerable size with deep clear pools in it of indigo blue in colour and as strong as brine, but we have not as yet crossed a single fresh water creek. There can be no doubts therefore of our being in the neighbourhood of the Lake, and we shall probably fall upon it tomorrow.

Sunday August 10th 1845

A short period, Dearest, was put to our chaining on Monday last. At about 6 miles we got on the brow of the ridge from which the country had appeared to dip and beyond which there seemed to be a great hollow, and immediately beneath us at the distance of about a mile and a half saw the dry shallows and sandy bed of an immense lake. It extended to the north-west and to the south further than we could see, and was about 12 miles broad. Beyond it the country appeared to be wooded and beyond the wood there was another great hollow towards the ranges now standing out boldly in the sky altho' still at a distance of from 40 to 50 miles. My first anxiety was to ascertain if I could cross the bed of this lake. I therefore rode down into it with Mr Browne, and found it to consist of patches of sand and salt and clay with gypsum (Plaster of Paris). It was exceedingly level and large masses of clay were scattered over it of fantastic shape, the deep furrows in which shewed with what violence the rains must at times fall there. It was sufficiently hard to bear our horses for two or three miles, but we were ultimately obliged to dismount, and, after walking a mile or two farther, to give up the attempt. I then tried to turn it by sending Mr Stuart my draftsman to ride 10 or 12 miles to the south and by going myself to the N.W. I thought that at that distance I should reach that part of it where it makes a turn to the westward but after riding 15 miles I seemed to have gained nothing, so deceptive was the mirage. I saw dark blue sheets of water fringed round with samphire bushes in detached parts of the lake, but no connected channel and I was obliged to turn in order to get back to the party before dark.

Mr Stuart on his part was equally unsuccessful, and saw no termination to the lake in the direction in which he went. It remained therefore for me to consider during the night what course next to pursue, and I thought that I could not do better than to devote a day to the examination of the neighbourhood before I decided.

I had had three objects in view, Dearest, in this excursion to Lake Torrens. The first was to ascertain if the country to the north and N.W. of it was practicable for the drays, as that was the direction in which it appeared to me Lord Stanley wished me to go. I was further in hopes that I should find Lake Torrens connected with some large internal body of water, the early discovery of which would facilitate my future movements, and lastly I was anxious to connect the ranges I had crossed with the Mount Serle Chain.

My examination of the country on the 5th July satisfied me as to the total impracticability of the country to the north of the lake. On a more minute survey of that basin also I felt assured that I was not on the main body of the lake but on an out-feature of it, and that the lake itself was in the hollow beyond the wood. I further became convinced that, however extensive Lake Torrens might be, it was not connected with any internal body of water, but that it owed its existence in former times to Spencer's Gulf. I was therefore disappointed in the two principal objects for which I had undertaken this journey and I had now only to return to the Depôt and try some other quarter. Before I did this, however, I connected the principal points of the Mount Serle Range with the end of my base line by an operation that you would not understand if I told you what it was, but the angles gave me 57 miles as the distance the hills were from me. I was a mile or two to the south of Mount Hopeless, but I could see nothing of it unless it forms part of a small flat-topped range rather more to the north than the main Range. However my knowledge of the locality is so imperfect that I will not venture to give any opinion. Perhaps Mr Eyre will recognise the shape of the hills, an outline of which I have drawn on the opposite page, from which you will judge that making such a show at such a distance they must be exceedingly lofty and rugged.

On the 7th, Dearest, we commenced our retreat which was more rapid than our advance, and was only remarkable for the muddy water we had to drink. The weather had been extremely warm at times although at times it was so cold that we had frosts in the morning before sunrise, but the noonday heat was always in proportion to the morning cold. Add to this that there was a constant high wind that by agitating the now shallow pools of water, that at no time were more than four inches deep, formed them into thick plaster. I would have given anything for a little alum to clear it, but we were obliged to drink it after precipitating as much of the dirt as we could by boiling. The country looks more miserable on our return than when we advanced and road seems interminably long. However we are now about [blank] miles from the Depôt and I hope that we shall reach it next week early. Till then, Dearest, Goodbye, May God protect you and all around you. I lay down my pen committing you to His blessing and care.

Sunday August 17th 1845

Last Sunday, Dearest, we halted within a few miles of the Depôt. On Monday morning, therefore, I left Mr Stuart to bring up the chainers and went on with Mr Browne to the camp, and I was glad to find every thing regular, the cattle properly attended to, the sheep right, and the camp in order, the garden dug and sown, and the place on the whole looking neat. In the afternoon Mr Stuart came up, and we were once more assembled only to separate in a day or two.

As I was now bent on a distant excursion, my first care was to put the camp in a state of defence in the event of its being attacked during my absence by the natives. I marked out and drew the place of a stockade that I directed Mr Stuart to erect without loss of time, and I ordered that all the firearms and ammunition should be deposited in the tent in the centre of it, that on the first indication of hostility the sheep were to be driven into the stockade, and that the men were not unnecessarily to expose themselves to the spears of the natives. On the 11th some natives came to the camp who I fed well and to whom I made some trifling presents. We had not seen many, but it was clear that at times they assemble in this neighbourhood in great numbers. Having given Mr Stuart detailed instructions for his guidance, and ordered Morgan to get the boat painted and prepared in the event of her being wanted, I again left the Depôt, Dearest, on the 14th accompanied by Mr Browne with Flood, Joseph and Lewis.

I took the spring cart, 4 pack horses, and 15 weeks provisions. This journey would in truth decide the failure or the success of the Expedition. If we find water I see no reason to doubt that we shall pass into the tropics in six weeks from this date, but unless rain falls our supply of surface water will be sure to fail, indeed it is already almost exhausted, in which case we shall be beat back. From what I saw of the neighbourhood of Lake Torrens, I fear that we may descend into a region where there will be a succession of shallow basins of dry lakes. That the whole of this region has been covered by the sea is evidenced by many things. By its exceeding low level, the level of the ocean, by the want of timber, by the salsolaceous character of its productions, and by the deposition of sands upon its surface, that are in truth so many land waves over an earth sea, so that if we fall to a lower level we may naturally expect a change for the worse. We must, however, take our chance and run all risks, adopting every prudent plan for our own safety.

From the Depôt, Dearest, I moved on a bearing of 335°, that is to say 25° to the west of north, or as a sailor would term it a N.N.W. course, the variation of the magnetic needle being 5° easterly. I found that I could not take a more westerly course from the impracticable nature of the country. For a few miles after we left the Depôt on the course I have taken up it was decidedly better than the country between the Depôt and Lake Torrens, but this improvement was only temporary, and at about 10 miles we found ourselves toiling over sand hills the number of which in the interval of another 10 miles I had the curiosity to cross, and they amounted to 63 that at the mean height of 30 ft gave 1890 feet of ascent for the horses in 10 miles. We halted at 20 miles without water. The sand ridges hereabouts ran N.E. and S.W., a fact you must bear in mind.

On the 15th, Dearest, we passed thro' a country similar to that of yesterday. At 6 miles from where we slept we found a small puddle of filthy water, but we breakfasted on it, and before we left I sank a well to catch any rain water that might fall. At 11 miles more we descended into a flat in which there was a good deal of water and here I halted for the night, and we employed our time in digging a large tank to secure our retreat, such were the expedients and shifts we had to make for our safety.

The night of the 15th was very cold with a S.W. wind. The morning temperature was 42°. We found the country more open as we advanced. The flats were broader, and of a mixed soil and some of them had fragments of stones scattered over them, but they were not deficient in grass. The sand ridges, or as I shall call them, the land waves, were much higher and of a fiery red covered with spinifex, gheum and a kind of polygonum, the acacia having been replaced by the scarlet banksia. We travelled 24 miles without seeing a drop of surface water and at length encamped by another of those muddy puddles, which circumstances alone forced us to drink, half clay and half water.

Today our road lay over a changeable region. The flats were of increased breadth and the land waves higher, but for some miles there was no scarcity of grass on the flats. They were however all subject to flood, and the piles of rubbish at the foot of ridges shews that at times they must be three or four feet under water. About noon, we crossed a polygonum flat, in which there were several fine pools of water from two to three feet deep with some of which we cleared our throats and washed ourselves. For the last 6 miles the country fell off in appearance, the flats were of a white clay without a blade of vegetation upon them, and they were full of deep holes. The view from the top of the land waves was over a most dreary region to whichever point of the compass we turned, and no poor travellers could have blanker prospects before them than we had, with a wild and difficult desert to traverse, threatened with a total failure of water, and no indication whatever of a change of weather. However, I thought that I observed a considerable fall of the country from the north to the south as I crossed some of the flats, and an apparent inclination in the land to form creeks, but I was very probably deceived. We have again halted, Dearest, without water for our horses, but having a two gallon cask with us we have some of the good water from the polygonum flat for our tea. We are living exclusively on 5 lb of flour and 2 oz of tea a week, for neither Mr Browne nor I can venture to touch salt pork. How long we shall do on such fare I don't know, but I hold out as yet tolerably. And now, Dearest Charlotte, adieu. I am writing by lamp light and it somewhat tires my eyes. God in his Mercy bless you and maybe enable me to compass my wishes, to ensure future comfort and tranquillity to you. God bless you and my dear, dear children.

Sunday August 24th 1845

I do not know why it should be so, Dearest, but my spirits have for the last few days been unusually depressed in so much that I cannot shake off the emotions that have seized me. If therefore my journal of this week should be tinged with any feeling of depression you will know that there is no apparent cause for it.

On Monday last we had a cold wind blowing from the eastward, and there were some heavy clouds about, an unusual appearance here where the vault of heaven is generally as clear as crystal. The clouds, however, were rising up from the west in direct opposition to the way they always do. On Sunday the wind was from the west and the few clouds that traversed the sky rose from the east. Today it is reversed the wind is in the east quarter and the clouds are rising from the west, but I suppose it will all end in nothing, tho' in any other part of the world one would have prepared for rain.

We started at 7 o'clock and after crossing three land waves of great height descended from the last to a plain of great extent extending to the north and south further than we could see, and about 3 miles broad. At the western extremity of this plain there was a thick line of gum trees running directly across our track, but as they were denser to the S.W. than in the direction in which we were moving, I sent Flood to examine the neighbourhood there. On reaching the trees Mr Browne and I found ourselves on the banks of a fine creek.$^{\varrho}$ There was a fine sheet of water 150 yards broad upon our right. The creek had a good deal of grass under open box forest on either side of it, and it promised well coming apparently from the north and falling to the south. Flood on rejoining me told me that he had not found any water but that below the trees to which I had sent him it appeared to spread over the plains, but he said there was an abundance of grass in its vicinity. Thinking that this creek might turn out to be of importance, I determined on stopping for an hour or two, and sent Mr Browne with Flood to ride some eight or ten miles up it.

In the meantime I looked about and found two native huts. At the fires near them were the claws of crayfish, similar to those on the Murray and I thought I recognised amongst the other bones the vertebrae of some fish. On Mr Browne's return he informed me that a little above where he left me the creek had no channel but spread over a grassy flat, then at 7 miles he came on a tolerably large pond of water, but that he did not think there was any water beyond, that the country to the north was very level, and the sand ridges much lower. He had seen three natives an old man and two women, the latter of whom, contrary to their usual custom, had their two front teeth punched out and the man like all the other natives we had seen was circumcised. They understood a few words Mr Browne spoke, and told him that there was both water and hills to the N.E. I did not however think possible on their information to alter my course, and as Mr Browne had had a long ride, I remained where I was for the day. When we started on Tuesday, Dearest, we had a mile of the plain thro' which the creek flows to cross, to get to a little hill that had served as a point of bearing. From its summit, the view to the north was over an exceedingly level country. Extensive flats, the dry beds of lagoons stretched farther than the range of vision in that direction which must during seasons of flood contain immense bodies of water. From this little hill we crossed a small plain to a lofty sandy pile, the abrupt termination of a land wave, and descended to a plain of great extent. Running along this plain for eight miles we crossed a polgyonum flat in which Mr Browne saw a new and beautiful parrot, but did not shoot it. We shortly afterwards crossed a dry creek but found a pond of good water under some box trees near it, and we ultimately halted at 18 miles, at another small water hole. Here we could see to an immense distance across the plain and we should most likely have had to stop without water if we had gone on.

On the 20th, Dearest, we left the little water hole at which we had slept at 8 o'clock and traversed plains of great extent, the fall of the country being to the N.W. longitudinally along them. These plains were bounded by sand hills entirely different from the heavy and fiery waves we have left behind us. The country was entirely denuded of trees, excepting a few box trees that grew round the edges of the flooded flats or on the banks of creeks. It was a most monotonous and dreary region, and I felt weary of toiling over so interminable a desert. At 10 miles we crossed a line of gum trees and a fine creek coming apparently from the N.E. but there was no water in it. Extensive plains having deep fissures and holes in them and perfectly destitute of vegetation lay to the westward of it, in crossing which I feared the horses would break their legs. At 3 miles we ascended a sand hill from which we saw at the further extremity of a plain between them and us and distant from five to six miles, a line of box trees, to which we crossed, and being fortunate in finding water, I stopped for the night. The trees masked a creek of some size that promised to be of considerable importance to us, as it appeared to turn in our course. Its bed was broad and grassy, and its banks were ornamented by a beautiful new and graceful tree in addition to the box tree.

Thus, Dearest, it appeared that these creeks were a peculiar feature in that region, occurring at intervals of from 10 to 15 miles. Most providential is it for us that such is the case, or I may now say was the case, for all the surface water left by the late rains has long since disappeared. Their watercourses are however of singular formation. They apparently rise in one plain to spread over and to terminate on another. They are only a few miles long so that a course a few degrees either to the north or to the west of the one I have taken up would have carried us wide of them. Equally providential therefore has been our striking them in succession as we have done been, as the fact of their existence in a low and level country far beyond the point at which the creeks from the hills have ceased. Their occurrence in truth is a puzzle to me that I must endeavour to make out.

In walking a little way down the bed of the creek Mr Browne passed two more water holes, and told me on his return that it was much broader below than where we were. I had myself been up the creek, and had come on a village of 18 huts, and I observed that there were broad native paths leading from angle to angle of the creek, as if at certain seasons the natives assembled in great numbers on it. I also passed some graves that had been made longitudinally from north to south and not from east to west as is the general custom.

I was disappointed on leaving our camp that at a mile and a half the creek turned too much to the westward for us to follow it. We therefore continued onwards over bare and blistered plains and at 6 miles crossed a branch creek with a large pool of water in it. We then ascended some broken sand hills grouped together in confusion and from there descended to a firm and grassy plain of about 4 miles in breadth. Crossing this we again ascended a broken mass of sand hills, and observing a line of gum trees a little to the westward of our course, and it being late in the evening, I turned towards them and finding that they masked a creek with several large ponds of water in it I halted for the night.

On Friday we started at 8 and crossed the creek about 100 yards below where we had slept. We then traversed a large plain obliquely and at 6 miles ascended some broken sand hills, this formation having succeeded the land waves more to the S.E. At a mile and a half we descended to a large plain at the western extremity of which we struck the dry but grassy bed of a large creek. Crossing this, we rose by a gradual ascent to the summit of some sand hills beyond it, and again descended to a large plain at the further extremity of which there was also a row of box trees running from north to south. The banks of this creek however were so steep that the cart could not descend into it and we had to run northerly along it for five miles before we found a convenient place to cross it. We had then left the last water hole about a mile below us, so that I continued to the north and at ½ a mile arrived at a nice clear little water hole at which we encamped. On tasting this water we found it as I suspected from its clearness to be slightly brackish but it was not disagreeable to the taste. I don't know what put it into his head but Mr Browne fancied there were fish in it, and getting Lewis to make him a pin hook, he rigged a line and went down to the water to try his fortune when he caught a dish of nice silver perch. How these fish could possibly have got into that hole I cannot imagine. They could not originally have dropped there from a cloud? There were none in the water above which was perfectly sweet, only in this brackish hole. It is one of those anomalies in this anomalous country for which I cannot see any satisfactory explanation.

Leaving this creek yesterday, Dearest, at immediately below where we had slept it spread over a plain, we ascended some hills of clay rather than of sandy formation, that continued for two miles. From these we ascended to a barren region of salt formation on which nothing but samphire and other salsolaceous plants were growing. At three miles we crossed the half dry bed of a salt lagoon and then for eight miles traversed the most desolate wilderness on earth, but at that distance we suddenly came on a line of box trees and passing through them found ourselves on the outskirts of some beautiful grassy plains studded with trees tho' surrounded by sand hills, and more like a nobleman's park than anything else. So rapid are the changes from good to bad and from bad to good in these regions. In crossing these plains we surprised 4 native women thrashing out seeds. One of them was of a jet black colour and had curly hair, and was evidently of a distinct race. Apprehensive, I suppose, that we should seize upon them, the other 3 offered us this fair damsel, but we declined the present. They were most earnest in assuring us that there was no water in the direction in which we were going but plenty in the opposite one. However, as I doubted what these ladies said, I pursued my own way and soon found out what had made them so anxious to turn us away. Their huts were close to an almost exhausted waterhole about a mile off and their little children were playing about. As soon as they saw us they crept into their huts and hid themselves, but I went round not to frighten the poor little things. I rode some way down the bed of the little creek in which the water was to find another hole that I might not encamp near them, but could not find one, and Joseph having met with an accident by cutting his eyelids in two with his whip, I was obliged to stop opposite to the native camp.

About sunset the chief came home, a fine handsome-looking fellow of about 30. He had his spears with him and other war weapons and had I suppose been to some corroborie, as he was painted all over. He was exceedingly indignant at our having taken up our quarters so near him and threatened to go and muster his tribe and to drive us away. We did everything we could to pacify him but to no purpose. On the contrary, our kindness seemed to impress him with the idea that we were afraid and as I was determined he should not entertain that notion, I soon gave him to understand that I cared very little for him and all his tribe and I soon cooled him down altho' he continued exceedingly sulky. We therefore left him to enjoy his ill-humour, intending to go back in about an hour and to give him a tomahawk, but when I did so I found he had decamped, and the only trouble it gave me was to be a little more watchful that night, or as I should have said last night but I go on writing as if I was writing of a distant past period, without reflecting that every day brings me nearer the present.

My mind, indeed, is oppressed with some weight and I fear I am making but a lame and sorry account of this, but it is for you Dearest Charlotte, and you will excuse its errors and imperfections I know. I write it only for your amusement and that you may be made aware of the nature of the service in which I have been engaged, and the difficulties that have or may beset me.

I had hoped from the nature of the sand hills we had lately crossed that we should not again encounter such terrific obstacles as the land waves I have already described to you. This morning we started with fair prospects, and for eight miles had an easy road through open box forest. We then ascended some sand hills that gradually changed their colour from that of sea sand to a fiery red, and became higher and higher the further we advanced.[R] The valleys were filled with sand, grass disappeared and spinifex alone covered the ground. At length the bare tops of the land waves became so precipitous that we could hardly get the cart over them. It is impossible for me, Dearest, to describe to you the character and appearance of these singular heaps. They were much steeper on the eastern than on the western side, and were the gigantic similitudes of the ripples left by the tide in its ebb and flow. We toiled over this heavy and dreadful country until the sun had set, and have halted without water in one of the valleys. Nevertheless, in strolling about after we had encamped, Mr Browne, from the summit of one of the ridges, saw a distant glimmering as of water, and after walking about two miles to ascertain if it really was water, or not, he arrived at a small pool, to which we shall remove in the morning, the horses being too tired to push on tonight. What our destinies will be next week it is difficult to say, but I cannot anticipate any favourable change.

Goodnight, Dearest,and may God bless you and all around you. Would I could only know that all was going well at my once happy home, I should care little for disappointments here.

Sunday August 31st 1845

Altho' I take up my pen only once a week to write to you, believe me, my Dearest Charlotte, you are never out of my thoughts. Whether I am pushing over deserts, or pouring over my chart, whether I am engaged in any occupation or am lying on my mattress it is all the same. A foreboding of evil tidings that await my return, if to return I am permitted, adds tenfold to the anxiety attendant on this difficult undertaking. Your eye may never glance over these pages. Some corner in the nursery may be unoccupied. Some untoward event had I am sure long since occurred to weigh thus heavily on my mind and to add the horrors of suspense to my other cares. Here I am day after day increasing my distance from that spot to which I would I had the wings of the eagle to cleave my way, but it may be that I shall never cross my threshold again, or shall only cross it in sorrow. Be that as it may, I must bow to the Chastener, and abide my time.

Last Sunday, Dearest, as you will have gathered from my journal of the preceding week, we stopped amongst high and broken land waves, without water, but with the certainty of relief early on the following morning. Tonight we have halted under still less favourable circumstances. However of that in its proper place.

As you will suppose, we started early on Monday morning to relieve our horses, and stopped at the water Mr Browne had found to breakfast. This water was the drainage from a flat that opened upon an immense plain the character of which I shall presently have to describe to you.

I had almost determined on halting for the day at this water as there was something the matter with the cart that made it draw heavy, but as there was not much feed for the horses we went on, but coming on some more water at about a mile, where there was also plenty of grass, I pulled up with the intention of digging a large reservoir. But one of the men fortunately made a discovery that spared us the trouble, who, whilst strolling over the ridges, fell on a beautiful little serpentine sheet of water in a secluded valley, round which a number of box trees were growing. It was in truth a perfect oasis in the desert. A pretty, romantic spot, that one would not have expected to exist in so dreary a region.

The land waves, Dearest, had become so formidable that I dreaded to encounter them. Happily, however, they here ceased for a time as we found on continuing our journey on Tuesday that they abutted upon and terminated in the great plain over which I am now about to take you.[R]

At starting I altered my course somewhat to the north to avoid a sand ridge, without being aware of the character of the plain before me. On clearing it however I was astounded at the dark and gloomy space over which we had to go. Half the circumference of the horizon from the south point of the compass westward round to north an immense stony plain extended without any visible limit. We had no point no object on which move, but the whole expanse appeared to be as level as the ocean, nor had it as far as we could see a single shrub or a blade of vegetation upon it. The stones indeed lay so thick on the ground, that it was impossible for any herb to have forced its way between them.[60] We steered our course over this dreary desert as a ship at sea, and at 20 miles halted upon it for the night, on a clear sandy spot of sand on which there were a few tussocks of grass and a few gallons of water. We did not tether the horses for there was no fear of their venturing over the stones in reach of anything. On Wednesday morning we started early and on our old course pushed still deeper into this wilderness, to which I believe there is no parallel on the earth's surface. There could be no doubt but that these fragments of what were once mountains had been deposited where they now lie during some tremendous convulsion of waters. They were mostly of the same size from 4 to 6 inches long, were rounded by attrition, were very evenly distributed over the surface of the ground, and being tinged with the oxide of iron, they give the whole plain a deep purple tint. They were all of the same rock as that composing the northern group on which I had been, indurated quartz, and altho' small they were so hard as to have resisted the elements for ages.

At 10 miles we descended from this plain some five or six feet upon a polygonum flat of about two miles in breadth, the stony plain there ceasing to the northwest, but still stretching north and south farther than we could see.

From the polygonum we debouched upon a bare plain apparently as interminable as the stony plain. When I say bare I mean it in the strictest sense of the word. There was not an herb of any kind upon it. It was a space evidently subject to inundation for it was blistered on its surface and was intersected by water channels all making to the northeast as to a common center. There was not a tree on the visible horizon but all was as level as the sea. We had advanced about 10 miles into this singular region, when at length we saw four box trees ahead of us, it being near sunset at the time. Also the evening refraction threw up some sandhills on the farther side of this dreary waste of which I took the bearings, and we halted at the gum trees for the night to which we secured our horses, having water but nothing to eat.

As the sand hills bore north from where we stopped, I made for them in the morning and reached them at 11 miles, but even on them there was but little grass. However I gave the horses two hours and then pushed on on my old course leaving the land hill on my left, these it appeared having commenced again. In truth they abutted upon and terminated in the flooded flat as they had done on the stony plains, so that they seemed to have been broken by the force of waters when they swept over those lower levels. At about 4 miles I crossed the land hill, and descended to a box tree flat. On our way along the sand hill however we had a polygonum flat on our right. As we were riding along, "What is that Sir?", said Flood to me in the polygonum, whose sharp eyes were always at work. I could not see but Mr Browne observed a dark object on the ground towards which he rode. It proved to be a native woman who had crouched behind her platter, a large dish they carry for putting their roots in. Finding that this did not conceal her she jumped up and ran away, so I called Mr Browne back. It appeared however from the native being there that these deserts were not altogether uninhabited as you will find presently, altho' we saw none.

In the centre of the box forest we struck a very large creek but it was dry.[5] In running it down however we arrived at a native well of unusual dimensions. It was about eight feet wide at the top and 22ft deep, and it was a work that must have taken the joint strength of a powerful tribe to perform. There was a small cave hollowed out for the water of which there was but little in the well and that little tho' good was brackish. Well-beaten paths from every point of the compass led to this golden mine but none of them appeared to have been lately trodden. But the forest was alive with birds of all kinds whose shrill clear notes were new to us who had been traversing deserts as silent as the grave, and that dived into that gloomy recess to drink the life sustaining fluid it contained. A sad evidence of the state of the interior!!!

On following up the largest of the paths, Mr Browne and I came on a native village consisting of 23 huts many of them double and even treble having smaller or sleeping huts attached to the larger or common apartment-like [covers?]. It had not been inhabited since the seed-season and it was clear that this is the only time when the natives collect in any numbers.

We remained at this well all night, and on the following morning pursued our way over a bare plain to the northwest, and fortunately at seven miles struck a creek that had a broad but shallow sheet of water in it, and as the well had not supplied sufficient for the horses, I determined on giving them the rest of the day to themselves.

I do not know whether it was from the irregularity of the supply of their food, or that they had eaten something that disagreed with them, but at this place soon after our arrival the horses were seized with inflammation of the stomach, four or five of them swelled greatly, and Flood's horse was so bad that we were obliged to blister and bleed him. The poor animal was in great pain, and rolled violently on the ground. I saw him about 10 lying close to my tent, but in the morning he was nowhere to be found. I was consequently obliged to stop another day at this water hole, but we could not get on Rodney's tracks (he was the horse I bought from Mr Metcalf, and recovered at Moorundi) and as the other horses were all well, I left him to his fate and this morning pursued my way into the interior.

From the creek we traversed a plain that might in truth be said to have been torn to pieces by solar heat so full was it of deep yawning rents and chasms six or seven feet in depth. Into these the earth fell with a hollow sound and it ws with difficulty that we got our horses over it. We then advanced over barren plains but of firmer surface into a low scrub, and at 23 miles halted for the day in consequence of the extreme heat. We could not, however, procure any water and are now this our fourth Sunday without. There is close to us one of those shallow receptacles for water so common on the plains, at the bottom of which the natives have dug a hole to secure the water as long as they could, and a little mud still remains in it, to which the unhappy birds that used to drink of its purer element still resort. The surface water however is becoming so precarious, and the land waves to the N.W. so terrifically high, that I contemplate tomorrow changing my course to north in the hope of finding a more practicable country for if I am not very cautious I shall have my retreat altogether cut off. To add to my anxieties, too, Mr Browne I observe is very unwell. He tries to hide it from me but sometimes forgets himself and I can evidently see that that horrid disease has again attacked him. Such being the case I have only to thank God that I am not worse.

We have now penetrated direct into the interior from the Depôt 347 miles, but we have seen no change in this fearful and unparalleled desert. I have now lost all hope of finding any body of water or of making my discovery, and I feel that I am subjecting myself and others to all this exposure and privation solely to discharge my duty conscientiously. It is a service I sought with how different anticipations! But I may not shrink from it under any circumstances. Poor Mr Browne attends me malgré soi, and is heartily sick of traversing such a wilderness. How much more then, Dearest, must I yearn to turn my back on so dreary a region to fly to you and to my home once more, but weeks have yet to transpire ere I can feel myself justified in giving up this most difficult and most anxious task.

Sunday September 7th 1845

After due consideration, Dearest, last Monday I turned to the north in the hope that by thus altering my course I should find a better country, and more surface water. We started early and at the end of the scrub ran up a flat with steep hills of sand on either side of us. At 9 miles, we came upon two small puddles of water, at which I stopped for the remainder of the day. On Tuesday we continued our journey up the flat, but at 2 miles had to cross a sand ridge into the succeeding flat up which we travelled 5 miles to the base of another sand hill, at which we waited for the cart. On its coming up Joseph told me that he had met about a dozen natives and had stopped a short time with them and he had good-naturedly given his knife to one of them. How we missed these people I do not know, but I was sorry for it, more especially as they were at too great a distance for me to turn back.

We travelled for the remainder of the day up flats on which there were a good many box trees, and halted at 22 miles at two small puddles of water that were hardly fit for our horses to drink much less for ourselves. I thought but I knew not why that there was an improvement in the country. On Wednesday we again started early on a north course and at 5 miles found a small supply of water in a small creek. At 5 miles more we struck a magnificent creek, with very lofty banks and of great width. It had large but shallow pools of water in it, and its bed was full of grass and what was still more fortunate it was running N.N.W., and S.S.E. our old course. We therefore turned from the north and ran along its banks for twelve miles when we halted at a fine sheet of water and the horses were in clover. On the following day, Thursday, we continued our journey up the creek and again halted at 24 miles under very favourable circumstances, altho' the creek had in places shewn a decreased size. You will understand, Dearest, that we were running it up to the N.W. On Friday we kept wide of the creek to avoid lateral channels falling into it, but at 12 miles found ourselves on its banks. It still retained an abundance of water and grass, but it no longer looked the same creek up which we had been travelling. At the point at which we struck it, it made a sudden bend to the north-east and in following it up, we had to ascend an isolated sand hill when directly below us we saw a beautiful sheet of clear water, in the bed of another creek apparently coming from the north-east. The water was too clear and too blue to be fresh, as we found on tasting it, but it was covered with wild fowl none of which we could kill, and there were the tracks of many natives along its margin. The general course of the main creek having been N.N.W. I hoped that by cutting across this apparently new creek I should again find it, and accordingly striking over we passed some beautiful grassy meadow land, and on the herbage of which there were the withered stalks of a native millet, but we could not procure any of the seed. From this grassy land we traversed plains but could see nothing of the creek. At 8 miles we passed the foot of a sand hill having gradually advanced, I was sorry to observe, into a country of salt formation. The rhagodea had given place to samphire bushes and the atuplex to schlerolisae. The sand hills again assumed a formidable character and red colour, and in the valleys there were small white patches of waterholes on the dry surface of which salt had crystalized. It was hopeless to expect to find water in such a region, so that we halted 13 miles from the creek for the night.

Still under an impression that the main creek was to our left, I sent Mr Browne before we started to the westward to examine the country, whilst I proceeded slowly onwards. When he overtook me he told me that he had ridden over a most dreadful country, that he could see nothing of the creek, but had been stopped by a salt water creek in the bed of which there were ship-loads of beautiful salt. He stated that this creek was running north and south and as that was also nearly our course, and I foresaw that we could not expect any favourable change as long as we kept it on our left. I determined on crossing it at once, and therefore turn us a little more to the westward. The bed of the creek, however, was too soft to allow of the passage of the horses, so that I was obliged to give it up and to look out for a place. Its channel was as white as the driven snow and a dark line of samphire bushes growing on either side of it made it shew still whiter and you will be enabled to form some idea of the quantity of salt it contained when I tell you that it hid the surface of the deep, deep blue water and coated it like ice to the thickness of an inch and a half, and so strongly was the water saturated with the muriate of soda that it was stronger than any brine. At 2 miles we came to the head of this creek or the place where it originated, at the base of a sand hill, but there it was dry. Still in this singular creek, as in others, there were the lines of high floods. Whence, however, so near its sources could the waters come from to inundate it here?

Crossing the head of the creek, we continued onwards over plains of samphire for about seven miles, when we rose to the summit of a sand hill *traversing* our course instead of running *parallel* to it. From the summit of this hill the country appeared to dip slightly to the N.N.W. There were long and terrific sand ridges close to each other running in that direction with valleys of about a quarter of a mile wide between them, with a dark line of acacia trees (of the kind that never grow near water) down their centre. Taking down one of these we rode on for eight miles, when I stopped to consider what I should do. The horses had already been one night without water, and the poor animals were not in a condition to endure privations in weather that was so hot as that which now prevailed. I saw that we were on a sandy table land of apparently interminable extent and on which there was not the remotest chance of our finding water. Grass had entirely disappeared and the horses wound about working their way through the pointed spinifex with which the ground was universally covered. Ascending one of the sand ridges I saw a numberless succession of these terrific objects rising above each other to the east and west of me. Northwards they ran away before me for more than fifteen miles, with the most undeviating straightness, as if those masses had been thrown up with the plumb and rule. How much farther they went with the same undeviating regularity God only knows, but I find it utterly impossible, Dearest, to describe the appearance of the country to you. As I have told you, the ridges were covered with spinifex but only to a certain height. Their summits and about ten feet down either side were perfectly bare, and the hue of vegetation and of barrenness were as strongly marked as the limits of perpetual snow on the sides of the Andes. There was a species of mesembryanthemum that happened to be in blossom and so thickly does it bloom that it gave to the ground its own purple and sulphureous tint between long lines of fiery red, whilst the valleys [were] occupied by dark masses of acacia trees. But I cannot describe the ground so that you must assist me when I get back. The scene was awfully fearful, dear Charlotte. A kind of dread (and I am not subject to such feelings) came over me as I gazed upon it. It looked like the entrance into Hell. Mr Browne stood horrified. "Did man", he exclaimed, "ever see such a place?!" "It is bad enough indeed," I replied, "and I fear we can hardly hope to do anything by going on." In truth, Dearest, I saw that Mr Browne was not in a fit condition for me to expose him to hardship. I expected every morning to hear that the fatal blackness had shewn itself on his legs, and I could [not] bear the thoughts of my kind and only remaining companion dropping beside me. I determined therefore to turn back to the creek and to try some other quarter. Accordingly we pushed back as far as we could and today reached a pool below the salt lagoon in which the water is fresh, and we have discovered to our astonishment that the salt lagoon is also in the bed of the creek, and that the creek continues beyond it.

Sunday September 14th 1845

You will have seen, Dearest, at the conclusion of my journal of last week, that I had been forced back to the creek in consequence of the dreadful nature of the country to the northward and westward. On Monday I determined to examine the creek more narrowly which I had found to continue on beyond the salt lagoon. Mr Browne and I accordingly mounted our horses, and rode up it to a distance of eleven miles, when we ascended the terminating point of a sand hill in the centre of a large plain, and from it surveyed the country. The plain was surrounded on all sides by sand hills, and it was clear that in it the creek took its rise. I saw therefore that there was no hope in that quarter. We therefore turned back, and I ultimately made up my mind to try a westerly course in the morning. Now we had invariably met the worst country to the westward, but baffled as I was at all other points, I thought that I might here be more successful. We started therefore on Tuesday on a due west course from the creek, and had soon to repent of the step we had taken. At a mile we encountered an immense sand hill that had been hid from our view by trees. From its summit we saw that we were already on the margin of the salt formation. The valley below us was dark with samphire bushes, and white with salt that blew into our faces and eyes like snow drifts before the heavy breeze that was blow[ing], and to the westward there were a succession of sand hills gradually increasing in height as far as the eye could reach. My heart sank within me at so hopeless a prospect. This was the journey on which we hoped to pass the desert, to make the centre, but all was apparently blighted. I continued onwards however for about 8 miles when I ascended the loftiest hill we had seen for some time from which too I had the same forbidding scene before. Joseph had enough to do to get the horses up it and when he did, he reported to me that the wheels of the cart were in such a state that it could go no further. On examining them I found that they were indeed in a shattered state, and I doubted how far we should be able to get the cart back to the creek. However by patching and cordage we managed it and once more took up our quarters on the water hole. Wednesday, Dearest, was devoted to the repair of the cart. In the meantime I resolved in my mind what I should do and I ultimately decided on trying a north-east course notwithstanding the unfavourable appearance of the country in that direction.

We started then on Thursday morning up the creek and at 18 miles came to a part of its bed that was very grassy, and there were some green polygonum bushes, near which there was, I had no doubt, some little water still remaining. I therefore stopped for the cart, and sent Flood to ascertain if there was any water or not, who after an anxious search found a small muddy puddle, so that I resolved on remaining where we were for the night.

On the morrow we again pushed on and at four miles got to the head of the plain in which the creek rises. We then ascended the sand hills by which it is surrounded, and immediately descended to a country of salt formation. Traversing a large plain covered with samphire we ascended some lofty sand hills at its opposite extremity, and found ourselves in a country exactly similar to that from which I had been forced back on a north-west course.

Gigantic red sand hills running parallel to each other for miles upon miles, dark and gloomy valleys, and a region overgrown with spinifex and mesembryanthemum. Nevertheless I pushed on, until at length I observed that Mr Browne was suffering very acutely. A sudden thought struck me on which I determined immediately to act. I gave up the attempt to push on and told Mr Browne that I had resolved on returning to the Depôt. That night our horses had nothing to eat or to drink. We fastened them to acacia bushes and there they stood all night.

Yesterday, Dearest, we kept more to the eastward on our return to the creek, and this morning found ourselves once more upon our old ground over the water hole near the lagoon.

I could have gone a few miles further than I did if I had left the cart, but we had seen 20 natives armed but by no means hostile, yet I did not like leaving the men under such circumstances as it would not have done for me to have found them killed on my return.

The furthest point we gained, Dearest, was latitude 24..40..00 S. and longitude 138 . . 00 . . 00 East.[T] We were then about 70 miles from the tropics but it is a most remarkable fact that I have to state to you – no alteration took place in the vegetation or natural productions of the country from the banks of the Darling to that distant spot. There were the same trees, the same shrubs and the same grasses as we had found both on the banks of the Murray and of the Darling, nor was there a single plant to be seen from the character of which we could have supposed that we were drawing near regions so marked for its vegetable productions.

The weather had been cloudy for several days and last night the vapours appeared to be low and we had partial and gentle rain during the night, altho' it was not sufficient to saturate our blankets. Still, Dearest, I was truly thankful even for such rain as it was. It might, I thought, have fallen heavier to the south, and would enable us to return to the Depôt without suffering or loss. At all events it cooled the air of that burning region and gave us one sateful day out of three hundred.

We started our return this morning knowing that our progress down the creek would be rapid and prosperous, and we had made about 20 miles and encamped somewhat below our third encampment on coming up the creek.

Sunday September 21st 1845

I had, Dearest, as I told you when I last took up my pen, determined on returning to the Depôt, but it would now have become a question how I should have effected that retreat. I could not have hoped for water for 140 miles after leaving the creek and, believe me, it would have been a difficult job to have got our poor exhausted animals over such a distance without water, but as I also told you, it pleased God, in this the moment of our difficulty, to send rain that was sufficient for our relief and no more.

We started on Sunday, Dearest, on our return. On Monday and Tuesday we make rapid progress, and about noon of the latter day having struck the point at which we struck the creek and given our horses a good drink of water, we left it and turned southwards. There was no water in the first water holes from it, but as we passed several rain puddles at which the horses always drank a little they did not require much. Fortunately we found a little water in the second water-holes on Thursday that altho' unfit for our use did for the horses, and at them we stopped for the night. On Friday we passed the little native well that had been so judiciously placed that it had been filled by the rain. Here our horses took a good drink and we gained a day on our outward journey by pushing on to the creek at which we left Flood's horse. On Friday we again gained a day by passing the large native well in the box tree forest and gaining our encampment on the muddy flats. On Saturday we encamped on the stony plain without water, and today, Dearest, we reached the valleys in which Mr Browne and Lewis found water as we went out. But the pretty little serpentine sheet was gone, and of the other two holes that on which we the least depended had the most water in it.

I forgot to tell you that as we again passed the polygonum flat in which we saw the woman crouched behind her platter, we saw a tribe of natives or I should rather say a family. They were at some distance from us. An old man, however, mustered courage to come over to us solely with a view to tell us that the horse we had lost was gone to the eastward. He called it a 'Cadli' as being the largest four-legged animal of such he knew. Mr Browne good-naturedly gave him a pocket handkerchief of blazing red with which he was delighted. We afterwards crossed the tracks of the horse going in the direction in which the old man said he went, but it is doubtful to me if he crossed the stony plain. No horse would willingly have faced that iron sea.

Sunday September 28th 1845

On Monday, my Dearest Charlotte, we had again to toil over the heavy and terrific sand hills, by which we were so much embarrassed on Sunday the[21st September]. It is a long and dreary road across them to the grassy plains, and it was full sunset before we halted about two miles short of our old encampment. We were a little delayed by our search for water in consequence of our seeing some blacks on the plains who all ran away from us. We found another of the large wells I have already described to you but there was not sufficient water in it to supply our wants. However, after we had encamped, Joseph stumbled on a little puddle, to which we removed and I gave the horses Tuesday to recover from their fatigues. On Wednesday we gained the fish pond^U where Mr Browne was luckier than ever and caught seven dozen nice little fish, that made no bad fry for us poor famished beings who had so long confined to 5 lb of flour a week and 2 ozs of tea, for all birds were so exceedingly wild that we seldom shot anything.

On Friday, Dearest, we made the third creek, and yesterday, instead of going to the creek at which we before stopped, we passed it knowing that we should not find any water, and made for a clump of trees to which I had sent Mr Browne as we came out and at which we found an abundance both of feed and water. As we were riding along some natives called to us, and on going up to them, they told us that they came from the north and were going to water, that all the water to the north was gone, and that they had been a long time without any. Their lips were parched and cracked and swollen, and they appeared reduced to the last extremity, and at length started off at a rapid trot. When I told them I had been to the north-west they shook their heads, and said there was no water there either. I really do not know what these poor creatures will do if the drought continues, as every water hole we have seen must shortly be dry. It is a most dreadful region.

Today, Dearest, we reached the first creek and are now only 76 miles from the Depôt. All my men are knocked up, my horses are very weak and Mr Browne exceedingly unwell. However we shall reach the camp in three days, I hope, when they will have temporary rest. There was one day in this week – there was one day, my Dearest and my Beloved Charlotte, that did not pass over unremembered by me. It was the 24th. A day which I ought to look upon as the happiest day of my life since it had placed within my grasp, every blessing that man may desire on this earthly stage, but whilst I acknowledged the goodness of Providence in thus having filled up the measure of its bounties, by giving me a good and an affectionate wife, and such children as were mine, I had to reproach myself alone for all the sorrow, and I will say affliction, of which I had subsequently tasted. I may not however trust myself on this subject. You will know from the little I have said, that even in this wilderness my thoughts are thrown back upon the past.

Sunday October 5th 1845

I am writing to you, my Dearest Charlotte, from the Depôt Camp at which on my arrival I was glad to find every thing regular. Mr Stuart reported to me that the men had been very attentive so that neither bullock [n]or sheep was missing.

We had a long and fatiguing journey on Monday, and halted at 26 miles without water. We had to cross a great many sand hills, but I was astonished at their comparatively low appearance when contrasted with the gigantic masses we had encountered to the north-west.

On the 30th we reached the flat in which we dug a well, and found it about a quarter full but the water was very muddy. However it partly relieved the horses and gave them a better chance of getting home safe. On Wednesday we started early having a journey of 37 miles before us, and about 9 got to the first well we had sunk in which I did not hope to find any water remaining. However to our astonishment there were three or four buckets of clear water still in it. I determined therefore on giving this to the cart horses alone, and on riding ahead with Mr Browne and Flood to gain the camp as soon as possible. I desired Joseph to give the cart horses a bucket of water apiece and then to turn them out to feed, to harness them in two or three hours, and after giving them what water might remain, to push on as far as he could so as to shorten his journey for the morrow.

We reached the tents just at sunset, and dismounted after an absence of seven weeks of as excessive exposure as any to which man was ever subjected. We had ridden from first to last a distance of 963 miles, and had generally been on horse-back from the earliest dawn to 3 or 4 often to 6 o'clock, having no shelter of any kind from the tremendous heat of the fiery deserts in which we had been wandering, subsisting on an insufficient supply of food, and drinking water that your pigs would have refused.

How I have stood it so well I know not, but although I feel that that horrid disease has still a hold of me, I have been free from the pains with which Mr Browne had been afflicted, and have returned certainly the least sufferer in the party. Joseph and Lewis came up on the following day, but they had evidently had great difficulty in getting the horses on.

Thus, my Dearest Charlotte, terminated an excursion that was to decide the success or failure of the expedition. A second time had we been forced back from the interior, conquered alike by the difficulties of the country, the severity of the season and the scarcity of water, and I had the painful reflection before me that whatever my exertions had been, I had made no discovery to entitle me to credit or reward, and that therefore I should fail in the only object for which I sought and undertook this tremendous and anxious task. Providence had denied that success to me with which it had been pleased to crown my former efforts, and I felt that instead of benefitting those for whose happiness and welfare I had made such sacrifices, I should only have inflicted an injury upon them. In vain had I prayed to the Almighty for success on this to me all important occasion. In vain had I implored for a blessing on you and on my children, if not on myself. But my prayer had been rejected, my petition refused, and so far from any ray of hope having ever crossed my path I felt that I had been contending against the very powers of Heaven, in the desperate show I had made against the seasons, and I now stood blighted and a blasted man over whose head the darkest destiny had settled. God knows Charlotte that I have not been influenced by any feeling of selfishness or of restlessness in that I have done. I thank God my own heart acquits me of that if you or the world will not. I sought this service to make atonement for the past, to make up to you for all the sorrow I had given you, and to obtain leisure that I might devote it to my children, but difficulties and disappointments have overwhelmed me from first to last, and altho' I have done twice as much perhaps as I should have done under more favourable circumstances, yet shall I fail in the attainment of these good objects because I have been unsuccessful.

Sunday October 12th 1845

When I last took up my pen, my Dearest Charlotte, I was at the Depôt. I am once again a wanderer from it having left it on the 9th with Mr Stuart my draftsman, Morgan and Mack, leaving Mr Browne in charge of the camp. But before I give you any account of my present movements it will be necessary for me to detail to you what has led to them.

I think I told you in its proper place that a sudden thought or determination had struck me, that induced me the more readily to turn back to the Depôt, from the extreme point to which we had gone.

I did not think it necessary to speak to Mr Browne on the subject until we should reach the camp, for I knew it would try his feelings, and I was uncertain in what state I should find the party to enable me to carry out my views. Having found everything regular, I one day sent for Mr Browne to my tent, and after he had sat down, I said that I had sent for him to speak to him on a subject on which I was most anxious. "I am about to make a proposition to you," I added, "that may startle you, but I hope you will see reason to concur in it. If indeed you have encouraged any kindly feelings towards me on account of our having been thus accidentally thrown together I am sure you will. I will", I said, "deal frankly with you Browne. I have returned from this excursion not only dissatisfied with its results but with my own exertions. My conscience tells me that I have fallen short in my former efforts, and altho' I am aware why I did not push my investigations further than I did, I cannot reconcile myself to the idea of returning back to Adelaide under existing circumstances, in truth I could not return. Mr Poole," I continued, "whether authorised by you to do so or not I will not enquire, often spoke to me about you, and assured me that our detention at the Depôt was equally injurious to your prospects and to your health. It was in consequence of this that I gave you at the time the option of going back with Mr Poole if you wished, but I did not press the matter because Mr Poole also told me that you hoped to find good land in the province to which you might raise your sheep. It has latterly," I said,"pained me to see you suffering as you have done and whether I acted on a right feeling or not I could not bear the idea of your sinking on this journey. It is enough for me that one has fallen, I would not that your loss should be added to it, and it was because I saw that your strength was not equal to the fatigues I should myself have undergone if you had not been with me that I returned to the Depôt. Now," I said, "what I would propose is that you should make the best of your way back to Adelaide. In two months you will be in the bosom of your family, and will have the rest you so much require. Leave me here with Mr Stuart, Morgan and Mack, and with the provisions you will be able to spare me, I shall have it in my power to make another effort to cross the desert and will then follow you home."

It was some time before Mr Browne made any reply. At length he said, "Have you considered the means necessary for carrying out your project – the quantity of provisions, the number of horses you will require?" "I have", I replied, "but with these matters I do not consider you have anything to do. I now wish to adopt that plan of operation which I think most conducive to the public advantage. All I wish to know from you is whether you will thwart those views or not." "You must give me an hour or two to consider," he replied, and left the tent.

In about two hours, Dearest, Mr Browne returned. He was evidently excited but he sat down and remained silent for some time. At last he said that he had been considering the proposal I had made and that he could not and would not desert me in such an infernal desert as this, that I had always treated him like a brother and that he would sooner die than return to Adelaide without me. "I am sorry," I said, "Browne that you have viewed the matter in such a light, and that you have come to such a resolution for it will only oblige me to order you to do that as a point of duty which I rather you did on the score of friendship." "Well", he said, "if you order me I will resign my post and then I may do as I please." "Excuse me," I said, "you cannot. If you were anywhere where I could supply your place you might but not here. It would be taking an unworthy and ungenerous advantage of your situation. It has," I observed, "been my curse through life to have friends instead of officers about me, to be taken care of, to be given in charge to instead of being looked upon as one who was leading a difficult and arduous service. But," I added,"you know what urged me to leave my home. You know that I have got my affairs confused, and that I undertook this fearful task in the hope of benefitting my family. What hope is there for me if I return to Adelaide now having literally done nothing, and with the means still in my power of doing more? How could I meet Captain Grey, how [could] my wife endure a consciousness that I had fallen short of my duty? How could I reconcile myself to Sir Ralph Darling or expect any reward from the Secretary of State? On the contrary I am sure I should not survive my return a year. I am not," I added, "like a young explorer, more will be expected from me than from such, and I am sure Browne your own breast will subscribe to the truth of everything I have said." "I admit it," he replied, "I admit it, but I cannot desert you. I owe you much for your great kindness to me, and I promised Mrs Sturt that I would remain by you to the last. I cannot and will not leave you," and bursting into tears he rushed out of the tent.

Now, Dearest, however much I might have acknowledged Mr Browne's generous devotion if I may call it, I could not see anything but ruin in it to us both, and I felt that I would not allow myself to be influenced by it. I therefore sent for Mr Stuart and gave him orders to warn Morgan and Mack to attend me with himself to the north on Thursday the 9th. I then sent for Flood and told him to have eight of the horses, 4 riding and 4 pack, ready for me to leave the camp on that day with ten weeks' provisions. Shortly afterwards Mr Browne came to me. "You are going out again," he said, "may I ask for what length of time?" "Why," I said, "I do not think you have any right to ask. It is not in your department, neither are you interested in the matter." "Will you then permit me to ask who you intend leaving in charge of the camp?" "You" I said, "have declined all responsibility, therefore I must leave it in charge of the individual in whom amongst the men I have the most confidence." "Captain Sturt," said Mr Browne, "you have misunderstood me. I have not wished to avoid responsibility but I have wished to avoid doing that which appeared to me to be a desertion of my friend. It was to tell you this that I came to you and I am sorry you hurt at what I have said. I will willingly take charge of the camp during your absence and do anything to serve you. I acknowledge therefore of what you have said and see the necessity of your satisfying your own mind, and therefore I will not try to dissuade you from your intended journey."

"Well then," I observed, "if such are your feelings I shall leave the camp more satisfied, and I will as soon as I have completed my arrangements make you acquainted with them. I propose," I said, answering his first question, "taking ten weeks provisions with me, but unless rain falls, you may expect me back before half that time has elapsed." I had in truth in starting from the Depôt 80 miles to go without water, and I knew not how soon it might fail us altogether.

I had had a small fortification or blockade erected of logs at the Depôt capable of a stout resistance and sufficiently large not only to contain the sheep but to give the men plenty of room to move about. It was on a rising bank on which there were when we came some native huts. There was a large sheet of water in front and the spot altogether was pretty enough. This I called "Fort Grey"[v]. It had not had any rain, if I except the partial shower on the 14th,

August since the two days rain that enabled us to move from the old Depôt now three months, whilst on the other hand the heat had been terrific. However I had every reason to anticipate rain either at the close of this or the beginning of the next month as we had had heavy rain in November 1844 and all the vegetable kingdom appeared to be waiting for this seasonable fall. Notwithstanding, I felt it necessary to make arrangements with Mr Browne before I left the camp for his retreat in the event of the water at the Depôt drying up. I left it discretionary with him to go over the hills or to take the direct road 61 miles to the old Depôt without water, and I directed that a large and deep well should be sunk in the creek for our use in the event of Mr Browne finding it advisable to retire.

Having given all necessary orders, and everything being ready I bid Mr Browne goodbye. It was the first time we had so separated, and with my party once more took my way to the north-west on Thursday the 9th inst, intending to make the first creek and then to run it up northerly. We halted at 32 miles without water and the next day at 30 miles under similar circumstances, but on Saturday we got early to the creek and turning north encamped at seven miles from where we struck it on a fine sheet of water. The pools of this creek were however dreadfully reduced and I was obliged to examine them carefully that I might calculate with the greater certainty on the probable time they would last.

This morning, Dearest, we left the creek on a north course as it spread over an immense plain, and traversing a very bad country for thirty-six miles have stopped under a small sand hill without water. Before we encamped, however, I ascended this hill, and thought that I could see large trees on the flats below, but it was so dark that I could not distinctly make out whether it was large timber or brush. We have during the day traversed immense plains from 15 to 20 miles in length and the country to the north appears to be level and in some measure free from the sand hills that were so heavy to the north-west. I do not know what to think of the country, however, with such intervals without either the vestige or the likelihood of water. However, we shall see what prospect is before us, and how far I shall be able to carry out my present views which are to run to the north, to ascertain if there are any high lands or any water or any change of country between me and the tropics. I expect sooner or later to be brought up by the stony desert but in this direction it may be narrower and I may find a more practicable country beyond it.

Adieu, Dearest, it is late and I have been exposed all day to a burning sun and am tired. Adieu May God bless you ever.

Sunday October 19th 1845

I told you, Dearest, in my journal of last week that from the little hill under which we stopped I thought I saw some gum trees in the flats below. On Monday morning when it was lighter I saw that I had not been mistaken. I likewise observed from the same hill high and broken ranges of mountains to the north-east but they were very distant. They had pics and perpendicular sides and greatly resembled the Mount Serle Chain. I descended from the hill to the trees on a bearing of 327°, and after crossing a small plain we entered some open box tree forest with an abundance of grass, and at about a mile we found ourselves on the banks of a fine creek with a large pool of water. Here we stopped to breakfast, after which I went on a course of 340° to a little hill I wished to ascend and from which I had a still clearer view of the ranges to the N.E. The creek trending to the westward I was obliged to cross and leave it, but at six miles I found myself under some more box trees.

I then crossed a native path of great breadth, and directly after stood on the banks of a most magnificent canal that rather deserved the name of a river than a creek. W It was 240 yards broad, was lined by lofty blue gum trees and the broad expanse of water stretched away to the eastward and to the northwest further than we could see. The feed in this bed of the creek was so beautifully green that I determined on giving the horses a treat and halted for the day. In the afternoon we had a sudden and sharp thunderstorm that lasted for about twenty minutes and absolutely wet us to the skin. On Tuesday we had to ride some way down the creek before we could cross it, and I thought we should have had to swim our horses over, but a convenient place offering itself, we were spared the trouble. I now held a north course over fine grassy plains for about eight miles keeping the river line of trees in view to my left. We then ascended a higher sandy table land that at first had but low sand hills upon it. Here we saw about a dozen natives but we did not stop to communicate with them. The country generally was grassy and a new tree species of ash prevailed.

As we advanced the sand ridges became higher, and we found ourselves in much such another country as that to the north-west, it being evident that the occurrence of the river and of the ranges had caused a temporary alteration in the features of the country. We halted at 34 miles under an immense land wave, near a puddle of water, and here sank our first well. On Wednesday, Dearest, having got wide of the creek or river we traversed a barren interior of alternate sand hills and flats. At 3 o'clock we came to the dry bed of an immense salt lake and keeping the ridge to the westward of it, rode along it for more than six miles, when seeing that the ridge terminated at about a mile before us, and that the bed of the lake swept round it, I was afraid to cross so suspicious and wild a looking place so late in the day, and therefore halted at about 31 miles at another puddle left by the late thunder storm and dug another larger well by moonlight. On Thursday we continued our course northwards and crossing the bed of the salt lake 5 miles, ascended a sand hill on the other side of it that suddenly terminated at 10 miles, when we found ourselves overlooking a beautiful lake of about 15 miles in circumference. It was literally covered with wild fowl and other birds, and it was surrounded on every side by sand hills except to the north in which direction the country was very low.

There were no samphire bushes or other salsolaceous plants growing round this pretty sheet of water, but there was a green and gentle slope between its margin and the sand hills so that I had great hopes that it was fresh. On descending from the sand hill I had to alter my course a little to the westward. At the foot of the ridge we crossed a broad native track, and following it down, we arrived at a village of nineteen huts, but they did not appear to be recently occupied. On tasting the waters of the lake I was vexed to find them half fresh and half salt and quite putrid. I dug to try and get fresh water, but I procured nothing but brine. I then rode along the western shore of the lake, under an immense sand hill about 200 feet high, and passing another village of 29 huts dismounted and scrambled up to the summit of a high point to overlook the country. To the eastward I saw another lake and low lines of hills of white sand. To the north the country was very low and appeared to be a white sandy and salty desert, and to the west were fiery sand hills of great height. I saw at once that it would be fruitless to attempt a northerly course as with a succession of salt lakes and low sandy deserts I could not hope to find water. I was now 87 miles from the main creek and had no water between myself and it on which I could depend for more than five days. It was essentially necessary therefore that I should find a supply of a less precarious nature before I went on any farther. To have faced the sand hills would have been impossible, so that I was forced to the north-west. We ran for about eight miles on that course, and stopped at a third small puddle at which we dug another well.

We had encamped at the termination of a small valley, and from a small hill near I observed some very extensive grassy plains to the south. Not doubting but that I should find water somewhere in their neighbourhood I turned towards them, and after riding about five miles got on a native path that led to two huts. I searched long and anxiously round these and at last found a small deep creek or channel almost covered in with long grass in which there was some clear water and in sufficient quantity to justify my pushing on. I therefore again took to a north-west course, and after crossing several extensive and beautiful grassy plains again got amongst sand hills and halted at 4 p.m. on a shallow and stagnant puddle of water at which we dug a fourth well. I had marked the progressive changes in the country and I feared that we were again approaching a salt formation. Moreover, we were now about the latitude of the stony desert and I started yesterday morning in anticipation that I should meet with some obstruction. Almost as soon as we started we had to cross the dry bed of a large salt lagoon,[x] and we subsequently traversed for eight miles a region of absolute barrenness. At length from the rise of a sand hill we saw the great stony desert stretching out before us like the ocean, apparently as boundless in it extent, and without a single object on the visible horizon to guide us over it.

Coming thro' such a wilderness as we had done to it, this dreary and dreadful place looked still more terrible. We were looking out for an object on which to take a bearing, when Mr Stuart thought he saw in the distant horizon the small point of a hill, and taking the bearing of it, we descended to the stony plain and commenced our passage across it. As they had done above, the sand hills abutted upon and terminated in it. Here, however, there was no vegetation of any kind, no clear patches of sand, the universal coating of the land was stones in which our horses' feet left no impression or track. At six miles the little point for which we were steering shewed itself, and six miles more brought us to the base of it where we found that it was the commencement of a sand hill on the opposite side of the desert that now stretched from N.N.W. to East on the one hand and from W.N.W. to South on the other without any visible limit. There was in truth nothing on the visible horizon but the sand hill before us, but we knew that at a certain distance the sand hills existed to the eastward of south.

We were sadly put to it for water as the day had been tremendously hot, and was doubly insupportable on the fiery furnace, but we at length found a small puddle of water that contained enough to quench our horses' thirst but none for them in the morning. This morning, therefore, I started early and at about two miles got to a kind of swamp in which we found several small channels containing water, and here we stopped to breakfast. Pursuing our journey we came to the top of the sand hill along the base of which we had been riding, and traversed a deep sandy country for seven miles. We then descended to a large plain the lower part of which we crossed and again ascending some sand hills pursued our way down a valley, but we have halted after a journey of nearly 40 miles without water. There are some dark looking hills in front of us but we cannot make out their character. I hope however to find some creek or other near them, for our situation is very uncertain. I am indeed doubtful how far a retreat is practicable even now.

However, Dearest, we must leave our fate in the hands of the Almighty, from whom whatever adversity may await me, I pray ever for a blessing upon you.

Sunday October 26th 1845

Last Sunday my Dear and Beloved Charlotte we were in no enviable situation as you will have gathered from what I said at the close of my journal of the last week. We were now 160 miles from the creek and had no permanent supply of water on which to depend in all that distance, not having crossed a single creek of any kind. My horses were worn out with fatigue and by weariness, and I myself began to feel the effects of constant exposure, incessant riding, scarcity of food and anxiety of mind. I started on Monday hoping to find water under the dark hills we had noticed the evening before, and I really thought that we had crossed the great stony desert. Judge of my astonishment, therefore, when on rising from the valley, I saw it again spread around me, and observed that the sand hills I had been crossing were as an island in the centre of it. Yet such was the case that adamantine, that iron shod plain, stretched before me in all its gloominess and monotony. At 11 miles I reached the hills, and here a fresh disappointment awaited me. Instead of finding them like ordinary hills or as at all indicative of a change of country, I found them to be no more than sand hills of greater height than any we had seen covered over with fragments that covered the plains. They were much larger, however, and appeared to have been an after deposit as their sharp points seemed to have been driven into the sand with great force. Gaining the crest of one of these hills I looked around me, and never saw such a view in my life. It was all – dark, dark, dark. Before me the same kind of hills as that on which I stood rose one after the other as far as I could see, and in no direction could I see a glimmering of hope.

I dismounted and sat down to consider whether I should go on or return. I felt quite convinced that if I went on and that we did not find water that night the whole party would perish. My horses had already been 34 hours without water, and they could not bear privation in their exhausted state. They were fast wearing their hoofs down to a level with their quicks being unshod, and their hoofs were so dry that splinters flew from them at every step. Men and animals could not indeed have been in a more fearful position for we were nearly 50 miles from any known water and Morgan having put the bungs into the little water kegs carelessly, we as well as the horses were without a supply. Yet an almost irresistible desire to push on took possession of me, but, an unknown and a secret influence prevailed and at length determined me to turn back.[Y] I slowly and sullenly led my horse down the hill, and when at the bottom could not but contemplate with amazement the force of the element that must have produced the effects around me. There was a plain as extensive as the sea covered over with the shivered fragments of former mountains.

The Departure of Captain Sturt,
August 1844, by S. T. Gill

Sturt's Reluctant Decision to Return,
by Ivor Hale

There were hills over which the floods must have swept clad if I may say so with the same imperishable materials. The heat from the stones was overpowering and a steady blush was parching our lips and skins.

We reached the place at which we had slept about 4, and as there was a little green grass there, I turned the horses out to feed. At 6 we again pushed on, but in going up the valley one of my horses fell to rise no more. He reeled to and fro for a moment, and then falling on one side with a heavy crash, almost immediately expired. I halted with the remainder at 12 at night about eighteen miles short of the little swamp, after a journey of more than 50 miles. Our rest, however, was of short duration. At 4 a.m. on Tuesday we were again on horseback, and Mr Stuart and I preceded the pack horses to the swamp, but judge of our feelings on arriving at it to find the water all gone. I stood for a moment or two doubtful of the fact, but it was too true. We now commenced a search for some but without success, until Morgan and Mack came up having left another of the horses behind. They had, however, been more successful than us and had found a small puddle at which they had quenched their own thirst and that of their horses, but they had left none for us. They had secured also a bucket full for the horse they had left behind, with which I immediately sent Morgan to him. We now recommenced our search for a further supply and Mack at last guided by a pigeon, the only bird we had seen for days, found a little pool in which there was sufficient water not only for the day but for the morrow also. I determined therefore to give the animals a day of rest.

I should have mentioned to you, Dearest, that when I stopped at the place where we slept on Sunday to give the horses a little feed none of them would eat but the brute we lost, all the others, but particularly the grey horse I ride, clustered round me in a ring as if imploring for water. They licked my face, tried to pull my hat off, and did everything to attract my attention but poor animals I could only pat them. I had not the wherewith to supply their wants. This work has made them tamer than dogs.

On Wednesday, Dearest, I halted for the sake of the cart horses, but it was no day of rest to me. Vexed at having been obliged to fall back nearly 50 miles, I determined to go to the N.E. to try if I could cross the desert in that direction. Early in the morning, therefore, I mounted my horse and with Mr Stuart proceeded across the plains. We had no object on which to steer but were like a ship at sea. We traversed a region for eleven miles that it is impossible for me to describe to you. Over the smoother deposit of stones that generally covers this fearful desert huge fragments of rocks and sand had been hurled by the force of waters whose pointed edges presented so many needles to our horses' feet and the whole span looked like a sea beach on which fragments of rocks of every size had been thrown. Still though we had gone 11 miles the same boundlessness of plain stretched before us nor was there a visible object on the horizon. Again there I was forced to turn back and to determine on going to the eastward to examine the ranges I had seen as the country in this direction was perfectly impenetrable.

On Thursday, therefore, we continued our retrograde movement, and crossing the remainder of the stony desert reached the last well we had dug about sunset, but here we found the water so putrid that it was unfit either for ourselves or for the horses. However, as I relied on a supply in the little channel by the native huts, I did not mind much. On Friday we pushed for that place, and gained it about 4 p.m.; another day would have dried that pond on which I would have depended for a month. So tremendous had the heat been, and so little rain had fallen to saturate the ground before the holes were filled, that the evaporation and absorption were now doubly rapid, and had well nigh cost us our lives. At this place, Dearest, we are nearly 90 miles from the creek and I could not hope for water in the interval, for altho' we had my three wells there was it appeared to me no chance of water in [any] of them, and I really doubted how far it would be practicable to get our horses on. However we could not stay where we were for there was no water, so that yesterday morning we started with the resolution of travelling by day and by night.

Our first well was dry, and passing it we gained the lake about 11. At 5 we got to our second well having travelled 35 miles, but it was dry also. Here I halted until 7 when we resumed our journey, and kept on our old track, but as night came on we could not see it, so that we lit a lantern and proceeded slowly over that dreary wilderness by its faint and uncertain light. At 3 o'clock this morning we gained our last well. How anxiously, Dearest, had I approached it! Our horses were all but exhausted; they could scarcely crawl for they had started without a sufficient supply, and had been altogether without the day before, but on looking into our well, to our inexpressible joy we found that a little water still remained altho' we knew not how much. Still, there was a little, and on examination we found there was enough to give the horses three gallons each. We therefore took their packs off and gave them rest until 8 o'clock when we again pushed on for the creek, and we are now, Dearest, contrary to my expectations, on its banks, having left only one horse, that roan Mr Campbell used to ride, behind us, with every prospect of recovering him in the morning. I am truly thankful for the mercy that has been extended to us and for the escape we have now so evidently had from destruction.

I am writing to you, Dearest, by the light of a blazing fire, and under circumstances that might have excused my taking up my pen, but I have determined whatever may be my situation to devote a certain portion of this day to you and I will not break through it. I am however very tired and fear I have ill described the country to you. But excuse it Dearest.

May God ever bless you,
Amen.

Sunday November 2nd 1845

I was truly thankful, Dearest, on finding myself once more on the creek, altho' I was again going to incur the risk of having my retreat cut off from it to the Depôt. It now became necessary for me to give the horses a couple of days rest. They were all of them fairly worn out and jaded. Poor Bawley the horse Captn Frome wanted was reduced to a skeleton, and I really grieved to see the animal in such a state. Mr Campbell's horse managed to crawl after the others during the night, but I question if I shall ever take him back to the camp.

On Monday I walked to a little hill about 2 miles from the creek to survey the country to the north east. From this hill I had a commanding view, and took bearings of different points in the ranges, that still bore the appearance to be a lofty and broken chain from 3 to 4,000 feet high. They stretched away to the north east peak after peak, and I really have some hope that they will lead me to a good country. I could see the line of the creek coming from the southward of east. It had a deep belt of trees on either side of it, beyond which were extensive plains.

As I should have to return to this place again, I determined on burying or hiding everything superfluous to relieve the horses as much as possible. I put aside for this purpose my own box containing many valuable things, taking out of it your Father's Bible only, which has been my companion and has rested under my pillow during the whole of this journey. I put aside as much provisions as would do us on our return from the creek to the camp, and put most of the ammunition and powder into the bag with the lamp and other things. On consideration I thought it would be better to hide rather than to bury these things, so I selected a large rhagodia bush, in the middle of which we put them all, and there placed other bushes so as to hide them the more effectively from the keen and searching eyes of the natives.

The horses were hardly recovered from their fatigues on Wednesday but I moved on that day about six miles up the creek and encamped on a large and beautiful sheet of water. On Thursday we found the wood so thick near the creek that we were obliged to traverse the plains. At 20 miles however I again struck the creek and passed for about seven miles the open box forest with plenty of grass, and ultimately we camped where the horses had excellent feed.

On Friday, Dearest, I kept nearer the creek as the ground was more open, and the scenery was picturesque to us. In the afternoon I ascended some stony ranges, and found that we were almost north of the main range of hills to which I was going. However I could not leave the creek, and I entertained no doubt that altho' it was now taking me a little too far to the south, it would come up again. We passed several parties of natives on the most friendly terms, and I observed that several had preceded us toward the more distant natives upon approach, which I was glad of as the signs of a dense population were becoming every moment more apparent to me. Yesterday as we rode along a broad pathway we saw an old native pulling down branches and as he was direct in our way and I did not wish to frighten him I called out, but he took no notice, so I rode quietly on until we got to within thirty yards of him when, still without noticing us, he shouldered his boughs and was about to cross to the creek. On this I gave a loud coohey. The old man turned round, down fell his boughs and he stood before me horror struck. At length he began shouting out when I dismounted and, leaving my horse, went and sat down in the grass and invited him to come and sit by me. This evidently pacified him. He had previously taken man and horse for one beast. However he was now joined by another native, a young man, and gradually gaining confidence came up to me, I made him a present of a knife, and did everything I could to soothe him, for he still trembled like an aspen leaf.

I was sorry to learn from him that this creek went to the S.E. and, as far as I could understand from his motions, terminated. He pointed to the north, however, threw himself into the attitude upon pulling a canoe, and extending his arm he drew it round from north to east when he repeated his former motions. Our progress in the afternoon was slow, as Mr Campbell's horse could hardly drag his hind legs after him. On examining his hoofs I found that he had worn them to a level with the quick which had been torn from them and you could see a large raw cavity up the heel. I saw at once therefore that it would be useless trying to take him on so I cast him adrift on a grassy flat and left him to his fate. That celebrated Hunter therefore is now wandering about in the desert, but so long as he sticks to the creek he will do well. Just before we stopped for the day I went down to a pool to water the horses, and was amazed at finding it brackish. I saw that melaleuca, the tea-tree on your creek, was growing on the banks of the creek, and the channel looked like an arm of the sea. The water was still drinkable, and, as I did not know what was before me, I stopped at the upper end of the pool for the day.

This morning I crossed the creek and rode along a broad native path. At five miles I again found myself on its banks just at the commencement of a long serpentine sheet of water as blue as indigo and as salt as brine. In the pool below there were thousands of fish similar to those Mr Browne caught on the furthest of the creeks to the northwest, but in this briny hole there were none.

Crossing the creek again at this place I traversed grassy plains of immense extent on an easterly course, but not seeing anything of the creek line of trees at eight miles, I turned to the south-east, and at seven miles struck a dry channel. From the appearance of the country I began to fear that I was approaching the head of this creek, and that after all the promise it had given it would disappoint me, and as I did not wish the horses to be without water, I turned a little to the westward of south to a belt of trees, and finding a small point with some beautiful green feed round its margin I have stopped at it. We had hardly completed our little camp arrangements when I heard a melancholy chant as from a body of natives. As last we saw a number of heads over a near bank approaching us, and the whole group soon stood on the brow. It consisted of an old blind man led by a younger one and seven women. I went over to them and brought them to the camp and made them sit down, and on their going away gave the old man the half of my blanket.

With that charitable deed, Dearest, I must close this week's journal. I do not feel very well, but I dare say that I shall be better in the morning.

One day, Dearest, in this week has past that called Napier to my

remembrance. The 1 day of the month. Will you tell him that his unhappy
father implored a blessing upon him from afar, and prayed to the Almighty that
he would make him a good man and enable him to realize the promise of his
youth. Neither, Dearest, did I forget you in my silent and heartfelt prayer to
Heaven.

Sunday November 9th 1845

We started on Monday last, Dearest, on a course somewhat to the south of
east along a native path, having small stony hills on our right, boundless plains
to our left, and the creek no longer retaining its broad character but split into
numberless channels. I should however have told you that altho' we left one
pool as salt as brine on our journey of Sunday last, the next we came to was
quite fresh. At six miles I crossed a branch creek and then a plain intersected in
every direction by native paths. At 2 miles I again struck the creek where there
was a large pool of water. Having neared the ranges on our right at this point I
turned to them to have a look at the country from their summit, but they were
so low that the view was unsatisfactory. To the eastward there were apparently
interminable grassy plains crossed in all directions by small water channels, but
I could see no broad belt of trees to mark the line of the creek and plainly saw
that I had got nearly to the head of it and that it was unconnected with the
ranges to which I was going.

As I descended from the range to the river again, I saw a body of natives
approaching to whom I sent Mr Stuart on foot, and as they were more
numerous than usual, followed him pretty closely. However when they saw us
approaching, they sat down, and on going up to them we found two chiefs
seated in front who absolutely wept most bitterly, whilst those behind were
laughing. I kept a grave face, however, and let them have their cry out, when
they raised their heads and spoke, on which all ceremony was broken through.
One of the chiefs was the finest native I ever saw. He stood about 6 foot 3 inches
high was well-made, muscular, and active but was hideously ugly. He
explained to me that we were going away from water, that there was no water
to the eastward but to the N.E., and that we should have to cross the creek and
go along a native path. I gave this Hercules a knife. On mounting our horses
they kept abreast of us and shewed us the way. After passing their camp we
crossed the creek and soon found a path leading to the north east. All now
remained behind but the two chiefs who continued to accompany us.

At about a mile we came to a native hut at which there was an old man, the
father of one of the chiefs, so I dismounted to speak to and notice him. At
about two miles further we came on a tribe of 24 natives, men, women, and
children to whom we were formally introduced,and then we passed four tribes
successively, receiving from each very polite invitations to stop for the day.
However I still went on, and shortly after leaving the last tribes saw that our
guides or envoys in truth trotted off to get ahead of us to a sand hill now distant
about a mile. I knew from the motions of these people that there was

something behind that sandy curtain. Accordingly on gaining the top of the bank we were saluted by a most tremendous shout, and looking into the flat below, I saw from two to three hundred natives who had an encampment on a rising piece of ground near. All was tumult and confusion – the shouts of the men, the screams of the women and the cries of the children. Amidst all this I rode quietly down the sand hill and having got within fifty yards of the natives dismounted, and giving my horse to Morgan, walked up to them followed by Mr Stuart who is an exceedingly cool and brave little fellow. All noise now ceased and the blacks crowded round us but not to annoy. As I passed each hut the owner smoothed away a piece of ground and asked me to sit down, and at last three or four elderly men came up and asked me to sleep at a fire to which they pointed, but having observed a more convenient place under some trees about fifty yards from their encampment, I told them I would sleep there on which they nodded their assent and cease to importune me. They now brought troughs of water for us to drink and asked if we wanted anything to eat, and really behaved in the kindest manner. After staying some time with them I went to the trees and we unloaded the horses, taking care not to leave things about.

After a short time a number of men came down to pay us a visit, and a finer race of men I never saw; many were six feet, several more than that in height they stood erect, with good broad shoulders and great muscular strength. They had not the pot bellies the natives of Australia generally have but were clean-limbed and without a blemish or scar on their bodies, having only the right

Aboriginal huts, a sketch by Charles Sturt
'*As I passed each hut the owner smoothed away a piece of ground and asked me to sit down. . . .*'

tooth of the upper jaw extracted. The custom of lacerating their bodies does not seem to prevail amongst them, neither does that of circumcision, which has obtained amongst all the other natives to the north west of the Barrier range. There was not any great disproportion in the numbers of males and females, and even the children appeared to me to be a fine race. I counted 69 able-bodied men as our first visitors, our second amounted to 53 and they were mostly young men. They left us at sunset and returned to their own camp, from which they sent two men with a quantity of wood for our fires, it being very scarce. When night closed in, the encampment of the natives presented a beautiful spectacle. The women were occupied bruising the seed they eat to make cakes, and the noise they made with their stones resembled the noise of machinery in a manufacturing town. Their figures were visible seated round their fires and above them the tall forms of the men, passing to and fro. At 10 all noise ceased and from that time to dawn everything was as still as death, nor would any one have known that such a mass of people was near.

We rose early and saddled our horses, and then bade the natives adieu. I had been at their water hole and found it contained so little that if I had allowed our horses to drink at it they would almost have exhausted it. At my own expense, therefore, I determined not to injure these people, so that I would not let my horses have any. The natives had assured me most positively that there was no more water to the eastward. They made signs that if I went on I should die. I could not understand from them that there was any body of salt water beyond them on which the natives used canoes. They motioned that the creek rose in the plains before me from all about and said that the waters were gone down to where I came from. Notwithstanding, I determined to satisfy myself and accordingly rode away to the north-east, the natives shaking their heads at my obstinacy. This, Dearest, will, I think, prove that the natives of this country can be passed with out much difficulty or danger. It is on the manner in which they are treated that their conduct to you depends. Had I terrified the little bands I met scattered over the country I should have found these people arrayed in arms against me; as it was I did not see a weapon displayed in the hand of any of them. I made a long circuit of the plains, Dearest, to satisfy myself that the creek really rises on them, but altho' I am inclined to think that it does, the features of this country are so anomalous that I will only answer for what I see. I observed, however, that it was taking me from the ranges, and there were many other considerations to induce me to leave it. I turned to the westward, therefore, at 21° and got back to the little grassy water hole about half an hour after sunset, where the old blind man paid me another visit. On Tuesday I ran down the creek and encamped about a mile from a branch creek from the ranges in which I hoped to find water as I approached them. On Wednesday I turned up this creek which was of considerable size, but of character that precluded the hope of finding water in its channel. The ground was nothing but sand and loose stones whose sharp points projected above the ground, and sadly annoyed the horses. At eight miles I entered a narrow pass between two low ranges, that I had all along noticed hid the more distant and lofty ranges from us. The channel of the creek was very large, vestiges of tremendous floods on every side, but not a drop of water to be seen. The bed of the creek was gravel, the banks of it were sand. It was indeed evident that no flood had occurred in the impetuous and momentary water course for many many months.

Proceeding up the pass I stopped where it opened out into a valley and ascended a point of about 500 feet elevation. To my astonishment I found that it was not like other ranges of solid rock but a mass of rocks and sand so loose that I could hardly scramble up it. Arrived at the summit, fresh disappointments awaited me. I saw indeed other ranges to the north and north-east, and recognised in them the shapes of the lofty and broken chain I had first seen from the creek but it was now clear that the effects of refraction had entirely misrepresented them to me, that the whole were similar to the hill on which I stood, and that the country was wholly impenetrable. My heart sank within me, Dearest, at seeing my hopes blasted one after the other in such a way. I stood long on that hill resolving what I should do and at length descended with the determination of ceasing to struggle with such difficulties and of returning to the Depôt.

As I mounted my horse I said to the men, "Now men, we are going to make our first step towards our homes." "Thank God, Sir," said Mack an old servant of Evelyn's,[61] "for that, for if you had not gone soon I believe we should have had to leave you." I was in truth beginning to feel very weak. I had been so long exposed had ridden so much, had drunk such filthy water, and had subsisted on such inefficient nourishment, that my iron constitution was beginning to give way. I found that it required a greater effort to rise into my saddle, and that I could not lift things with the usual facility. I was, moreover, only skin and bone, as indeed one of the natives of the large tribe found out with evident sympathy, for he turned to another native and spanning his wrist pointed to my arm, and both said something that from their murmurs appeared to be indicative of sorrow. However I need not trouble you with this. We got late back to the creek.

The next day we got to our encampment of the 29th ultimo, and there found seven natives, one of whom was so forward that I really thought they had found the things we had hid. As soon therefore as I got them away I went to see with Mr Stuart. On approaching the bush we at first thought that everything was snug, but coming nearer we saw that one of the bags had been pulled out but none of its contents had been extracted. There were no tracks of the natives, but of a wild dog and the fact of his having smelt our oil lamp explained why the animal had pulled this bag out in preference to any other article. Every thing was safe, so that when the natives came again I made them some trifling presents.

Yesterday we moved to the place at which we first struck the creek a distance of 4 miles, where I remained all day for the horses to rest for I doubted how far some of them poor Bawley [the horse of?] of Mr Frew's and the colt would stand the morrow's journey. Indeed so weak were they that I was obliged to abandon 75 lb of flour, all my heavy stores, and one of the packsaddles. Stupidly it never occurred to me or the men to give the horses the flour to eat.

This morning we started having thirty six miles to go to the upper water holes of the first creek when we should be only 88 miles from the Depôt Camp. The day, Dearest, has been burning hot, and well was it that I relieved the animals or they would never have performed the journey. Still better was it that I had turned back and had resisted the importunities of the men to give them another day of rest at the big creek. That day would have been fatal to us all. Sufficient water only remains at this place to supply our wants tonight and tomorrow morning. I could not if I would stay another day here. I must move early therefore to the lower water hole, altho' I have doubts whether any water remains in it. If there should I shall remain there all tomorrow to prepare the horses for their long journey to the Depôt.

In this uncertainty I must close the proceedings of the week, placing every thing in the hand of that Good Providence which altho' it has refused me the success for which I prayed has yet been visible in my destinies.

God ever ever bless you Dearest. Every step I now take is one nearer my home. Shall I ever reach it? I pray I may whether it be to meet sorrow or joy.

Sunday November 23rd 1845
You will no doubt, Dearest, be anxious to know the events of the past week. There is nothing I am sorry to say cheering in them, and I fear that the close of my journal will cause you additional anxiety, as last Sunday I was unable to take up my pen to write to you as usual.

Last Monday fortnight, then, I moved to the lower water hole in the first creek that originally was 150 yards broad by 300 long. It was now reduced to as many inches, and so little water was there in it that I was obliged to dig a pit for the horses to drink out of, and to prevent their drinking any until the morning of Tuesday, when they drained it to its last drop, and I took a gallon of water to give any of the horses that might be tired. We started at 6 in the morning, but before I inform you of the particulars of our journey to the Depôt it remains for me to tell you that Monday turned out one of the most fearful days I ever remember.

At 9 a hot wind set in from the north-east that I thought would have burnt us up. I was seated under the shade of a gum tree at noon, and taking the thermometer out of a zinc case in my box found the mercury up to 125°, the instrument being only graduated to 127°. Thinking that it had been unduly affected I put it in the fork of the tree, a very large one five feet from the ground, and on going to look at it at 2, I found that it had risen as high as it would go, and the expansion of the mercury had burst the bulb, a fact that I believe no traveller ever before had it in his power to record, and one that will give you some idea of the terrific heat to which we were almost daily exposed, unless some fluctuation of temperature and a fall of 60° made the matter worse. We could not have moved on such a day, but fortunately at sunset, we had a thunder shower that cooled the air altho' it did not lay the dust and the wind shifting to the south-west, brought on a refreshing night.

On Tuesday therefore we started under rather favourable circumstances, and continued to push on from 6 am to 6 pm. I then stopped on some tolerable feed to let the horses eat which they did sparingly. At this time none of them shewed any symptoms of flagging. At 9 the moon rose when we again mounted our horses and went on. At midnight Morgan called out to me, "One of the horses down Sir", and on going to see which it was I found it to be poor Bawley, whose hollow flanks and protruding ribs, shewed by moonlight more strongly than in the day the condition to which that spirited animal was reduced. We managed however to get him on his legs again and went on. In about an hour after he fell again, and as the moon was nearly down and I thought he might get better by an hour's rest. I halted and gave him the gallon of water, but foreseeing that the men would have great trouble in getting him on, I determined on riding forward with Mr Stuart to the Depôt to send them assistance. I therefore told them to abandon all his load and to bring him quietly on.

I thought, Dearest, that I should never get to my journey's end, but we reached the Depôt at 11 on Wednesday and found it silent and deserted. No dogs gave notice of our approach, no tent caught our eyes, but all had departed. I then went to the tree under which I think I told you I had arranged with Mr Browne that he should bury a bottle with a letter in the event of his being obliged to retreat before my return. Having found the bottle, I read the letter he had put in it, in which he informed me that he had reluctantly left in consequence of the men having been seized with dysentery and blight of the eyes from the putridity of the water; that he should go to the gum tree flat as I ordered six miles from the old Depôt, but that if the water there was not good he should move to the upper water hole of the Depôt Creek. He expressed great doubts as to my safety, told me where he had sunk a well, and implored me to hasten back. Thus poor Bawley's fate was sealed. I had not the means of sending water to him. Mr Stuart and I made a fire, but had nothing to eat. At midnight Morgan and Mack came up having succeeded in getting Bawley to a stony plain within eleven miles of the Depôt on which he had finally dropped as the colt had done about four miles back, and they had left everything behind them. Mr Browne had left a leather bottle for holding water, and early in the morning I sent Mack and Mr Stuart with it full, the former to go on to Bawley, the latter to bring up the colt, but the poor animal making his appearance just as they started, Mr Stuart was saved his ride. Mack however went on with the pack horse, to bring up our eatables, and found Bawley in a hopeless state and unable to raise his head from the ground, so that he was obliged to leave him to his fate.

He returned to us about 7 when we got something to eat. Mr Stuart when up at the Stockade Fort Grey observed a crow scratching in one of the garden beds, from which he pulled a large piece of bacon and flew away. This induced Mr Stuart to examine the spot when he rooted up another piece of bacon and two pieces of suet which the dogs had buried there, but which he took it into his head Davenport had left for Mack. These Morgan cleaned, and, bringing me a small piece of the bacon certainly not larger than a five shilling piece, told me that it was perfectly clean and good, that he had cut it out of the centre, and that he had brought it to me as I had had nothing for so long a time. I took it malgré moi I wanted it not, relished it not, my appetite was sunk below that but I took it because I felt that I wanted nourishment and I did not dream of so small a piece of such meat doing me any harm. The very next day, however, I was seized with shooting pains in my legs, that increased towards the evening, and were worse the next morning.

I had, however, arranged to start and follow Mr Browne at 5 pm on this day, Sunday, Dearest, and therefore it was that I had not time to write you as usual. I had 64 miles to go a distance that the pack horses would not have gone without assistance. I told Morgan and Mack therefore to start at 5 on the following day and that I would sent a dray load of water to meet them. At 5 Mr Stuart and I left for the box tree flat which we reached at 8 on Monday morning, but Mr Browne was not there. We next went six miles to the upper water hole but neither was he there. I then rode down the creek past the old Depôt and at 4 miles got to the tents, having been eighteen hours on horseback in absolute torture. Great was the joy of all at seeing me. Mr Browne came running up, and Flood with tears in his eyes, for in consequence of the drought they had given me up as lost. I dismounted, Dearest, having ridden 917 miles in five weeks and three days. When I got off my horse I felt as if the old dog had put his head between my legs as is his wont in welcoming any one and was pushing me forward. I turned round therefore to chide him but no dog was there. It was the jerking of the muscles of my thighs, and was the forerunner of something worse. My two journeys combined made up 1878 miles that I had travelled since the 14th of August that day being the 17th of November out of which time I had been stationary and halted about fifteen days, so that I had so many days to take off from the time I have stated during which I had travelled such a distance. I had tired and worn out every man in the party and started on my last journey with entirely new hands. I had been exposed from sunrise to sunset to a scorching sun and at night had slept under the canopy of heaven alone. No wonder then that I was at length reduced, but the object I had in view made me reckless alike of exposure and privation. The day after I arrived in the camp, I lost the use of my left leg, the main muscles contracted and I lost all power of straightening the limb. Gradually my right leg became affected until at length I am stretched on my mattress a helpless and prostrate being. However, Dearest, I complain not.

The long continuance of the drought now made me apprehensive that our retreat to the Darling from which we are distant 260 miles was cut off. I had calculated on rain both in October and this month, the same as last year, but none fell and that ground which at this time twelve months had ripe grass waving over it was as bare as the streets of Adelaide, and that spot which teemed with animal life was as deserted as Tyre.

I had sent Flood the moment I arrived in camp to meet Morgan, and had therefore to await his return before I could send back to ascertain if there was water to enable us to move. He came up, however, on the following day, and on Tuesday I sent him off to a creek in which when we passed it there was an abundance of water, but he returned with the intelligence that it had long been dry. I now sent him to the eastward thinking I might get round by the back of the ranges, but here again we were disappointed. The only place in which I could now hope to find water was in Flood's Creek distant 107 miles, but that distance and back was too far for any horse to go without water supposing that creek should also have failed. Mr Browne, whose kindness and anxiety I cannot sufficiently appreciate, had gone to the south-west.

No time was to be lost. A hot wind and a temperature of 110 daily was fast licking up the water around or rather near us. How to send to Flood's Creek occupied my early and my nightly thoughts. At last I decided on sacrificing some of the bullocks, and on turning their hides into bags for the conveyance of water. On Thursday one of them was shot and prepared. In the afternoon Mr Browne also returned unsuccessful. But he insisted on starting again in the morning to Flood's Creek. I therefore arranged with him to send a bullock dray 30 miles with a supply of water for his horse. He proposed going with Flood in the cart, giving the horse as much water as he would drink when the dray stopped, then to take on 36 gallons of water in the cart as far as he could, to give the horse one half, leaving the remainder for his return and then riding on to the creek. With this object in view he left me on Friday, and is still absent. Jones returned yesterday with the bullocks, leaving the water which had kept perfectly sweet. You may fancy, Dearest, how anxiously I am looking for Mr Browne's return. His success or failure will either put us free or seal our doom. It grieves me to be in such a state at such a moment, but I cannot help it.

Sunday December 7th 1845

It was not until late on Tuesday, Dearest, that Mr Browne returned with the welcome intelligence that water still remained in Flood's Ck, altho' it was as black as ink with gum leaves. It now remained for us therefore to adopt plans to get to it. The skin I had prepared for Mr Browne having answered so well, I ordered two more bullocks to be shot, and we have been all the week busy preparing them and repairing the drays. I find that by abandoning the boat, and the case of bacon still containing 270 lbs, I can put up three skins with 600 gallons of water independently of the water we shall carry in casks, and altho' this is not half a day's consumption for our stock, I yet hope to get the cattle over this heavy journey with it. The only thing I dread is the continuance of the dreadful weather we have lately had. Nothing could have been more trying, with the thermometer at 106° before 9 in the morning and at 112° and 115° at noon accompanied by a hot wind that has kept us in constant dust. Should this continue and at this moment there does not appear to be any hope of a change, I fear we shall have great trouble and loss, but there is no time for hesitation. The men are now busy filling the skins and we start at 7, Dearest, this being Sunday. I only pray we may be fortunate, and that we shall reach Flood's Creek in safety. I must ride in the cart instead of being able to cheer the men on, and even in that I fear my poor bones will be shaken to pieces, but what most grieves me is the thought of returning so helpless a state to Adelaide. But God knows that this affliction has been brought on by the severity of the duty to which I have been subjected and therefore I ought to be resigned.

Mr Browne is just come in to speak to me about some of the arrangements prior to our starting. I must therefore lay down my pen, Dearest, for the present, commending you to the protection of that Good Being whose favour and protection you have ever sought. May it please Him to give a happy issue to this fearful enterprise, and enable me to make up to you for all the past sorrow and anxiety that I have occasioned you.

Sunday December 14th 1845

Last Sunday, Dearest Charlotte, we were in the midst of doubt, today we are quietly established at the foot of the Barrier range, and shall please God next week descend from them to the plains of the Darling.

We started last Sunday with a fearful hot wind blowing, but at midnight the wind shifted to the south and it became cool. By 3 o'clock on Monday morning we had advanced 24 miles and were within 18 of the pine forest in leading us thro' which Mr Poole, poor man, made such a sad business last year, but last December indeed. I continued moving until 3 in the afternoon when I halted on the edge of the scrub to rest the cattle and to water them, but at first they would not drink. Having picked a little however they were not so nice and we got the most of them to take a little. I then threw away the remainder of the water in the skins, one of which I however should have told you had proved defective. I foresaw indeed that all we had now to do was to perform the rest of our journey with all possible expedition. I therefore lightened the drays as much as I could, reserving only a few gallons of water to give any of the animals that might knock up. Instead of taking our old line I took the bearing of a distant hill in front and ran direct for it, by which I avoided almost all the pinerys and had a beautiful road. We journeyed on all Monday, and we had during the day a sharp shower, the most providential thing that could have happened to us. It moistened the herbage and left a very little surface water which the cattle eagerly drank. At 3 o'clock on Tuesday morning I stopped until day light and then again starting reached Flood's Creek[z] at midnight. Mr Browne came up with the drays two hours after me. Thus, Dearest, we performed this long journey of 115 miles, from 7 pm on Sunday to 2 am of Wednesday, without losing an animal, travelling night and day we brought horses bullocks and sheep in safety to our destination. On Wednesday, we remained idle but on Thursday morning Mr Browne started with Flood for the Rocky Glen 49 miles, between which and us I knew there could be no water. On Friday I followed with the drays to meet Mr Browne half way, to proceed if he had succeeded in finding water in the Rocky Glen, and to turn back if not. Fortunately he found water so we went on yesterday and reached this place yesterday afternoon at 5 pm.

We are now, Dearest, about 120 miles from the Darling. I am giving both men and animals a day of rest today and tomorrow we shall ascend the hills. Still if there is not water at the Boonbaralba Pass, we shall have some difficulty in getting to the river. Flood goes on ahead tomorrow morning and I shall stop for him under the little trap rock where I found the spring last year.

In five days more and I trust our labours will partly have closed. How anxiously, Dearest, shall I approach the Darling where tidings of you are no doubt awaiting us. I fervently pray that all may have gone on well with you and that I shall have no trial to bear after the severe ordeal through which I have passed. If it should please God to unite us once more, Dearest, it may be that even this heavy punishment, I can see it in no other light, that even this heavy punishment may have been intended for my ultimate benefit – to make me bend more submissively and view more calmly those trials and afflictions which it may be are my portion of human trials and afflictions. It may be this has been as a lesson to me to teach me moderation, to oblige me to limit my wants to the means I may have of attaining them, to stoop to gather the blessings of this life, and to cast from me those oppressive and irritable feelings which so sear the heart and deprive the man who gives way to them of all mental tranquillity. If such has been the merciful object even of this severe punishment I shall be truly grateful.

God knows I repine not even now.

Sunday December 21st 1845

Last Sunday, Dearest, we were on the north side of the ranges; today we have gained the south side and are established on the banks of the Darling near our old ground at zz Williorara. My little journal is therefore drawing to a close.   On Monday, as I told you, Flood went on to the Boonbaralba Pass whilst I took the party up the hills. I waited for him on Tuesday at the little trap spring and again drank of the cooling waters it contained. In the afternoon Flood returned with information that there was only just enough water for a day. So we started early the next morning. The drays did not arrive until after midnight. I rested them on Thursday, being then 68 or 70 miles from the Darling without the hope of any water in the intervening space. We had a large tribe of natives with us all day but they were very quiet and well behaved, so I gave them a sheep.

On Friday we started at 6 in the morning and travelled until 2 in the afternoon when I halted for the men to have their dinners. We pushed on again at 4 and got to the edge of the plains at 3 am on Saturday, and I then halted for an hour. At 4 we again started and reached Cawndilla at 7 in the evening, that being 9 miles from the Darling, but the bullocks were so tired that I was forced to stop and this morning pushed on to join Mr Piesse's party who had been doing all he could to ascertain our fate, and had stuck letters against every tree informing me that he had seen you and that you was well.

Thankful indeed, Dearest, was I for the news, and having read one or two of your letters I have determined on sending in to Adelaide express by natives to relieve your anxiety. I will therefore close this for other business, only regretting that the hurry in which it has occasionally been written will scarcely render it intelligible to you. Yet if it affords you gratification I shall have attained my end.

God bless you

Amen

[1] Grange was Sturt's second Adelaide house, built in the early 1840s on land known as Reed Beds on Port Adelaide River. He chose the site because the sands reminded him of his childhood holidays at Poole Harbour, Dorset. The house is said to have been inspired by that of George Macleay at Brownlow Hill near Camden. Sturt described it in 1844 as 'a very pretty home about $\frac{1}{4}$ mile from the sea, and I take a great deal of pride in my garden.' When Sturt went to England in 1847, he left it in the hands of W. Newland, who accidentally set on fire the fruit trees and the fences around the house. In 1895 Napier Sturt wrote to John Harris Browne, asking him what had become of the old home. Browne replied that all five acres had been incorporated into the township of Grange, with the decaying house in the centre. On 17 February 1956 a decision was taken at a Council meeting of the Henley and Grange Corporation to purchase Grange and restore it. This work had been undertaken by the Charles Sturt Memorial Museum Trust.

[2] When Sturt left on 15 August 1844 to join the rest of the party who had gone ahead five days earlier, Colonel Robert Torrens, 1780–1864, and his wife gave a small but lengthy farewell breakfast.

[3] For writing and drawing, Sturt had with him two quarts of ink, twenty-five goose quills, half a pound of sealing wax, crow quills for etching maps, and two quires of blotting paper.

[4] Napier George Sturt was born on 1 November 1836 in Bargo Brush Cottage, New South Wales. Bearing a paternal family first name in honour of his uncle, and 'George' after George Macleay, he inherited his paternal grandmother's mild temperament and was Sturt's especial favourite. He shared his father's love of flowers and went to his town office four times a week for lessons. Sturt took Napier to the Central Australian Expedition's farewell breakfast. Educated at Rugby and Woolwich, Napier served in the Abyssinian War in 1868, in 1876 married Beatrice Muirhead, who was to become her father-in-law's biographer, retired as a Colonel in 1889, and died on 11 November 1901. He had three children.

[5] Stanley, Edward George Godfrey Smith, 1799 – 1869, was Secretary of State for War and the Colonies 1841 – 45.

[6] Charles Sheppey, 'Sheppey' after his maternal grandfather, was born on 22 September 1838 at Varroville, between Liverpool and Campbelltown. His father described him as a sturdy, rosy-cheeked child, full of fun and with an eye like a

hawk, but very fickle. Educated first at a local school with the young O'Hallorans, Hawkers and other sons of English settlers, he went on to Cheltenham and Addiscombe. He entered the Indian army, served in Abyssinia and Burma, married in 1868, retired as a Major General in about 1885, and died in December 1910, survived by his wife and one daughter.

[7] Evelyn Gawler Sturt, named after Sturt's eighth and youngest brother, Evelyn Pitfield Shirley, and the Governor of South Australia, George Gawler, was born in 1840 in the Sturt's first South Australian home in East Street, Adelaide. Educated at Cheltenham and Sandhurst, he joined the army in May 1859 and died on 29 May 1864. He was considered by his parents the most fearless of the children.

[8] Sturt's active service has been questioned by Beale, *Sturt*, Ch. 4. Sturt fought the Americans in Canada, and served in France and Ireland. Promoted to captain in 1825, he came to Australia in 1827 with the 39th Regiment on the convict transport *Mariner*. Shortly after his arrival, he was appointed military secretary to Governor Darling and major of brigade to the garrison, but soon grew to dislike the restrictions of military duty.

[9] Sturt also wrote to Napier, stressing that he must obey his mother. 'You must bear in mind that she is your best Friend, better even than me, for to your Mama you owe everything.' Depôt Camp, 12 July 1845.

[10] Although Sturt had orders to return within a year, the journey was to last seventeen months and consisted roughly of six stages: (1) from 10 August 1844 when the largest group left Adelaide to 10 October when the party reached Menindie; (2) from 10 October to 10 December when they explored the Barrier Range area north of the modern town of Broken Hill and made camp at Flood's Creek; (3) from 10 December to 27 January 1845 when they made short excursions from Flood's Creek, and noticed the first signs of scurvy; (4) from 27 January to 18 July when they were trapped at Depôt Glen by lack of water; (5) from 18 July to 6 November when the party was based at Fort Grey (the name Sturt finally decided on after first calling it 'The Park', a change designed to win Grey's favour) and from where three separate journeys were made: to what Sturt believed to be Lake Torrens (in fact Lake Blanche), the area where the mountain range was supposed to be (and which has since been identified by geographers, though it is well worn down), and to the area where Cooper's creek was discovered; (6) finally, the journey to Adelaide, arriving home on 19 January 1846.

[11] John Harris Browne and James Poole.

[12] Charles Calton was the hotel-keeper of The Spot at Gawler Town.

[13] Possibly Ridgway William Newland who had conducted services at Sturt's survey camps.

[14] Francis Stacker Dutton of Anlaby.

[15] James Hawker was a neighbour of Eyre at Moorundi. In a boat, he accompanied Sturt's party up the Murray.

[16] Captain George Hall owned property with William Mein in the Lyndoch Valley.

[17] Captain Charles Harvey Bagot, 1788-1880, had 12,000 sheep on his station Koonunga in January 1845, and was one of the first to use Ridley's reaping machine. Sturt mentions Bagot's absence in 1844. He was probably attending a meeting of the Legislative Council. J.C. Hawker and Francis Dutton are two of many who acknowledged the Bagot family's warm hospitality to any who passed their station.

[18] Angas Park, the property of George Fife Angas, was, in 1844, under the management of his son, John Howard Angas.

[19] Anna Browne married Joseph Gilbert of Pusey Vale in 1848.

20 Elizabeth Bagot, née Clibborn.

21 Mary Bagot was married to William Jacob of Moorooroo.

22 Dust Hole was a sheep station. Sturt says it was deserted. Brock notes it was occupied by Jeffery.

23 Frederick Hansborough Dutton who owned Anlaby with his brother Francis as overseer.

24 Edward John Eyre, 1815–1901, had undertaken a similar expedition in 1839 but had turned back, convinced there was no inland sea in that parched land.

25 Camboli, described by Sturt as 'active, light-hearted, and confiding', and Nadbuck, 'restless, and exceedingly fond of the *fair* sex. He was a perfect politician in his way, and of essential service to us.' Sturt, *Narrative*, Vol. 1, pp.44-5.

26 In 1839 Eyre had come across a natural avenue of trees and declared that one day he would build a house at the head of it. This he was able to do when he was appointed Protector of Aborigines at Moorundi in 1841. He took out a special survey, and had a small township laid out in half-acre allotments.

27 James Chambers who later patronised expeditions conducted by John McDouall Stuart.

28 James Poole was a red-headed Irishman who previously had been employed by Sturt on survey work. He was a short man and, in the Aborigines' eyes, resembled N.S.W. Surveyor-General, Sir Thomas Mitchell, especially when he wore a blue foraging cap similar to that sported by Mitchell. The Aborigines who remembered conflicts with Mitchell's parties in the 1830s were anxious about Poole's identity until he changed his cap for a straw hat.

John Harris Browne, 1817–1904, who in the course of local exploration had discovered and occupied the sheep-grazing land Booboorowie, accompanied the expedition as surgeon, botanist and naturalist.

John McDouall Stuart, 1815–1866, was a short wiry man with auburn hair. After arriving in the colony in 1839, he had been employed on survey work.

Louis Piesse had also been employed by Sturt in early survey work.

Thirty-three year old Daniel George Brock was a Methodist, and judging from the diary he kept of the expedition, was fairly well educated. Financial troubles prompted him to join the party. Although Brock is listed as armourer, Sturt put Sullivan in charge of the arms and so Brock spent most of his time looking after sheep and collecting and skinning birds. There was little love lost between Brock and Piesse because Piesse had once tried to court Brock's wife, Delia, who had come to Australia on the same ship as Piesse.

Robert Flood, who had a good reputation for handling horses, had been head stockman of Sturt's overlanding party of 1838.

George Davenport was an ex-convict who claimed he had been wrongly convicted of cowardice at Waterloo. He was Sturt's cook on Norfolk Island, was present at Napier's birth, and had accompanied Sturt down the Murray as his personal servant.

Joseph Cowley, a youth whom Sturt praised for his moral courage, devoted half his pay to the support of his aged parents.

David Morgan, after serving in the navy, arrived in Adelaide in 1837, had worked on the survey under both Light and Sturt.

James Lewis (called William in Sturt's *Narrative. . .*, Vol. 1 p.46) was a sailor who it was hoped would come into his own when an inland sea was discovered. Brock describes him as stubborn, foolhardy, but very useful at odd jobs.

John Mack had previously worked for Sturt's brother Evelyn.

Hugh Foulkes [Ffoulkes] was described by Browne as an old soldier 'who was all through the wars with Spain and received three wounds for which he receives a pension. He is now past sixty years old and quite decrepid (sic).' One of the first medical tasks Browne performed was to draw a tooth for old Foulkes. H.J. Finnis, 'Dr John Harris Browne's Journal...' pp.24,26,47.

Adam Turpin was another old man. Browne wrote of the party, 'I am sorry to see that there are several amongst them who look anything but able bodied and robust. Several of them I am sure are old convicts.'

John Kirby (Kerby) was the cook, said by Brock to be 'missing a shingle' but, like John Sullivan, was reported by Sturt to be 'getting along well.'

29 To this list should be added 200 sheep, 4 kangaroo dogs, and two sheep dogs.

30 Samuel Stuckey, who in 1859 found a passage through the supposed horse-shoe of Lake Torrens and discovered Lake Hope. Stuckey brought a number of camel drivers to Australia in 1866. Had camels been imported earlier, Sturt's task might not have been so difficult.

31 John Bentham Neales worked as an auctioneer under the title of Neales Bentham to avoid confusion with another agent called Neale, and later followed a political career in both the upper and the lower houses in South Australia.

32 Although Daniel Brock complained that Sturt worked the men on Sundays and that his prayers were perfunctory, Sturt, like most Australian explorers faced with a hostile environment, leant hourly on God's mercy. Every night he slept with a Bible that had belonged to his father-in-law under his pillow, keeping it even in favour of an oil lamp when he had to discard possessions in the desert.

33 Although he had already undertaken several gruelling journeys, Eyre was still looking for another opportunity to lead an expedition. Writing to Sir George Gipps on 28 November 1844, he pleaded, 'I cannot willingly divest myself of the hope of doing so until the very last, and most tenaciously cling to anything that affords even the slightest prospect of my wishes being gratified.'

34 Part of this letter read, 'With every deference for the opinion of so intelligent and experienced a traveller as Captain Sturt, I must confess that I cannot... see any data from which to infer either the existence of a fine country ... or of a deep inland sea.' The full text of this letter appears in *Historical Records of Australia*, Series 1, Vol.XXIV, p. 51. Mr E.J. Eyre to Lord Stanley, 22 August 1844.

35 Sturt was correct in thinking that Eyre's plan to conduct an expedition overland from Moreton Bay to Port Essington would not be supported. Eyre sailed for England on 20 December 1844, planning to state his case more forcefully to the Colonial Office, but he was unsuccessful, and his days of Australian exploration had ended.

36 Sturt described Tampawang (Tamp-pi-vam) or Bob as a good, inoffensive lad and a capable shepherd.

37 Kusick was a mounted policeman.

38 Judge Charles Cooper was criticised in the press for his timidity in making decisions but his gentleness and conscientiousness were also widely acknowledged. Miss Cooper helped make the flag Sturt hoped to plant in the centre of Australia.

39 Edward Charles Frome, 1802–1890, who had replaced Sturt as Surveyor-General also assumed, unpaid, the duties of colonial engineer. He offered to lead the 1844 expedition if Sturt were not available.

40 Tenbury knew Sturt from an earlier meeting at the fossil cliffs of the Murray. Although old, Tenbury was an invaluable guide.

41 Henry Bryan, the eighteen year old son of an Essex rector, perished in 1840. Charlotte Sturt accompanied this expedition.

42 Named by Eyre after Charles Bonney who, with Joseph Hawdon, was the first to bring cattle overland from New South Wales to Adelaide.

43 Eliezer Levi Montifiore, a commission and shipping agent, and later a leading patron of the arts.

44 Polygonum. A large genus of plants more familiarly known by names such as knotgrass and snakeweed, characterised by swollen stem-joints sheathed by stipules, and small flowers.

45 Major Thomas O'Halloran was Chief of Police in Adelaide and chaired the Expedition's formal farewell breakfast on 10 August 1844. There is a comment in the Sturt family papers about O'Halloran and Grey that typifies the family's attitude to Grey. Sir George Grey told Lady Fox Young that Major O'Halloran had been his only friend in South Australia. 'He really had no friends at all there', commented Lady Fox Young.

46 Sturt is referring to one of a series of bloody encounters between overlanding parties and Aborigines in the early 1840s. Grey was anxious to defuse the tense situation and when he heard that volunteers were organising a group to protect Langhorne's party, he forbade the private venture but substituted an official expedition under O'Halloran and the Protector of the Aborigines, Dr Matthew Moorhouse, with thirty-one volunteers sworn in as special constables. Unfortunately Langhorne's party was attacked before its protectors arrived. Four Europeans were killed and the sheep were carried off and slaughtered. O'Halloran rescued the survivors and some head of cattle but, as ordered, did not attack the Aborigines. In August 1841 there was another serious clash with William Robinson's overlanding party, and this time, contrary to orders, the natives were fired on and about thirty were killed.

47 Miller was formerly a soldier in Sturt's 39th Regiment. The old, white-haired Aborigine had accompanied Sturt for a few days on his Murray River expedition of 1830 and became the self-appointed guide for the parties that followed. He also accompanied Sturt overland from Sydney in 1838.

48 In the *Narrative* ... Sturt spells it Pulcanti.

49 See footnote 46.

50 Sir Richard Bourke who succeeded Sir Ralph Darling as Governor of New South Wales in 1831.

51 Camboli.

52 Sturt left the Council meeting to farewell Gawler as he embarked on his voyage to England.

53 Eliza Lucy Grey. Grey hoped that his wife's visit would be seen as a measure of his concern.

54 Lieutenant Lushington (later Captain Lushington of the 9th Foot) was a member of Grey's Western Australian expedition, an expedition which Sturt felt was poorly conducted.

55 John Alexander Jackson was appointed Colonial Treasurer and Accountant-General in 1839. During Grey's investigations into the colony's finances he was criticised for his methods of accounting, and although his character remained intact, he became so incensed by Grey's suspicions of his work that he resigned his posts on 10 June 1843. He went to London to clear his name but to no avail, and he was refused employment in the colonial service. He was not exonerated until 1847.

56 Milvus affinis, Gould.

57 These pigeons were safely delivered alive to his daughter, Charlotte Eyre. Born on 19 January 1843, she died unmarried on 11 December 1928.

58 Georges L.C.F.D. Cuvier, 1769–1832, French naturalist.

59 Sturt has left the date blank because he has confused the events of these days. The party left on the 14th not the 15th.

60 This stony plain was later called Simpson Desert.

61 Evelyn Pitfield Shirley, 1815–1885, Sturt's brother.

Charles Sturt in the heroic mould of the text book.
'*No one could question the skill or experience of so renowned an explorer as Captain Sturt.*'
E. J. Eyre

'*I . . . stood blighted and a blasted man over whose head the darkest destiny had settled.*'
Charles Sturt

APPENDIX

Captain Charles Sturt to the Right Honourable Lord Stanley, 16 March
1843
(This plan was amended by Lord Stanley)

My Lord

On the 25th of January last, I addressed a letter to your Lordship, through General Sir Ralph Darling, with whom I formerly served as Military Secretary and Major of Brigade in the which I venture to offer my services to your Lordship to explore the Australian Continent, and I requested Sir Ralph Darling to forward my letter to your Lordship with such remarks as from an intimate knowledge of my dispositions and habits he might be pleased to make. Having left the matter in his hands, I should not again have troubled Your Lordship on the subject, but, that it has occurred to me, that, from circumstances, which will come to Your Lordship's knowledge about the time you may receive my communication through Sir Ralph Darling, Your Lordship may be led into the belief that I have been induced to make this offer without a due consideration of the magnitude and difficulty of the Undertaking. I feel therefore that even supposing Your Lordship should decline my proposals, I still owe it to myself to remove from your mind any impression that I have been influenced by waywardness or inconsistency.

Had it not been for the tardy progress I made towards the recovery of my sight, I should long ere this, I am to assure Your Lordship, have thus made an offer of my services to the Colonial Office and volunteered the general exploration of this Continent, and with that object in view I took with me when I returned to New South Wales in 1834 Transit and other valuable Instruments to assist me in my labors. Your Lordship will not therefore imagine that I have recently applied myself to the subject or that disappointment has urged me inadvisedly to come forward and volunteer a service of great risk and responsibility. Interested as Your Lordship will readily believe me to be, in the progress of internal discovery, I further consider that there is no greater geographical Problem remaining unsolved than the nature and character of Central Australia. I deem therefore that I could not be employed on a more honorable service than that on which I seek to be employed, or one from which, if successful more important results are likely to spring.

As I stated to Your Lordship in a former letter in a conversation I had with Sir John Barrow some years ago I expressed my opinion that no party from Europe would succeed in any effort to penetrate this continent from the Coast. I was aware from experience that altho' Men of Spirit enterprise and ability could be found, the necessary elements of an Expedition such as ought to be employed on so gigantic a work could no where be put together except in the Australian Colonies. The Men My Lord should be habituated to the Bush and confident in meandering about it, accustomed to and fearless of the Natives, uncomplaining under privations, and vigilant and steady in the performance of their duties, for their labors end not with the day's march. The very animals should have been trained to the service required of them and fit for draught or for the Pack saddle for Your Lordship cannot conceive the anxiety and danger attendant on a want of proper qualities in either Men or Animals, or the great difficulty there is in keeping even the best trained Cattle from wandering at night in search of water and feed when they have been for days without either; for Australia has large tracts of barren land like Africa, between the more fertile portions of it in crossing which it requires precautions which experience can alone suggest.

I have enclosed for your Lordships examination an Estimate of the expense of an Expedition such as I would recommend. I stated in my former letter that I thought it would be about £4000, but Your Lordship will see, that it is rather under that sum even with the liberal allowances I have made. The provisions are calculated to last for two years, for I am of the opinion that a less period would not suffice for the full and satisfactory attainment of the objects in view. The recent discoveries of the Beagle have disclosed to us Rivers of considerable size both in the NE and NW angles of the Continent tending, as Your Lordship will observe, to a common centre, in corroboration of the opinion I have ever entertained of there being an available country in our central inter-tropical regions. The tracing up of these Rivers would give us a knowledge of the country on their banks but it would necessarily be to a limited extent, and the veil would still hang over those parts of the Interior which could not under such circumstances be attained. It is for this reason that I would most respectfully urge your Lordship to sanction an Expedition of such a character as should leave nothing undone. It is an enterprise worthy of Your Lordship's support. I would propose to go into the interior with such supplies as would render me independent for I know too well the loss of time in seeking for an appointed rendezvous, where every moment of time is valuable. I would propose to Your Lordship to organise an Expedition here upon the spot. Many of those who accompanied me on former occasions would gladly follow me now. Men who have sustained privations and fatigue without a murmur, and whose past experience admirably qualifies them for the task. I would propose to proceed along the line of the Darling, to the northward of the latitude of Moreton Bay, in the event of its being found impracticable to penetrate to the westward from that River before gaining the 27th parallel of Latitude. Your Lordship will be aware that all the streams of the Interior to the Northward of Sydney are tributaries to the Darling, but about the 29th parallel that central river approaches close to the Mountains so that it is reasonable to presume that its basins are at no great distance, but that other streams may be found beyond them leading to the NW. I suggest this route because it appears to me that it would be of infinite importance to unite the North with the East and South Coasts. Thousands my Lord have been spent in enterprises less worthy the attention of Government, nor can I doubt the generous view Your Lordship will take of such a design. If I did not feel myself equal to its execution I would not seek employment, for I have established my reputation as an Explorer, and am not called upon to enter the field of Discovery again, but it often happens that we follow an irresistible impulse which in most cases leads to successful results. Altho' I am not personally known to Your Lordship I believe my family is not unknown to you. I have not the means my Lord which they have of being useful, and I would therefore fain make up for this, by endeavouring by personal and honorable exertion to benefit my Country and mankind. In these great objects I look to your Lordship for support, and I would only assure Your Lordship that if it should please you to employ me, I trust that I shall justify the confidence you will repose in me. I will leave little to be done after me, if God gives me strength and affords me the same protection he has afforded to me on former occasions. It is no idle, no common employment I seek but one which if successfully carried out, would add even to your Lordship's credit. I have ever endeavoured to seek honorable distinctions and I owe it to my own exertions that Sir Ralph Darling reposed a confidence in me which I did not abuse.

The instruments I have enumerated are at Houghton and Simms' prices, and might be sent direct to South Australia. Your Lordship will see the necessity of such being provided where the safety of the Party will depend on accuracy of observations, and there might be points which it would behove me to be critically correct in fixing.

Considering that with an Assistant to succeed me in the event of any untoward accident to myself, and an Individual to collect Specimens, a Black, an Overseer and twelve men, I could move safely thro the most populous districts. I would confine the strength of the Party to that number and it may not be necessary to trouble Your Lordship with minute details.

If the Instruments and other Articles in Schedule A* were forwarded from England, I should have no occasion to call on Your Lordship for a greater sum than £1700 until the return of the Expedition and I should forward to your Lordship a regular account of the Expedition as it took place, and implicitly follow such instructions as Your Lordship might give for my guidance.

I have availed myself of the present opportunity to communicate with Your Lordship because any reply with which you may be pleased to honor me, will be received by me in about twelve months from this date, and in the event of Your Lordship's accepting my offer will give me time to equip an Expedition so as to start at the most favorable season of the year, the end of June.

I beg to subscribe myself etc.

(Signed) Charles Sturt.

* This was a list of instruments and supplies, including lined tents for the

gentlemen and bell tents for the men; hatchets, knives, fish-hooks and blankets as presents for the aborigines; and , of course, a boat and boat-carriage for use on the inland sea. The 1844 Expedition set off with a similar list of provisions.

INDEX

Aborigines, assistants on expedition:
Jackey (Camboli), 18, 23, 31, 32, 36,
40, 103, 105; Nadbuck, 18, 23, 30, 31,
32, 33, 34, 40, 103; Pulcanta(i), 29-30,
105; Tampawang, 23, 24, 43, 56, 104;
Tenbury, native constable at
Moorundi, 24; 25; 29; 104; Topar, 38,
39, 40, 41; Toonda, 32, 33, 34, 39;
encounters and relationships with:
Eyre, E. J., 30-1; Inman, Mr, 28;
Langhorne, Mr, 28, 105; Miller, Mr,
28-9, 105; Mitchell, T. L. 31, 38-9;
O'Halloran, T., 28; Robinson, W., 29,
105; Sturt, C., 36, 39, 41, 46, 54, 59-60,
67, 89-90, 91-3, *passim*; instructions
concerning, 21, 62; encourage idea of
'great water', 49, 54, 64; diet, 25, 28, 31,
59-60, 67, 72, 93; affected by drought,
77; graves, 30, 39, 66; physical
appearance, 35, 65, 67, 92-3;
encampments, 30, 32, 46, 54, 59, 64,
66, 67, 70, 81, 84, 91-3, *passim*; wells,
70, 71, 76, 77
Angas, George Fife, 102
Angas, John Howard, 102
Bagot, Charles H., 17, 18, 102
Bagot, Elizabeth, 17, 103
Barrow, John, 107
Beagle (ship), 108
Bonney, Charles, 104
Bourke, Sir Richard, 36, 105
Brock, Daniel G., 3, 8, 9, 10, 19, 20, 21,
103, 104
Brock, Delia, 103
Browne, (Dr) John Harris, 8, 9, 10, 17, 18,
20, 24, 28, 29, 31, 33, 34, 35, 36, 38, 39,
40, 42, 43, 44, 54, 55, 56, 57, 60, 62, 64,
65, 68, 69, 70, 73, 75, 76, 78, 82, 90, 97,
99, 100, 101, 102, 103, 104; asked to

return to Adelaide, 79-81; buries
bottle at Fort Grey, 96; fishing
successes, 66, 77; good relationships
with Aborigines, 59, 77; praised by
Sturt, 58, 98; scurvy, 45, 51, 52, 53, 71,
74, 77, 80
Bryan(t), Henry, 2, 25, 104
Calton, Charles, 17, 102
Cameron, Mr, 28-9
Campbell, Charles, 5
Central Australian Expedition, *see under*
Sturt, Charles Napier
Chambers, James, 19, 103
Charles Sturt Memorial Museum Trust,
101
Cooper, Judge Charles, 24, 104
Cooper, Sarah A., 104
Cowley (Colley), Joseph, 10, 20, 21, 46,
52, 56, 62, 72, 75, 77, 78, 103; accident,
67; praised by Sturt, 45
Cuvier, G. L. C. F. D., 49, 105
Darling, Sir Ralph, 5, 8, 81, 105, 107, 109
Davenport, George, 10, 19, 20, 21, 31, 97,
103
Dutton, Francis, 17, 18, 102, 103
Dutton, Frederick H., 18, 103
Eyre, Edward John, 7, 8, 9, 18, 19, 20, 21,
24, 25, 29, 34, 36, 37, 38, 40, 42, 61, 102,
103, 104; belief in inland sea and
expedition hopes, 8, 22-3; good
relations with Aborigines, 30-1
Fauna, birds, 25, 40, 46, 47, 49, 70, 71, 72,
94, 105; fish and crayfish, 66, 77, 25;
jerboa, 58, 59-60; kangaroo, 28; wild
cattle, 28, 32
Flood, Robert, 10, 18, 20, 21, 24, 28, 29,
40, 42, 43, 45, 46, 47, 52, 62, 64, 70, 74,
75, 78, 81, 97, 98, 100, 103; accident, 33
Foulkes (Faulkes), Hugh, 20, 103

112

Frew, (J?), 45
Frome, Captain Edward Charles, 4, 8, 24, 89, 104
Gawler, (Colonel) George, 2, 3, 4, 37, 102, 105
Gawler Town, 17, 102
Gilbert, Joseph, 102
Gipps, Sir George, 23, 104
Gregory, Hon. Augustus Charles, 10
Grey, Eliza Lucy, 7, 37, 105
Grey, Captain George, 1, 4-7, 8, 9, 10, 22, 23, 24, 28, 30, 32, 37, 38, 40, 81, 102, 105
Gouger, Robert, 4
Hall, Captain George, 17, 102
Hawdon, Joseph, 104
Hawker, James, 17, 18, 26, 27, 102
Horses, Bawley, 9, 89, 95, 96; Colt, 96; grey [Duncan], 87; Punch, 45, 46; Roan, 88, 89, 90; Rodney, 71, 76; extreme suffering, 44, 47, 71, 86, 87, 89
Inman, Lieutenant, chief of police, 28
Jackson, John Alexander, 38, 105
Jacob, Mary, née Bagot, 18, 103
Jones, John, 20, 98
Kenny, Mr, police-constable, 21, 104
Kirby, John, 20, 21, 104
Kusick, Mr, mounted policeman, 24, 104
Langhorne, Mr, 28, 105
Lewis, James (sometimes recorded as William), 10, 20, 62, 66, 76, 78, 103
Light, Colonel William, 3, 103
Lushington, Lieutenant, 105
MacDonnell, Sir Richard, 10
Mack, John, 9, 20, 28, 33, 43, 79, 81, 87, 94, 96, 97, 103
Macleay, George, 101
Mein, William, 102
Miller, Mr, discharged soldier, 28-9, 105
Mitchell, Major (Sir) Thomas L., 9, 31, 35, 36, 38-9, 40, 58, 103
Montifiore, Eliezer L., 105
Moorehouse, Matthew, 105
Morgan, David 3, 10, 19, 20, 21, 28, 40, 42, 43, 79, 81, 86, 87, 92, 96, 97, 103; paints boat, 62
Neales, John Bentham, 20, 104
Newland [Ridgway William?], 17, 18, 101, 102
Nichol(l)s, Fanny, née Conway, 9
O'Halloran, Major Thomas, 28, 105
Piesse, Louis, 3, 9, 17, 18, 20, 21, 49, 56, 101, 103; praised by Sturt, 57

Poole, James, 3, 9, 17, 18, 20, 21, 24, 26, 27, 28, 29, 32, 33, 35, 40, 42, 43, 44, 45, 49, 80, 99, 102, 103; relapses and death, 51-7; reports sighting of large body of water, 36, 38
Robe, Colonel Holt, 10
Robinson, William, 29, 105
Scurvy, 45, 51-7, 64, 71, 74
Stanley, Rt Honourable Lord, later Earl of Derby, 5, 7, 15-16, 22, 23, 30, 49, 61, 101, 104, 107
Stuart, John McDouall, 3, 10, 20, 45, 46, 56, 58, 59, 60, 61, 62, 78, 79, 81, 84, 87, 91, 94, 96, 97, 103; praised by Sturt, 92
Stuckey, Samuel, 20, 104
Sturt, Charles Napier, career to 1844, 1-7, 37-8; career after 1845, 10, 12; *Central Australian expedition*: reasons for, 1, 6, 8, 30, 49, 57, 61, 78-9, 80-1; anxiety and disappointment during, 6, 21-2, 37-8, 49, 68, 74, 75, 78-9, 80-1, 85, 86, 94, 95, 100, 107-110; physical suffering, 44, 45, 47, 51, 64, 71, 78, 85, 88, 97, 98; extreme heat, 44, 51, 94-5, *passim*; salaries paid during, 9; *progress of*; Grange, 15; St Clare, 17; Gawler Town, 17, 24; Captain Bagot's property, 17-8; White Hut, 18; Dust Hole, 18; Moorundi, 19-24; orders and prayers, 19; Murray River, 24-6, 28, 32-3; Lake Bonney, 27; Hawker's Creek, 27; Rufus, 28-31; Fort O'Halloran and Hornets' Nest, 28, 31; Lake Victoria, 31-2, 40; Ana-branch, 29, 33; Darling river, 34-6; Williorara, (Laidley's Ponds), 36-9; Poole reports sighting large body of water to north, 36; visit Major Mitchell's 1836 camp, 38; *Cawndilloa*, 39-41, some major excursions from vicinity of: Sturt, Browne, Flood, Morgan, Topar, 40-41; Browne and Flood, 42; Browne and Poole, 42; Sturt, 44; Sturt, Browne, 44; *Depôt Glen*, 44, 49, 51-7; some major excursions from: Sturt, Stuart, Flood, Cowley, 45; Sturt and Cowley, 45-6; Flood, 46; Sturt, Stuart, Flood, 46-7; Sturt, Stuart, Flood, Cowley, 47; Sturt [and others], 48; Sturt, Browne, Flood, Cowley, 52; Mt Poole (Red Hill), 54; Sturt, Browne, 54; Piesse, Stuart, chainers, 56; *Second Depôt (Fort Grey)*, 57, 58-9, 62, 78-82;

some major excursions from: search for Mt Hopeless, 58, 59, 61; Lake Torrens (supposed), 56, 58, 59, 60, 61, 62, 63; Stuart, Browne, chainers, 58-9; immense dry lake bed (Lake Blanche) 60-1; Sturt, Browne, Stuart, 60; Mt Serle, 61; Sturt, Browne, Flood, Cowley, Lewis, 62-78; Stony desert, 69; Furthest point north, 75; Sturt, Stuart, Morgan, Mack, 79, 82-97; Stony desert, 82, 84-8; Browne and remainder of party at upper waterhole, Depôt Creek, 96-8; Flood's Creek, 98, 99; Barrier Range, 99; Depôt Glen, 100; B(C)oonbaralba Pass, 100; Darling River, 100, 101; Williorara, 100; Summary, 102; *see also*, Fauna; Horses

Sturt, Charles Sheppey, (Sturt's second son), 2, 12, 16-17, 101-2

Sturt, Charlotte Christiana (Sturt's wife), 1-3, 6, 7, 9, 12, 15, 22, 25, 37, 104, *passim*

Sturt, Charlotte Eyre (Sturt's daughter), 2, 6, 12, 46, 105

Sturt, Evelyn Gawler (Sturt's youngest son), 2, 12, 16-17, 102

Sturt, Evelyn Pitfield (Sturt's brother), 3, 5, 94, 102, 103, 105

Sturt, Napier George (Sturt's eldest son), 2, 6, 9, 12, 15-17, 37, 90-1, 101, 102, 103

Sullivan, John, 19, 20, 21, 103, 104

Torrens, Colonel Robert, 2, 15, 101

Turpin, Adam, 20, 104

Victoria, Queen, 12

Young, Lady Augusta Sophia Fox, 6, 105

AN ACCOUNT

OF THE

SEA COAST AND INTERIOR

OF

SOUTH AUSTRALIA,

WITH

OBSERVATIONS ON VARIOUS SUBJECTS CONNECTED
WITH ITS INTERESTS.

(Facsimile of Charles Sturt's *Narrative
of an Expedition into Central Australia*,
Volume 2, 1849, pp 145-286).

CHAPTER I.

DUTIES OF AN EXPLORER — GEOGRAPHICAL POSITION OF
SOUTH AUSTRALIA—DESCRIPTION OF ITS COAST LINE—SEA
MOUTH OF THE MURRAY—ENTERED BY MR. PULLEN—
RISK OF THE ATTEMPT—BEACHING—ROSETTA HARBOUR—
VICTOR HARBOUR—NEPEAN BAY—KANGAROO ISLAND—
KINGSCOTE—CAPT. LEE'S INSTRUCTIONS FOR PORT ADE-
LAIDE—PORT ADELAIDE—REMOVAL TO THE NORTH ARM—
HARBOUR MASTER'S REPORT—YORKE'S PENINSULA—PORT
LINCOLN—CAPT. LEE'S INSTRUCTIONS—BOSTON ISLAND—
BOSTON BAY—COFFIN'S BAY—MR. CAMERON SENT ALONG
THE COAST—HIS REPORT—POSITION OF PORT ADELAIDE.

No mariner ever shook the reefs from his sails,
on the abatement of the storm, under the fury of
which his vessel had been labouring, with more
grateful feelings than those with which I turn
from the dreary and monotonous wastes I have been
describing, to the contemplation of fairer and more
varied scenes. My weary task has been performed,
and however uninteresting my narrative may have
proved to the general reader, I would yet hope, that
those who shall hereafter enter the field of Australian discovery, will profit from my experience, and
be spared many of the inconveniences and sufferings to which I was unavoidably exposed. They

L 2

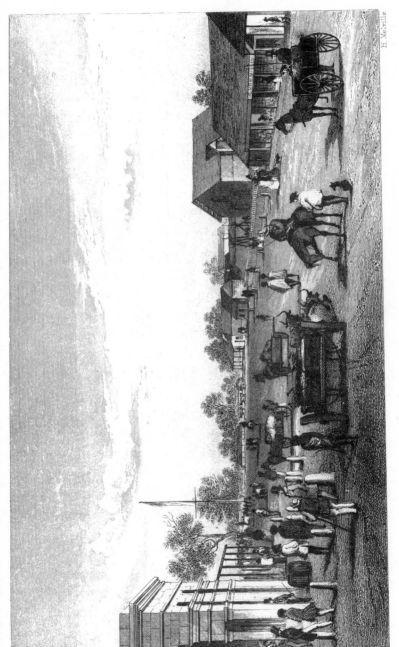

KING WILLIAM STREET.

H. Melville.

may rest assured, that it is only by steady perseverance and unceasing attention, by due precaution
and a mild discipline, that they will succeed in such
an undertaking as that in which I was engaged.
That unless they are fortunate enough to secure such
an assistant as I had in Mr. Browne, their single eye
must be over every thing, to study the features of
the country through which they are passing, to keep
their horses and cattle always within view, to prevent disputes in their camp, and to husband their
provisions with the utmost care, to ascertain from
time to time the quantity they may have on hand,
and to regulate their consumption accordingly. Few
difficulties present themselves to the explorer in
journeying down a river, for that way is smooth
before him ; it is when he quits its banks, and tra-
verses a country, on the parched surface of which
little or no water is to be found, that his trials commence, and he finds himself obliged to undergo that
personal toil, which sooner or later will lay him
prostrate. Strictly speaking, my work should close
here. I am not, however, unmindful of the suggestion I made in my Preface, that a short notice of
South Australia at the close of my journal would
not be out of place.

In the following pages, therefore, it is proposed
to give some account of that province, from whence,
as the reader is aware, I took my departure, before
commencing my recent labours. Its circumstances
and prospects have, I know, of late, been frequently

brought before the public, but, I trust, nevertheless, that my observations will carry something of novelty, if not of interest, and utility with them.

South Australia, then, the youngest of the colonies that have been established round the shores of the Australian Continent, is situate, as its name would imply, upon its southern coast. It extends from the 132nd to the 141st degree of longitude east from Greenwich, and runs up northwards into the interior to the 26th parallel of latitude. The district of Port Phillip bounds it on the east, for which reason, the fixing of the eastern boundary line between those two fine provinces has of late been a point of great interest and importance. Mr. Tyers, an able and intelligent officer, was employed by the Government of New South Wales, primarily to determine the longitude of the mouth of the Glenelg, and from his triangulations and observations it would appear that the 141st meridian falls on the coast about a mile and a half to the eastward of it. Subsequent observations, taken by Captain Stokes, in command of Her Majesty's surveying ship, the Beagle, differ slightly from the result of Mr. Tyers' observations, but they prove beyond doubt, the care and accuracy with which the latter officer carried on his survey. The point, has since, I believe, been finally recognised by the governments of Sydney and Adelaide, and the boundary line been marked to the distance of 123 miles from the coast. The party employed in this useful undertaking, however, was obliged to relinquish it for a time, in consequence of heavy rains ; but it is not probable that any dispute will hereafter arise on the question. If the line could have been extended to the Murray river, it would have been as well, but the desert country beyond it is valueless to civilised man. Taking it for granted, then, that the S. E. angle of the province of South Australia has been fixed, we shall in the first instance proceed along its sea line, and notice any thing worthy of observation, before we enter into a detail as to the character of the country itself.

From the mouth of the Glenelg the coast of South Australia trends to the westward as far as Cape Northumberland in long. 140° 37' and in lat. 38° ;* from Cape Northumberland it turns to the N.N.W., keeping that general direction for more than 100 miles. Between the last mentioned Cape and Cape Morard des Galles in lat. $36\frac{1}{2}$°, there are several bays, two only of which, Rivoli Bay, immediately to the north of Cape Lannes, and Guichen Bay, a little to the south of Cape Bernouilli, have more particularly drawn the attention of the local Government, rendered necessary in consequence of the rapid settlement of the back country. Recent surveys have enhanced the value of these two bays, and townships have been laid out at each. That at Rivoli bay being called Grey Town, that of Guichen bay Robe Town. At the latter, there is a resident magistrate and a party of mounted police. Many allotments have

* The reader will be good enough to bear in mind that the Longitudes in this work are all east of Greenwich, and that the Latitudes are south.

been sold in both towns, and although the bays offer
but little protection to large vessels, they are of great
importance to the colonial trade and to the settlers
occupying the beautiful and fertile country in the
neighbourhood of Mounts Gambier and Shanck.
From Cape Morard des Galles, a low dreary and
sandy beach extends for five leagues beyond the sea
mouth of the Murray, a distance of more than 100
miles. This beach, which varies in breadth from one
to three miles, conceals the waters of the Coorong,
and the depressed and barren country beyond it is
completely hid from view by the bright sand-hills on
this long and narrow strip of land.

The sea mouth of the Murray, famous for the
tragical events that have occurred near it, and which
give a melancholy interest to the spot, is in long.
138° 56′ and in lat. 35° 32′. No one could, I am
sure, look on the foaming waters of that wild line
of sand-hills through which it has forced a channel,
without deep feelings of awe and emotion. Directly
open to the Southern Ocean, the swell that rolls
into Encounter Bay, is of the heaviest description.
The breakers rise to the height of fifteen or eighteen
feet before they burst in one unbroken line as far
as the eye can see, and as the southerly is the
most prevailing wind on that part of the Australian coast, it is only during the summer season, and
after several days of northerly wind that the sea
subsides, and the roar of breakers ceases for a
time. The reader will perhaps bear in mind that
the channel of the Goolwa connects Lake Victoria

with Encounter Bay, the sea mouth of the Murray being the outlet through which its waters are discharged into the ocean.

The channel of the Goolwa (now called Port Pullen, in compliment to an officer of that name on the marine survey staff of the province, who succeeded, after several disappointments, in taking a small cutter through that narrow passage, and navigating her across the lake into the Murray River, as high as the settlement of Moorundi) is to the westward of the sea mouth as the Coorong is to the eastward.*

But although Mr. Pullen succeeded in getting into the Goolwa, it was only under the most favourable circumstances, nor will the sea mouth of the Murray ever, I fear, be available for navigable purposes. How far it may be practicable to steamers, I would not hazard an opinion, nor is the subject at the present moment one of much importance, for the country to the eastward of the ranges is not yet sufficiently located to call for such a speculation.

The sea mouth of the Murray is about the

---

* The compliment thus paid to Mr. Pullen, who is now employed on the expedition to the North Pole, in search of Sir John Franklin, by Col. Gawler, the then Governor, was well merited, as a reward for the perseverance and patience he had shewn on the occasion—for those only who have been at the spot can form an idea of the disturbed and doubtful character of the place, and the risk there must have been in the attempt to enter such a passage for the first time.

third of a mile in breadth, and when the river is flooded a strong current runs out of it with such rapidity, that the tide setting in at the same time causes a short and bubbling sea. It took Captain Barker nine minutes and fifty-eight seconds to swim across it on the fatal occasion on which he lost his life —but he was obliged to go somewhat above the outlet, as the stream would otherwise have carried him amidst the breakers. The western shore is very low, but the eastern one is marked by a large sand-hill, now called Barker's Knoll, after that talented and amiable officer. From seaward, nothing but a wild line of sand-hills meets the view, such as few mariners would venture to approach, and through which fewer still could hope to find a passage into the calmer waters of Lake Victoria, so completely hidden is the entrance. It was only by patient watching indeed, that Mr. Pullen seized the opportunity by which he entered the Goolwa. He was not the first, however, who did so, as Captain Gill, the master of a small cutter that was unfortunately wrecked on the strand at some distance to the eastward of the outlet, was the first to come down the Coorong in his boat, in which he ultimately reached Victor Harbour, but he also had to remain three weeks under the sand-hills before he could venture forth. Some years prior to this, however, Sir John Jeffcott, the first judge of South Australia, and Captain Blenkensorf, the head of the fishery, both found a watery grave in attempting to pass from the Goolwa into Encounter Bay.

I speak more particularly on the point, however, because, in 1838, during my first visit to the province, I went with a party of hardy seamen, with the intention, if possible, of passing into the Goolwa from seaward. At Encounter Bay, Captain Hart, who had the superintendence of the fishery there, gave me his most experienced steersman, and a strong whale-boat. In this I left Victor harbour for Freeman's Nob, a small rocky point in the very bight of Encounter Bay, where I remained until three A.M. of the next morning, when I started for the outlet under the most favourable auspices. A northerly wind had been blowing off the land for several days, and the sea was so tranquil that I had every hope of success. I had five leagues to pull, and keeping about a mile from the shore, swept rapidly along it. We were still about four miles from the inlet when the sun rose over it, as if encouraging us onwards. On approaching it at low water, I tried in vain to enter. The sea was breaking heavily right across the entrance from one side to the other, and after several ineffectual attempts to run in, I came to an anchor, close to the outer line of breakers, hoping that the sea would subside at high water and that we should then have less difficulty. We had not, however, been in this position more than half an hour, when a heavy southerly swell set in ; from a deep blue the water became green, and the wind suddenly flew round to the S.W. Before we could weigh and stand out from the shore, several seas had broken outside of us, and in less than ten minutes

the whole coast, to the distance of more than a mile
from the shore, was white with foam, and it seemed
clear that a gale was coming on. Under these circumstances I determined on returning to the little
harbour from which we had started in the morning,
but the wind being directly against us, we made
very little head. " We shall never get to the Nob,"
said Mr. Witch, who had the steer oar, to me; " it
blows too hard, Sir." " What are we to do, then?"
said I. " Why, Sir," he replied, we must either
beach or run out to sea," " We will beach, then," I
said ; " it is better to try. that than to do any thing
else." Mr Witch evinced some surprise at my
decision, but made no remark. " You had better
select your place," I observed, " and be careful to
keep the boat's head well on to the seas." " You
need not fear me, Sir," said the hardy seaman; " I
am accustomed to such work. It looks worse than
it really is." The sea, however, was now breaking
full a mile and a half from the shore, and in looking
towards it I observed a solitary horseman riding
slowly along, as if watching our movements. At
length Mr. Witch said that he thought we were opposite to a favourable spot, on which I directed him
to put the boat's head towards the shore, and to keep
her end on as he went in. Round we flew, and in
a moment after we were running at railway speed
on the top of a heavy wave. " Steady, men," said
Mr. Witch: " Steady all," and on we went; but
looking round him a moment after — " Back,
all. Back, all," he cried. The men did as they

were ordered, and the boat's way was stopped.
Her stern rose almost perpendicularly over the prow,
and the next moment fell into the trough of the sea.
The wave, transparent as bottle glass, rushed past
us, and topping, as it is called, burst at our very
bow, in a broad sheet of foam. " Give way, my
lads," was the next order of the watchful steersman,
as he again cast his eyes behind him. " Give way,
my lads. Give way, all." " Steady, men," he
called, as if doubtful of the result of the coming
wave. I thought I saw paleness on the face of the
rowers, but they pulled regularly and well, and a
thundering sound soon told us we had escaped the
threatening sea that had come so rapidly up. I do
not know if I am doing justice to the occurrence.
There was more of apparent than real danger in it,
and I myself was less nervous, because I had not
long before been accustomed to the heavy surf of
Norfolk Island. It was, however, a moment of great
excitement. We had literally shot towards the
shore, and were now within fifty yards of it, when
Mr. Witch said to me, " Take care of yourself, Sir;
we shall catch it at last."

I turned round, and saw a large roller close upon
us, just on the point of topping—I had scarcely time
to stoop and give my back to it when it came upon
us, and I never had such a thump in my life. The
boat was filled in a moment and we were all thrown
out—Mr. Witch, who had been standing, was hurled
to a great distance, but the men were up in a
moment, the water being about four feet deep, and

with admirable dexterity ran her on the beach.   I
do not remember ever having been in so strong a
breeze.   The reader may form some idea of it when
I assure him that the wind rolled the boat over and
over as if she had been as light as a carpenter's chip,
and the sand and pebbles came with such violence
in our faces, that we were obliged to retreat behind
the sand hills until it moderated.

It was my friend Mr. Strangways who had accompanied me from Adelaide, whose figure we had seen
on the beach, and he assured me that we seemed to
fly as we approached him.

The wind having apparently flown permanently
round to the south, and it being hopeless to expect
that the sea would subside for many days, I hauled
the boat over the sand hills, and launching her in
the Goolwa, tried to row through the outlet to sea,
but after remaining for eight days, and having my
boat four times swamped, I was forced to give up
the attempt as I had no time to spare.   The distance
between my outer and inner points might have been
a cable's length.   In endeavouring to pass out I
shoaled to a quarter less one, having kept the lead constantly going.   I abandoned the task therefore under
an impression that the outlet was not navigable, yet
Mr. Pullen succeeded in taking a small cutter into the
Goolwa with perfect safety.   I cannot but conclude
therefore that it has a shifting bar, and that it will
present difficulties to regular navigation that will
only be surmounted by a better knowledge of its
locality, and in all probability by artificial means.

From Freeman's Nob the coast line turns southwards to Rosetta Head, a bold and prominent conical hill, from the summit of which the whalers look for their game. Under the lea of Rosetta Head there is a small harbour called Rosetta Harbour. It is separated by a rocky island called Granite Island, and a reef that is visible at low water, and connects Granite Island with the main land from Victor Harbour, so called after H.M's ship Victor, when surveying in that quarter. Neither of these harbours however are considered secure, although they are protected from all but south-east winds.

It was in Rosetta Harbour, that during the early settlement of the Colony the South Australian Company's ship South Australian, was driven on shore and lost. The John Pirie, a strongly built schooner, also belonging to the Company, had well nigh shared her fate. This little vessel was lying astern of the Australian when she went ashore, with the reef close astern of her. In this fearful position her anchors began to drag, and her destruction appeared inevitable, when her commander, Captain Martin, determined on attempting to take her over the reef, it being high water at the time. He accordingly cut his cable, set his sails, and ran his vessel on the rocks. Four times she struck and was heaved as often over them, until at length she floated in the deeper water of Victor Harbour, and found her safety under the lea of the very danger from which she expected destruction. It was a bold resolve and deserved the success that attended it. I always feel a pleasure in recording such events, not only from feelings of admiration, but because they are examples for men to follow when placed in equally hazardous circumstances, and shew that firmness and presence of mind are equal to almost every emergency. The anchorage in Victor Harbour is under the lea of Granite Island, but I believe it is foul and rocky, and until both it and Rosetta Harbour shall be better known, the seaman will enter them with caution. Encounter Bay indeed, is not a place into which the stranger should venture, as he would find it extremely difficult to beat out to sea with a contrary wind. Still no doubt vessels may find refuge at these places from strong west and south-west winds, but I have always understood that it is better for a ship encountering a gale at the entrance of Backstairs Passage rather to keep at sea, than seek shelter in any contiguous harbour.

There is room for two or three tolerably sized vessels in Victor Harbour, which is in longitude 188° 38′ 00″ and in latitude 35° 32′, and in certain seasons of the year it may be deemed secure, if it were not liable to other objections, but I have heard it stated by an experienced seaman, one whose intimate knowledge of this part of the coast of South Australia is indisputable, that there is anchorage under the lea of Freeman's Nob, and a small island off it, sufficient for two or three vessels of 250 or 300 tons, altogether preferable to either of those I have mentioned, as being more sheltered, and having better holding ground—but we must not forget that

it is deeper in the bay, and there would consequently be a greater difficulty in beating out ; but
the truth is that the importance and capabilities of
these harbours will only be developed as the wants
of the colonists render it necessary for them
to have ports in this vicinity. When the country
to the eastward of the mountains shall be more
thickly peopled, and when the rich and fertile valleys
of the Inman, the Hindmarsh and Currency Creek,
and the available country between the two last,
be more generally cultivated, and when the mines
at the Reedy Creek and other places are at full
work, the want of a harbour at Encounter Bay will
be sufficiently apparent.

The principal whale fishery on the coast of South
Australia is in Encounter Bay, and has, I believe,
of late years proved as advantageous a speculation
to those who have carried it on as could be expected ;
profits are of course dependent on contingencies, as
the nature of the season and the number of whales
that may visit the coast : but the fishery at Encounter Bay has certainly been as successful as any
other on the coast, and would have been more so if
the ground had not been intruded upon. As a source
of colonial industry, and as a proof of commercial
enterprise, I should regret to see this bold and hardy
occupation abandoned. See Appendix.

From Rosetta Head the line of coast again trends
for a short distance to the west, and forms, together with the opposite shore of Kangaroo Island, the

Backstairs Passage, or eastern entrance into St. Vincent's Gulf, of which Cape Jervis is the N.W. point. It is here that the more important navigation of the South Australian seas commences. The line of coast I have already described is not sufficiently known to be approached by the stranger without caution, nevertheless the several bays and harbours I have mentioned may offer better shelter and greater convenience than I am able to point out.

One of the first establishments, if not the very first, of the South Australian Company was on Kangaroo Island, on the shores of Nepean Bay. Here the town of Kingscote was laid out, and some very good houses built, which are now falling to dilapidation and decay, since it has been abandoned by the Company's servants for some years. Nevertheless Kingscote is a very pretty sea-port town, and the harbour is undoubtedly good. The bay is large enough to hold a number of ships, and is secure from all winds, being almost completely land-locked. The water inside moreover is smooth, since the bay is protected by a long spit of sand, whereby the roughness of the outer sea does not affect it, and vessels consequently lie there during heavy weather without any apparent motion. It is to be regretted, that, with such advantages, Kingscote Harbour should have any drawback, but when we have given credit for its capabilities as a harbour, we have done all, and even as a harbour, sailors are divided in opinion, whether or not American River, or a small bay, five miles to the south-east of it, are not to be preferred. In Nepean Bay there is a deficiency of water, which is not the case in either of the last mentioned places. The soil is equally good in the neighbourhood of all three, but Kingscote having been occupied, the ground has been cleared of the dense brush that grew on it in a state of nature, and some of the most productive gardens in the Province are to be found there. It is astonishing what quantities of the finest onions are sent from Kingscote, with other produce, to Adelaide. The island is, however, so generally and so heavily covered with brushwood, that although the soil is good in many places, it has been found impracticable to clear. On the general character of Kangaroo Island, I would observe, that, from the reports of those best acquainted with it, nine-tenths of the surface is covered with dwarf gum-trees, or heavy low brush, that there are no plains of any consequence, no harbours excepting those I have already mentioned, — that water is generally scarce, and the best land is most heavily wooded and perfectly impenetrable; but, if it is thus useless and unavailable for pastoral and agricultural purposes, Kingscote, being so short a distance from Adelaide, holds out every inducement as a watering-place to those who, desiring change of air and sea-bathing, would wish to leave the heated neighbourhood of the capital during the summer months. It is a disadvantage to them that there are few places on the shores of St. Vincent's Gulf, on which bathing places could be established, but the change of air at Kingscote would be as great a benefit as sea-bathing itself, for hot winds are not felt there, but a cool and refreshing breeze is almost constantly blowing. As a watering-place therefore, it may, one day or other, be of importance, when the convenience of steam-boats shall render the passage from Adelaide to Kangaroo Island, like a trip across the Channel. But it is to be observed that whatever disadvantages the island may possess, its natural position is of the highest importance, since it lies as a breakwater at the bottom of St. Vincent's Gulf, and prevents the effects of the heavy southerly seas from being felt in it. There is, perhaps, no gulf, whether it is entered by the eastern or western passage, the navigation of which is so easy as that of St. Vincent, and so clear of dangers, that it can only be by the most fortuitous circumstances, or the most culpable neglect, that any accident can befal a ship in its passage up to Adelaide.

Anxious to make this portion of my work as useful as possible, and feeling assured that the remarks I have hitherto made will only lead the seaman to adopt those measures of precaution in approaching any of the harbours and bays I have mentioned, our knowledge of which is still limited, I shall here quote a passage from a small book of Sailing Instructions for South Australia, published some years ago by Captain Lee, an experienced mariner, for the guidance of commanders of vessels bound to Port Adelaide.

I shall only observe that, in running up the Gulf it is extremely difficult to recognise the peak of Mount Lofty ; but a pile of stones has been erected upon it, which is easily visible through a good telescope, and that the pilot station spoken of by Captain Lee as being five miles from Glenelg has been abandoned, and the pilots now board ships from the light vessel moored off the bar.

" Vessels from England bound to Port Adelaide, should, after leaving the Cape of Good Hope, run to the eastward in 37° or 38° south latitude, until they arrive in longitude 132° east, when they may haul to the northward, so as to get into latitude 36° 25', in longitude 135° 30' ; then steer to the north-east, and make Kangaroo Island, passing between which and a small island named Althorpe's Island, they will enter Investigator's Straits. These Straits form the western entrance to St Vincent's Gulf, and are so free from danger, that it seems almost wonderful how any vessel can get on shore without gross negligence. The only danger that can possibly affect a vessel is the Troubridge Shoal, and this, by a little attention to the lead, may be easily avoided, as on the south side of the shoal the water deepens gradually from four to seventeen or eighteen fathoms. The shores on the side of Kangaroo Island are bold and rocky, whilst on the north side, on Yorke's Peninsula, they are low and sandy. In working up in the night, stand no nearer to the north shore than nine fathoms, or to the southward than twelve fathoms. You will have from sixteen to twenty fathoms in the fair way—fine grey sand, mixed with small pieces of shell. In working up St. Vincent's Gulf, you may stand to the eastward in six fathoms, and towards the Troubridge Shoal in nine fathoms. The prevailing winds are from the south-west to south-east, especially in the summer months, when the sea breeze sets in about nine o'clock. The strength of tide in the Gulf is very irregular, with a strong south-west wind, the flood runs up at the rate of about two miles an hour, whilst with a northerly wind it is scarcely perceptible. The anchorage in Holdfast Bay is hardly safe in the winter months, as it is quite open to north-west, west, and south-west winds, which, when blowing hard, raise a short tumbling sea. The ground is a fine sand, almost covered with weeds, so that when the anchor once starts, the weeds being raked up under the crown, will in a great measure prevent its again holding. In the summer months it may be considered a perfectly safe anchorage, if due caution is exercised in giving the vessel cable in time. The best anchorage for a large vessel is with the summit of Mount Lofty, bearing east in six fathoms. A small vessel will lay better close in, just allowing her depth of water sufficient to ride in.

"The pilot station for Port Adelaide is about five miles north of Holdfast Bay. In running up keep in five fathoms, until abreast of the flag-staff on the beach, when a pilot will come on board. It is always high water in Port Adelaide morning and evening, and consequently low water in the middle of the day. In the present state of the harbour, no vessel drawing more than sixteen feet water ought to go into the port. Several very serious accidents have befallen vessels in this port, for which the harbour itself ought certainly to be held blameless."

"Vessels," he adds, "from Sydney, or from the eastward, bound to Port Adelaide, having arrived at Cape Howe, should shape a course for Hogan's Group in Bass' Straits, when off which, with a northerly wind, the best passage through the Straits is between Redondo and Wilson's Promontory, because should a gale of wind come on from the north-west, as it almost invariably does commence in that quarter, they would have more drift to the south-east than if they passed through near Kent's Group or Sir R. Curtis's Island. It is also a great saving in distance. Having arrived off King's Island, with a north wind, stand well out to the west or south-west, so as to keep well to the southward of Cape Northumberland, as the heavy gales from the north-west seldom last more than forty-eight hours, when they veer to the south-west, and fine weather ensues. Being abreast of Cape Northumberland, a south-west wind will be a favourable wind to proceed to Adelaide. Steer directly for the east end of Kangaroo Island, which you may pass at a distance of one mile; and if the wind is from the south or south-east, you may then steer across Backstairs Passage to Cape Jarvis; having arrived off which, proceed as directed before : should the wind be strong from south-west or west-south-west, keep Kangaroo Island close on board until abreast of Cape Jarvis, when you will have the Gulf open. Should it be night time or thick weather, and you have sighted Cape Willoughby at the entrance after passing that Cape, steer north-west fifteen miles, and you may lay to or run up north-east by east under snug sail until daylight. There are four rocks at the entrance of this passage, called the Pages; with a beating wind, you may pass on either side of them, but with a leading wind there is no necessity to approach them at all, as it is best to pass close round Cape Willoughby. Should the wind be so strong that a vessel could not carry sufficient canvas to fetch through the passage, it would be better for a stranger to stand out to the southward, rather than attempt to run into Encounter Bay. The anchorage in Encounter Bay is close round Granite Island, where a vessel may lay sheltered from all winds, save from south-east. There are several good anchorages where a vessel may run to, should she be caught in a gale of wind in Bass' Straits : one behind Wilson's Promontory, the corner inlet of Flinders; another in Western Port; two under King's Island, besides several on the Van Diemen's Land side, as Circular Head, George Town, Preservation Island, &c., the whole of which may be attained by a proper consideration of the chart ; but it is always better, provided a vessel has sufficient sea room, to keep at sea than to run for an anchorage, as the sea will seldom hurt a good ship properly managed, and she is always ready to take advantage of any change that may take place.

" Should a gale of wind come on when a vessel is far to the westward of King's Island, she may run for Portland Bay. In going in, you pass to the eastward of the St. Lawrence Islands, and haul directly in for the land west-north-west ; keep along the

H Melville

PORT ADELAIDE.

south shore of the bay, at a distance of one mile, until you see
the flag-staff at Mr. Henty's ; bring that to bear west, and you
will have six fathoms water about three-quarters of a mile from
shore."

From Cape Jarvis the coast line tends to the
north along the eastern shore of St. Vincent's Gulf.
The scenery, as you turn the point, is extremely
diversified. Dark cliffs and small sandy bays, with
grassy slopes almost to the water's edge, succeed
each other, backed by moderate hills, sparingly
covered with trees, and broken into numerous
valleys. Thus you pass Yankelilla, Rapid Bay, and
Aldingis; but from Brighton the shore becomes
low and sandy, and is backed by sand hummocks,
that conceal the nearer country from the view, and
enable you to see the tops of the Mount Lofty
Range at a distance of from eleven to twelve
miles.

Port Adelaide, a bar harbour, is about nine miles
from Glenelg, and situate on the eastern bank of a
large creek, penetrating the mangrove swamp by
which the shore of the Gulf is thereabouts fringed.
This creek is from ten to eleven miles in length. Its
course for about two miles after you cross the bar is
nearly east and west, but at that distance it turns to
the south, and runs parallel to the coast; and there
is an advantage in the direction it thus takes, that
would not be apparent to the reader unless explained. It is, that, as the land breeze blows off
the shore in the evening, and the sea breeze sets in

in the morning vessels can leave the harbour, or run up to it as they are inward or outward bound.

The landing-place of the early settlers was too high up the creek, and was not only the cause of great inconvenience to the shipping, but of severe loss in stores and baggage to the settlers; but at the close of the year 1839, Mr. McLaren, the then manager of the South Australian Company commenced and finished a road across the swamp to a section of land belonging to his employers, that was situated much lower down the creek, and on which the present Port now stands. The road, which is two miles in length, cost the Company £12,000. It has, however, been transferred to the local Government, in exchange for 12,000 acres of land, that were considered equivalent to the sum it cost.

The removal of the Port to this place was undoubtedly a great public benefit ; and whatever perspective advantages might have influenced Mr. McLaren on the occasion, he merited all due praise for having undertaken such a work at a time when the Government itself was unable to do so. Both the wharf and the warehouse belonging to the Company are very creditable buildings, as is the Custom House and the line of sheds erected by the Government ; but the wharf attached to them is defective, and liable to injury, from the chafing of the tide between the piers, which are not placed so as to prevent its action. Mr. Phillips' iron store is also one of a substantial description ; but there

was not, when I left the province, another building
of any material value at the Port.   Numerous
wooden houses existed in the shape of inns, stables,
etc. ; but the best of these were unfortunately
burnt down by a fire a few days before I
embarked for Europe.   Whether it is that a
misgiving on the minds of the public as to the
permanency of the Port has been the cause of, and
prevented the erection of more substantial and better
houses at Port Adelaide, it is difficult to say ; but
any one might have foreseen, that as the colony
progressed, and its commerce increased, the Port
would necessarily have to be moved to some part
of the creek where there was deeper and broader
water, for the convenience of the shipping.   I felt
assured, indeed, that the removal of the Port would
take place sooner than was generally supposed.
The following extract from the South Australian
Gazette of the 4th of December last, will prove that
I judged truly :—

" New Road to the North Arm.—This road was commenced last Tuesday week ; and at the rate at which the work
is progressing, will be completed (except as regards the subsequent metalling and ballasting) within four months from the
present time.   The line adopted is the one which was proposed
by Mr. Lindsay in 1840, as requiring less outlay in the original
construction than either of the other lines proposed.   Taking
Adelaide as the starting point, the course will be either along the
present Port Road between Hindmarsh and Bowden as far as
section No. 407, thence along the cross track between that
section and section No. 419 (preliminary), as far as the south-

east corner of Mr. Mildred's section, No. 421; then in a
straight line through the last named section and Mr. Gilles's, No.
2072, after leaving which it passes through an opening in the
sand-hills, and then winds along the highest ground between
the creeks, leaving the South Australian Company's road about
a mile on the left, till it joins the main road or street running
through section G. at the North Arm; or through North
Adelaide and along the road at the back of Bowden, parallel with
the main Port Road as far as Mr. Torrens' residence, to the
south-east corner of Mr. Mildred's section, thence through that
section as before. The soil of the so-termed swamp, or rather
marsh, is of the most favourable description for embanking and
draining operations, consisting at the part of the line where the
work has been commenced, of a good loam for the first spit, and
then clay to the depth of eighteen inches or two feet, resting
upon a stratum composed for the most part of shells of numberless shapes and sizes, which extends to the bottoms of the
drains (four feet), being the level of high water at spring tides,
and at about the same above the low-water level. The shelly
stratum continues below the bottoms of the drains to an
uncertain depth. From the commencement of the "Swamp"
to the Great Square or public reserve at the junction of the
North Arm with the main channel of the Creek, the distance
along the line of road is 4800 yards, or nearly two miles and
three-quarters. The breadth of the road between the ditches
will be 114 feet, or between three and four times the breadth of
the Company's road."

If there is anything more justly a subject of
congratulation to the Province than another, it is
the commencement of the work thus notified. The
road is now, in all probability, finished, and that
part of the creek rendered available where these
permanent improvements may be made, without

the fear of any future change; and when the shores of the North Arm shall be lined by wharfs, and the more elevated portions of Torrens' Island shall be covered with houses, few harbours will be able to boast of more picturesque beauty. There was something dreary in sailing up the creek with its dense and dark mangroves on either side, and no other object visible beyond them save the distant mountains; but the approach to the new Port will not fail to excite those pleasurable feelings in the heart of the stranger which give a colouring to every other object.

The removal of the port to the proposed locality will bring it within three miles of the bar, and will be of incalculable advantage to the shipping, since there will no longer be any delay in their putting to sea. The following letter, addressed by Captain Lipson, the Harbour-master, to the Colonial Secretary, in reference to the improvements that have been effected at the bar, will best explain its present state, and the description of vessels it will admit into the Port.

" Port, 6th July, 1847.

" Sir,—In answer to your letter of this day's date, requesting that I would report to you, for the information of the Legislative Council, what beneficial effects have been produced by the use of the mud barge in deepening the bar at the entrance of Port Adelaide, since the commencement of its operation, in the year 1845, up to the present date, also what additional depth of water, if any, has been obtained by the work alluded to.

" I have the honour to state, that at the commencement of
the colony, her Majesty's storeship ' Buffalo' was brought out
by the then governor, Captain Hindmarsh, to be detained here
nine months for the protection and convenience of the colonists.
It was, therefore, much wished to have her inside the bar ; but after
attending and carefully watching successive spring-tides, it was
given up as impracticable, she drawing fifteen feet. The Governor
then appointed a board to examine the bar, consisting of the
masters of the ' Buffalo,' ' John Renwick,' and another, who, in
their report, stated as their opinion, that no vessel above 300 tons
ought to be brought into the harbour ; however, last week two
vessels exceeding 600 tons have been brought up to the wharf.
But the most beneficial effect is now felt from a ship being able
to cross the outer bar so much sooner on the tide than before,
thereby having sufficient time to take her round the bar, and, if
moderate, to beat up and anchor at the North Arm the same
tide. Ships may now be brought in on the springs in winter,
drawing seventeen or eighteen feet, as the time of high water is
in the day, and the wind generally fair to beat in, but not so in
going out, from the difficulty of reaching the bar at the time required, and the tide leaving so quickly after the ebb is made
great care is required ; and I find it unsafe to allow any vessel
to load deeper than 15 or 16·6 inches at most. With a tug,
there would be less difficulty and danger in loading to 18 feet
than there now is to 15.

" There is now three feet more water on the bar than there
was previous to its being deepened, and if the work be continued
next summer, to enlarge a cut which has been made, there will
be five feet.

" I have the honour to be, Sir, your obedient servant,

" THOMAS LIPSON, Harbour Master.

" The Honourable Colonial Secretary."

It is not clear to me, however, that the admission
of larger class shipping into the Port will be of any
great advantage. I am led to believe that ships of

smaller tonnage than those drawing 16 to 17 feet,
have been found to be most convenient for the
ordinary purposes of commerce. However, it is
evident, that if Captain Lipson continues the same
praiseworthy exertions he has hitherto used, he will
deepen the bar for vessels of any tonnage. Under
existing circumstances, it may be as well to state
that any ship arriving off the bar when there is
not sufficient water on it for them to enter the
port, will find good anchorage all round the light-
ship, particularly a little to the westward of it.
The whole Gulf, indeed, from this point, may be
considered as a safe and extensive roadstead. As
regards Port Adelaide itself, I cannot imagine a
securer or a more convenient harbour. Without
having any broad expanse of water, it is of sufficient
width for vessels to lie there in perfect safety,
whether as regards the wind or the anchorage.

The head of St. Vincent's Gulf is in latitude
$34\frac{1}{2}°$. Between that point and Port Adelaide, the
shore is either lined by mangroves, or is low and
sandy. There are, nevertheless, several inlets
similar to, but much smaller than Port Adelaide,
and other commodious anchorages for small craft
along it. The principal of these is the inlet connected with the Gawler, of which I shall hereafter
speak. York Peninsula forms the western shore
of St. Vincent's Gulf, and separates it from that of
Spencer. It is a long, low tongue of land—Cape
Spencer, its southern extremity, being in 35° 17′,

and in long. 136° 52'. Though embracing a considerable area, the character of the Peninsula is unfavourable to the growth of nutritive herbage; the surface soil is a species of calcareous limestone, the rock formation of a tertiary description, although, at the lower extremity, granite and trap rock are known to exist. The surface of the country is undulating, covered in many places by scrub, and the trees being very short-lived, the whole is matted with dead timber, and difficult of access. A deficiency of water renders York Peninsula still more unfavourable for location; nevertheless, several sections of land have been purchased on that part which is immediately opposite to Port Adelaide, and it is said that indications of copper have been found there, a fact I should be inclined to doubt. In 1840, a company applied for a special survey on the shores of the Peninsula to the southward of Point Pearce, and gave the name of Victoria Harbour to the locality; but the survey was subsequently abandoned in consequence of the unfavourable character of the interior, from the great deficiency of water.

If we except the results of a survey made by the late Lieut.-Governor, Colonel Robe, of the upper part of Spencer's Gulf, during which, as is the case in the same part of the neighbouring gulf, his Excellency found convenient bays and inlets, but little is known of the eastern shore of that splendid gulf, beyond this point. Double the size of St. Vincent's

Gulf, it runs up to the $32\frac{1}{2}$ parallel, and was at one time or other very probably connected with Lake Torrens. The higher part is backed by a range of mountains, the more prominent of which were named by Captain Flinders—Mount Remarkable, Mount Browne, and Mount Arden. On the first of these there were so many indications of copper, that a special survey of 20,000 acres was taken by a company for the purpose of working any lodes that might be found. The country round about Mount Remarkable is stated to be exceedingly picturesque and good; so that independently of any value it may possess as a mineral survey, it possesses both agricultural and pastoral advantages. After passing the Mount Remarkable Range, however, the country falls off in character. A dreary region extends round the head of the Gulf, and, it is to be feared, to a much greater distance. The description given by Mr. Eyre, and the reports of those who have endeavoured to penetrate to the westward of Lake Torrens both agree as to the sterile and inhospitable character of the remote interior. Little improvement takes place in it on following down the western shore of the Gulf. Several individuals, indeed, have perished in endeavouring to take stock round the head of the Gulf to Port Lincoln, either from the want of water, or from having wandered and lost themselves amidst the low brush with which it is covered. The whole of the country, indeed, lying to the westward of Spencer's Gulf is, as far as I have been able to ascertain, of very inferior description. There are, it is true, isolated patches of good land, and a limited run for sheep, but the character of the country corresponds but little with the noble feature for which Spencer's Gulf is so justly celebrated. In reference to this magnificent basin, Captain Lee, from whom I have already quoted, observes—

"The harbour of Port Lincoln, including Boston Bay, is situated near the extremity of the Peninsula, which forms the west side of Spencer's Gulf in the Province of South Australia, and from its great extent, and the number of its safe anchorages, is capable of containing the largest fleets, and as a depôt, is not, perhaps, to be surpassed by any port in the world. Vessels from England, bound to Port Lincoln, should run along in about 35° 20′ south latitude, until they arrive in 135° 20′ east longitude, when they may haul up to the north-east, and make Cape Catastrophe. After arriving near the Cape, they may then shape a course to pass between it and Williams' Island. There are strong tide ripplings here, which, to a stranger, would present the appearance of reefs; but as the channel is perfectly clear, no danger need be apprehended. Having passed through the channel, should night be approaching, it would be advisable for a stranger to keep the main land aboard, leaving another Island (Smith's Island), on the starboard hand, and bring up in Memory Cove, a perfectly safe anchorage, in about five fathoms, and wait for day-light. Proceeding then along shore to the northward, he will arrive at Taylor's Island, which may be passed on either side; after which he may run along shore at a distance of one mile, until he arrives at Cape Donnington. This Cape may be known by its having a small islet laying about half a mile from the point. Rounding this islet, at half a cable's length, in about nine-fathoms' water, and hauling to the westward, he will open the magnificent harbour of Port Lincoln, stretching to the south-west as far as the eye can reach. Should the wind be fresh from the south or south-west, it would be better if bound to Boston Bay, to beat up between Boston Island and the promontory of Cape Donnington. The shores are steep on both sides, so that a vessel may stand close in on either tack. Should the wind be so strong as to prevent a vessel beating in, she may run up under easy sail to a bay on the north-east end of Boston Island, and bring up in seven fathoms opposite a white sandy beach, three-quarters of a mile off shore. There is also excellent anchorage at the entrance to Spalding Cove, bringing the western point of the promontory of Cape Donnington to bear north by east, and the northernmost of Bicker's Island west by north, you will lay in seven fathoms, muddy bottom. Having arrived at Bicker's Island and bound for Boston Bay, stand directly over to the westward, passing the south end of Boston Island, until you open the bay, when you may choose a berth according to circumstances, and in any depth from ten to four fathoms.

" The positions of the various points and islands are so correctly laid down on Flinders' chart, that the skilful navigator will at once know his exact situation by cross-bearings.

" The anchorage in Port Lincoln itself is not so safe as in Boston Bay, and more difficult of access, especially in the winter months, when the winds are strong from the south-west, and in the summer months it is quite open to the north-east. In working up, a vessel may stand close in to the eastern shore, and to within half a mile of the western, but should not attempt to pass between the two Bicker's Islands, as there is a reef running from the northernmost island nearly across to the other.

" Vessels from Adelaide, bound to Boston Bay, after arriving at Althorpe's Island, should shape a course so as to pass between the Gambier Islands and Thistle's Islands. There is a small island bearing west five miles from the south end of Wedge Island, the largest of the Gambier group, which is not laid down in Flinders, which should be left on the starboard hand. Bring

the highest part of Thistle's Island to bear west, distant about
six miles, and in twenty-two fathoms water, and a north-west
half-west course will carry you through midway between the
Horse-shoe Reef and the rocks which lay off the north-west end
of Thistle's Island, and in the direct track for Cape Donnington.
The passage between the reefs is about three miles wide, and
ought not to be attempted in the night, as the tides set directly
across the channel.   There is very good anchorage on the north-
east side of Thistle's Island, well sheltered three-fourths of the
year.   Bring the rocks before-mentioned to bear north-north-
west, and two remarkable sand hills south by west, and you will
lay in five fathoms, one mile off shore—north end Thistle's
Island west by south. Should the wind be so strong from south-
west or west-south-west, so that a vessel from the eastward
cannot carry sail sufficient to fetch up to Cape Donnington, or
under Thistle's Island, it would be advisable to bear up for
Hardwick Bay ; passing to the eastward of Wedge Island,
come no nearer to the shore of York's Peninsula than two
miles, until you arrive within five miles of Corny Point, when
you may haul in for that point, rounding it a distance of half a
mile, you may bring up in five fathoms, one mile from shore :
Corny Point bearing west.   Vessels from Sydney, bound to
Port Lincoln, may pass through Backstairs Passage, and proceed
according to the foregoing directions, or by keeping well to the
southward, pass outside Kangaroo Island, until they arrive in
longitude 136° E., when they may shape a course either to pass
between Gambier's and Thistle's Islands, or else for Cape Catastrophe, taking care to give the Neptune Islands a wide berth,
and then proceed according to either of the foregoing directions."

To this extract which refers exclusively to the
navigation of Spencer's Gulf, I may add, that
Boston Island lies immediately opposite to the bay,
and that there are two channels of entrance round

the island, through which vessels of the largest size can pass with any wind or in any weather, for the harbour is so sheltered by the headlands forming the entrance, that the swell of the sea is broken before reaching it.

The high ground which almost surrounds Boston Bay, protects it in like manner from the winds, more especially those coming from the west and south-west, in which directions some of the hills attain the height of several hundred feet.

The depth of water in the central parts of the Bay is about twelve fathoms, varying from five to seven at the distance of less than a quarter of a mile from the shore all round; whilst at Boston Point, where the town of Boston has been laid out, there is a depth of two, three, and four fathoms, at about a boat's length from the land. The bottom consists in some places of mud, in others of shells and sand, so that the anchorage is safe.

The tide sometimes rises seven feet, but that is considered a high tide, the ordinary rise not being more than five; this depends, however, on the outward state of the Gulf, and the quarter from which the wind may happen to be blowing.

In the summer season, the land and sea breezes blow very regularly, for three weeks or a month at a time. They are then succeeded by strong winds from the south-west, that last for three or four days, and are sometimes very violent. In winter these

N 2

interruptions to the usual calm state of the weather
are more frequent, but the harbour is little influenced by them ; taking it altogether, indeed, as a
harbour, it is unquestionably as safe and commodious as any in the world, and it is deeply to be
regretted, that its position, of which I shall have to
speak, and the nature of the country behind it,
should be any drawbacks to its becoming one of
the most important ports on the Australian Continent.

In the vicinity of Port Lincoln, the land is of
very varied character. To the west and south-
west it is poor and scrubby, covered with a diminu-
tive growth of she oak (Casuarinæ) or dwarf gum-
trees (Eucalypti), or it is wholly destitute of timber ;
but along the line of hills, stretching to the north, at a
short distance from the shores of the Gulf, there is
an improvement in the soil. The pasture is well
adapted for sheep, and there are isolated valleys in
which the soil is very good and fit for cultivation; but
this kind of country only occupies a narrow strip of
about ten miles, and although tracts of available
land have been found in the interior, and it has
been ascertained that water is not deficient, it must
still, I fear, be considered as a very inferior district.
As regards Port Lincoln itself, the inhabitants procure their water from a spring, on the sea-shore,
which is covered by every tide. This spring does
not appear to undergo any sensible diminution,
even in the height of summer, and is stated to be

so copious, that it would yield a most abundant
supply.

It has been reported, that strong indications of the
presence of copper have been found in the neighbourhood of Port Lincoln, and this report may be correct.   The discovery of mines there, would at once
raise the harbour to importance, and make it the
resort of shipping.   Mines might be worked at Port
Lincoln with more advantage perhaps to the province, than where they have been already in opera
tion, for it admits of great doubt whether the
benefit from the distribution of wealth from mining
speculations, makes up for the interference of such
speculations with other branches of industry.   Unless
some local advantage, of the kind to which I have
alluded, should give this noble harbour an impulse
however, it would appear to have but little prospect
of becoming a place of importance, for although
Spencer's Gulf penetrates so deep into the northern
interior, the country is altogether unprofitable, and
although there is depth of water sufficient for the
largest ships to the very head of the Gulf, yet, as
far as our present knowledge extends, it is not probable that it will be the outlet of any export produce.   It is to be remembered, however, that if there
should be minerals in any abundance found on the
Mount Remarkable special survey—the ore must
necessarily be shipped, from some one of the little
harbours examined by the Lieutenant-Governor
during his survey of that part of Spencer's Gulf—

In such case, Port Lincoln will be brought more immediately into notice.

From Port Lincoln, the shore of the Gulf still trends to the south, as far as Cape Catastrophe, in lat. 35°.   It then turns with an irregular outline to the N.N.W., and several bays succeed each other. The first of these is Sleaford Bay, sometimes occupied as a whaling station, but of no other importance. Coffin's Bay, almost immediately behind Port Lincoln, is rather an inlet than a bay, and runs so far into the interior, as to approach Boston Bay, to within 16 miles.   Coffin's Bay is exceedingly wide, and objectionable for many reasons, but as it is a whaling station of some importance, and visited by numerous whalers, I shall quote Captain Lee's remarks upon it, and give his directions for going to it.

" This is a very large bay, perfectly secure from all winds, save from north to east, but unfortunately a great portion of it is rendered useless by the shallowness of the water.   The best anchorage is with Point Sir Isaac, bearing north-north-west, about one mile and a half from the western shore in four or five fathoms. In working in with a southerly wind, you may stand to the eastward until you bring the above point to bear south-west by west, after which it would be better to make short tacks along the western shore.   You must be careful to keep the lead going, as the water shoals from five and four fathoms to one and a half at a single cast.   This bay seems well adapted for a fishing station.   The inner part of the bay extends a long way back into the country, at least thirty miles from Point Sir Isaac, and contains two or three secure harbours and excellent anchorages, a new chart of which is in course of publication.

" Vessels from Sydney bound to Coffin's Bay, should proceed as if bound to Port Lincoln until arrived off the Neptune Islands, when they should steer for Perforated Island, having passed which, steer for Point Whidbey, giving it a berth of at least two miles. In running along shore from Point Whidbey to Point Sir Isaac, come no nearer the shore than two miles, until you get the latter point to bear east-south-east as the rocks lay a long way from the shore. Having arrived at Point Sir Isaac proceed as directed before.

" Althorp's Island is of moderate height, situated at the entrance of Investigator's Straits ; may be passed close to on the south side. Several other islands and reefs lay between it and York's Peninsula, rendering that passage highly dangerous.

"Wedge Island, one of the Gambier Group, may easily be known by its wedge-like form, sloping from south-east to north-west. There are two peaked rocks off the south-east end, one mile off shore, also a small island, bearing west five miles from the south end, not laid down in Flinders' charts.

" Thistle's Island, is low at each end but high in the middle, it lays in a north-west and south-east direction. There are some rocks which lay off the northern point about three miles, which being connected with the island itself, forms a good anchorage behind, secure from all but north and east winds, another good place for a fishing party. See Port Lincoln directions.

" Neptune's Islands are low, three in number, and having numerous rocks and reefs amongst them; ought not to be approached too closely, there being generally a strong swell from the south-west, the sea breaks over them with great violence.

" Liguanea Island is of moderate elevation, and may be passed on the south side at a distance of two miles.

" Perforated Island, as its name imports, may be known by its having a hole through it near the north end and close to the top of the island, it may be passed close on any side. *Four Hummocks* may easily be known from their appearance answering to their name.

" Greenly Island, this is a peaked island, rather high, and may

be seen ten leagues off. There is another island laying south and
by west, seven miles, not laid down in Flinders', and two other
reefs between them, rendering the passage unsafe.

" Proceeding along shore to the northward you will fall in with
Flinders' Island. This is a large island, covered with wood,
with plenty of fresh water, possessing a secure anchorage on the
northern side, and is admirably adapted for a whaling station.
In going on from the southward, keep outside the top Gall's
Island, and steer directly for the north-east point, rounding
which, you will open the anchorage, and as there is no danger,
but may be seen, you may choose a berth according to circumstances.

" Waldegrave's Island, close to the main land, has good anchorage on the northern side, secure from south-east and south-west
winds.

"The shore, from Waldegrave's Island to Point Weyland is low
and sandy. There is a large body of water running in a direction parallel to the coast, all the way from Point Weyland to the
northward of Cape Radstock, having an entrance at both points.
It appears as if the action of the sea from the south-west, had
broken through the coast range and filled up the valley immediately behind. Indeed the whole coast from Kangaroo Island to
as far to the north-west as has been visited by the author, bears
evident marks of the encroachments of the sea. In some places
marked down as small islands in Flinders', there are now only
reefs, other places which were formerly points of land, are trans-
formed to islands."

In the year 1840, I was instructed by the then
Governor of South Australia, to send an officer of
the survey in a small vessel, with a supply of provisions for Mr. Eyre, who was at that time supposed to have reached Fowler's Bay, during the
first of his expeditions; I accordingly selected Mr.
John Cannan, in whose zeal and ability I had every

confidence. This officer left Port Adelaide the 9th
September, 1840, with instructions from me, in addition to the immediate object he had in view, to
survey such parts of the coast along which he was
about to sail, as had only been partially examined
by Captain Flinders. Unfortunately it was during
the winter time, and the task I had assigned him
would, I knew, be attended with considerable risk
in beating along that dangerous and stormy coast.
Mr. Cannan arrived at Streaky Bay on the 27th
September, but was disappointed in finding Mr.
Eyre, or a letter he had buried for him under Cape
Bauer, he therefore proceeded to the examination of
the coast, as I had instructed him to do; and the
following extract from his report will not only enable the reader to judge how he performed that
service, but will give him the best information as
to the character of the several bays and inlets he
examined.

" I send you a chart of Streaky, Smoky, and Denial Bays, by
which you will be better able to judge of the capabilities of the
harbours they contain, than by any description I can give. I
may mention however, that the entrance to Smoky Bay, between
the shoals of St. Peter's and Eyre's Islands, is dangerous, for
with any swell on the sea breaks right across. In the inlet, on
the west side of Denial Bay, there is a salt water creek with two
fathoms of water ; and adjoining some high sand-hills, among
which we found fresh water by digging. Our vessel being the
first, I believe, that ever entered Smoky Bay, on finding an
island at its southern end, I named it after that enterprising traveller Mr. Eyre. I also found an island and reef not laid down
by Flinders, to the southern of St. Francis Islands. There is

also an island 10 miles west of the rocky group of Whidbey's Isles, and about 12 miles from Greenly's Isles. The captain of a French whaler also informed me, that a sunken rock lays 6 miles N.W., off Point Sir Isaac, on which the sea breaks in heavy weather.

"The desert country surrounding these bays has been sufficiently explored, and so correctly described by Mr. Eyre, as not to require to be mentioned. The absence of any rise that can be called a hill, from Mount Greenly to Mount Barren, the eternal limestone cliffs, the scarcity of water and grass, surely prove this coast to be the most miserable in the world, whilst the harbours are as good as could be wished for, and it must be owing to the deficiency of charts, that whalers do not frequent these bays, for there are generally two or three French or American vessels in the neighbourhood during the season. I found no bones or carcases of whales in Streaky, Denial, or Smoky Bays, but the shores of Fowler's and Coffin's Bays, I found strewed with their remains. In the latter place, Captain Rossiter, of the Mississippi shewed me his chart, and told me there was no shelter for a vessel on this side of the Bight, except at Fowler's Bay, and that was indifferent. The great extent of smooth water at Denial and Streaky Bays, and a well of water on St. Peter's, dug by a sealer who lived on it many months, afford more advantages for fishing, and more especially to a shore party, than are to be found any where else in the Province.

"From the general flatness of the country, it may be presumed that its character does not alter for a great distance inland. I observed nothing in the formation of the island, differing from the mainland, and I may mention that the rocks of the isles of St. Francis presented the same appearance as the Murray Cliffs."

It will appear from the above, that Mr. Cannan did not proceed farther to the westward than Fowler's Bay, and that he did not therefore prolong his survey to the western limits of the Colony, by a distance of about five leagues, since the 132° meridian falls on that coast a little to the westward of Cape Adieu, and between 12 and 15 leagues from the bottom of the Great Australian Bight.

Although some of the bays and harbours I have described in running along its coast, are not so good as might be desired, yet it is evident that, as a maritime country, South Australia is particularly favoured, not only in having anchorage of the safest description, but also in possessing two or three known harbours, capable of containing ships in any number or any size, and as safe and capacious as any in the world. Looking indeed at Port Adelaide, one cannot but admire its appropriate and convenient position. Had such a harbour not existed there, the produce of that fertile portion of the Province would hardly have been available to the inhabitants in the shape of exports, so difficult would it have been to have found another harbour of equal security, or of equal size, for the commercial wants of the settlers. Added to this, it has the double advantage of being close to the capital, being so easy of access, and in so central a position, as to be able to communicate with the neighbouring colonies with the greatest ease.

It will be remembered that I stated in the former part of my work, that the remarkable wall forming the Great Australian Bight, was thrown up simultaneously with the great fossil bed of the Murray.

As the principal object of the Expedition into Central Australia was to ascertain the past and present structure of the Continent, I have been led to allude to the subject again, in consequence of two or three remarks in Mr. Cannan's letter, which has been quoted above, bearing strongly upon it, and corroborative of the hypothesis I have entertained as proving a striking uniformity in the rock formation of those two localities. To those remarks I would beg to call the attention of my readers. They will be found at the commencement and termination of the last paragraph.

CHAPTER II.

PLAINS OF ADELAIDE—BRIDGES OVER THE TORRENS—SITE
OF ADELAIDE—GOVERNMENT HOUSE BUILDINGS AND
CHURCHES—SCHOOLS—POLICE—ROADS—THE GAWLER—
BAROSSA RANGE—THE MURRAY BELT—MOORUNDI—NA-
TIVES ON THE MURRAY—DISTANT STOCK STATIONS—
MOUNT GAMBIER DISTRICT—ITS RICHNESS—ASCENT TO
MOUNT LOFTY—MOUNT BARKER DISTRICT—SCENE IN
HINDMARSH VALLEY—PROPORTION OF SOIL IN THE
PROVINCE—PASTORAL AND AGRICULTURAL—PORT LIN-
COLN—CLIMATE OF SOUTH AUSTRALIA—RANGE OF THE
THERMOMETER—SALUBRITY.

HAVING, in the preceding chapter, run along the
coast of South Australia, and noticed such parts
as have been sufficiently examined to justify our
observations, it remains for me to give an account
of its interior features, of its climate, soil, mineral,
and other sources of wealth, and lastly of its fitness
as a colony for the peculiar habits of an English
population.

The city of Adelaide, the capital of South Australia, stands on the eastern shore of St. Vincent's Gulf,
and is about six miles from the coast. Any one
landing either at the old or new port, and proceeding to the capital for the first time, would perhaps
be disappointed at the description of country through
which he would pass. It consists indeed of extensive level plains, over the eastern extremity of which
the Mount Lofty Range is visible. They are
bounded southwards by a line of trees, marking the

course of the river Torrens across them, but extend
northwards for many miles without any visible termination. Their monotony however, is, at the
present date, in some measure broken by belts of
wood, and the numerous cottages that have been built
upon them, with their adjoining corn-fields, have
changed their aspect, and removed the appearance
of loneliness which they first exhibited. Still neither
the gloomy swamp over which the stranger has in the
first instance to travel, on landing at the Port—or the
character of the plains themselves, are calculated to
raise his anticipations, as to the beauty or fertility
of the interior. The first town through which he
will pass after leaving the Port, is Albert Town,
which has been laid out on the first available ground
near the swamp. When I left the colony in May
last, several tolerable buildings had been erected in
Albert Town, but it was nevertheless a wretched
looking and straggling place, and will never perhaps
advance beyond its present state.

On his nearer approach to the capital the traveller
will pass between the villages of Boden and Hindmarsh, in both of which he will observe numerous
kilns of bricks. He will then enter on the Park
Lands, by which North and South Adelaide are
separated from each other. On this land the scene
at once changes, and he will find himself riding
through an open forest, shading rich, alluvial, and
grassy flats; and, strictly speaking, will then be
traversing the Valley of the Torrens. In May, 1847,

there were four bridges over that little river. The
Company's bridge a little above the city. The
Frome bridge, a light wooden structure, built by
the sappers and miners, under the direction of Captain Frome, the Surveyor-General, after whom it
was called. The City bridge, constructed of stone,
but then incomplete, and a rude wooden bridge between Adelaide and Hindmarsh, erected by an inn-
keeper, with a view of drawing the traffic from the
Port past his door. The City bridge, which was
undertaken by contract, promised to grace the approach to Adelaide, and was intended to be the
principal bridge to connect the north and south
portions of the city, as well as to form the chief
line to the Port and to the north. The occurrence
of an unusual flood, however, in the latter part of
the year 1847 deprived the good citizens of Adelaide of these necessary means of communication
with the country on the right bank of the Torrens,
by the injury it did to them. The Company's
bridge suffered less than any other, but was so
shaken as to be impassable for several days. Aware,
as I am, of the general character of the Australian
streams, and seeing no reason why the Torrens
should differ from others, taking into consideration,
too, the reports of the natives as to the height to
which the river had been known to rise in former
years, and the fact that no rain had fallen since the
establishment of the Colony to cause any very great
or sudden flood, it appeared to me, that the place

selected for the City bridge was too low. Ordinary
floods so completely change the channel of the
river, and make such devastation in its bed, that it
is hardly to be recognised when the water subsides,
so that unless the banks are high, and the soil of
which they may be composed stiff enough to resist
the impetuosity of the stream, I fear no bridge
across the Torrens will be permanently safe.

The position and ground chosen by the first Surveyor-General of South Australia, as the site of its
future capital is a remarkable instance of the quick
intelligence of that officer. For although he had
but little time to make his selection, a more intimate knowledge of the coast has proved that no
more eligible point could have been found. Fault
has, I am aware, been found with Colonel Light in
this matter, but without just grounds, I think, for
in no other locality could the same quantity of
water have been found, or the same facility offered
for the construction of those reservoirs and other
works so necessary to the health and comfort of a
large metropolis. A principal objection raised to
the situation of Adelaide is its distance from the
Port, but that we must remember is a disadvantage
common to many other large and mercantile cities.
The Surveyor-General seems to have been fully
aware of the responsible duty that devolved upon
him, and to have acted with great judgment. Port
Lincoln, indeed, is a splendid harbour, one with
which Port Adelaide, as far as size goes, cannot be

compared, but having said this nothing farther can be advanced in its favour, for it is not only deficient in its supply of water, but the contiguous country is far from rich, whereas Adelaide is backed by one of undoubted fertility.

Established where it is, the city of Adelaide stands on the summit of the first elevated ground, between the coast and the mountain ranges.

It is separated, as the reader will have learnt, by the valley of the Torrens, and occupies the northern and southern slopes and brows of the hills on either side. The view to the westward from the more elevated parts of the city commands the whole of the plains of Adelaide, and St. Vincent's Gulf; to the eastward, it extends over the rich and dark wooded valley of the river, the lighter wooded country at the base of the Mount Lofty Range, and the peaks and elevations of that beautiful mountain chain.

South Adelaide is on flat ground and twice the size of the northern part of the town. It has also been more extensively built upon, and is the established commercial division of the city. The Government House and all the public buildings and offices are in South Adelaide, and the streets in the vicinity of the North Terrace, have assumed a regularity and uniformity greater than any street in North Adelaide. Hindley and Rundle streets, indeed, would do no discredit to any secondary town in England. Every shop and store that is now built is fo a substantial and ornamental character, and

those general improvements are being made which
are the best proofs of increasing prosperity and
opulence.

There is scarcely any article of European produce
that cannot be obtained in Adelaide, at a very little
advance on home prices, nor is it necessary, or indeed advisable that Emigrants should overload
themselves in going out to any of the Australian
Colonies.   Experience, the best monitor, leads me
to give this advice, which, however, I am bound to
say, I did not adopt when I went out to New South
Wales; but the consequence was, that I purchased
a great many things with which I could have dis-
pensed, and that I should have found the money
they cost much more useful than they proved.

King William Street divides Hindley from Rundle Street, and is immediately opposite to the gate of
Government House, which is built on a portion of
the Park lands, and is like a country gentleman's
house in England.   It stands in an enclosure of
about eight or ten acres; the grounds are neatly
kept, and there is a shrubbery rapidly growing up
around the House.

The Public Offices are at the corner of King William Street and Victoria Square, facing into the latter. The building is somewhat low, but a creditable edifice, to appearance at all events, although not large enough for the wants of the public service.

I am not aware that there is any other public building worthy of particular notice, if I except the

gaol, which is a substantial erection occupying the north-west angle of the Park land, but is too low in its situation to be seen to advantage at any distance. Like Government House, it was built with a view to future addition, but fortunately for the colony, Government House is the first which seems to call for completion.

The number of Episcopalian Churches in Adelaide is limited to two, Trinity Church and St. John's. The former was originally built of wood, and may be said to be coeval with the colony itself. It has of late however been wholly built of stone, and under

o 2

the active and praiseworthy exertions of Mr. Farrell, the colonial chaplain, an excellent and commodious school-room has been attached to it.

Trinity Church stands on the North Terrace, and is a prominent object as you ascend from the Park lands. St. John's is situated on the East Terrace at a greater distance, but it has a commanding view of the Mount Lofty Range, and the intervening plains. Perhaps considering that the city has not extended much in the direction of East Terrace, it may be a little too far for public convenience, but this is a question that admits of doubt. It is a neat and unostentatious brick building, at which the Rev. Mr. Woodcock performs service, whose exertions amongst the natives in the West Indies have stamped him both as a christian and a philanthropist. The two churches are calculated to hold about 1000 sittings, and the average attendance is about 900.

It may appear to the reader that the number of churches in Adelaide, where there is a population of between 8000 and 10,000 souls, is not sufficient, as is the case. Ere this however, a third church, to be called " Christ's Church," will have been erected in North Adelaide, where such a place of worship was much required. £500 had been subscribed for the purpose in December last, and it was confidently anticipated that the further contributions of the colonists would enable the committee to commence and finish it. The arrival of the Bishop on the 24th of the above month, of which accounts have been received had given great satisfaction, and his Lordship was to begin his useful ministry on the following day (Christmas Day), by preaching at Trinity Church.

However few the Episcopalian churches in the capital of South Australia, we cannot accuse the Dissenters of a similar want of places of public worship, of which there are 9, the whole number throughout the province being 31 ; whilst the number of churches is 6. The Congregational chapels are calculated to accomodate 4700 communicants, the average attendance being about 2300, and are, generally speaking, good looking and ornamental buildings, and do no discredit to those who superintended their erection, and approved the places.

There is a Roman Catholic Bishop of South Australia, but he had, during the latter period of my residence in the province, been absent in Europe. The Catholic Church stands on the West Terrace, and is, perhaps, in one of the most healthy situations that could have been chosen. There is an excellent school attached to the church, which is equally open to all denominations of Christians, and is, I have understood, more numerously attended than any other in the capital. The total number of Sunday-schools in the province, in 1841, was 26, at which 617 boys and 582 girls attended. The average number of Sunday and other schools in 1845 was 55, at which 780 males and 670 female children attended.

In the year 1846, when His Excellency Colonel

Robe laid the estimates on the table of the Legislative Council, its attention was drawn to the state of education and religion in the province, and after a long discussion on the subject, a grant of 2s. per head was voted to the different sects in aid of religion and education. It was left to the ministers of the Protestant Church, and to the proper officers of the other persuasions to appropriate the sum received by each, according to the last census, as they deemed best, for the promotion of one or the other of the above purposes, with the sole condition that they should render an account yearly to the Council of the manner in which the several sums had been appropriated. Yet this provision, which without interfering in the slightest degree with any religious sect, gave to the heads of each the greater power of doing good, caused very great dissatisfaction. All I can say is, that it was an instance of liberal and enlightened views of government, of which the Council of South Australia in having set the example ought to be proud.

The Legislative Council of New South Wales has since, I believe, followed its example, and I sincerely trust the good that is anticipated, will result from this proof on the part of both Governments to raise the moral and social character of the people.

In addition to the schools already noticed, there is a school for the natives on the Park lands. At this school there were in 1847, thirty-five boys and twenty-nine girls. The establishment being entirely under the superintendence of the Government, is kept in the very best order; the apartments are neat and clean, the master is patient and indulgent, and if we could hope for any improvement in the moral and social habits of the aborigines, it would be under circumstances so promising, but as I propose, in another place, to make some observations on the natives generally, it may not be necessary for me to add to the above remarks at the present moment.

Of other public buildings not under the immediate controul of the Government, the Bank of South Australia is certainly the first. It stands on the North Terrace and is a prominent and pleasing object from whatever point of view it is seen. There are, however, several other very creditable buildings in different parts of the city.

Had the city of Adelaide been laid out in the first instance on a smaller plan, it would now have been a compact and well-built town, but unfortunately it was planned on too large a scale, and it will necessarily have a straggling appearance for many years to come.

North and South Adelaide are, as I have already stated, separated from each other by the valley of the Torrens, than which nothing can be prettier. Its grassy flats are shaded by beautiful and umbrageous trees, and the scenery is such as one could not have expected in an unimproved state. The valley of the Torrens is a portion of the Park lands which run round the city to the breadth of half a mile. Nothing could have been more judicious than the appropriation of this open space for the amusement and convenience of the public, and for the establishment of those museums and institutions which tend so much to direct the taste, and promote the scientific improvement of a people.

Beyond the Park lands, the preliminary sections, of 134 acres each, extend to a certain distance— many of which have been laid out into smaller sections, and the city is surrounded by numerous villages, few of which add to its appearance. This certainly may be said of Thebarton, Hindmarsh, Boden, and several other villages, but those of Richmond, and Kensington, embosomed in trees, and picturesque in scenery, bear a strong resemblance to the quiet and secluded villages of England.

In Hindmarsh, Mr. Ridley, whose mechanical genius has been of such public utility, and whose enterprise is so well known, has established his steam flour-mill, which is the largest in the province. In addition to this, the South Australian Company has a steam-mill at the upper bridge; there are several of a smaller size in the city, and the total number of flour-mills in the Colony, including wind and water mills is twenty-two.

This general description of the capital of South Australia will perhaps suffice to shew its rapid growth during the eleven short years since the first wooden dwelling was erected upon its site.

It may be necessary for me to state that its peace

and order are preserved by a body of police, whose vigilance and activity are as creditable to them as their own good conduct and cleanliness of appearance; and whilst the returns of the supreme court, and the general unfrequency of crime, prove the moral character of the working classes generally, the fewness of convictions for crimes of deeper shade amongst that class of the population from whose habit of idleness and drinking we should naturally look for a greater amount of crime, as undoubtedly proves the vigilance of the police. From the return of convictions before Mr. Cooper the Judge, it is clear that the majority of those who have been brought before him are men who have already suffered for former breach of the laws, and who, having escaped from the neighbouring Colonies, have vainly endeavoured to break themselves of former evil habits. The eyes of the police are however so steadily kept on such men, that they have little chance of escaping detection if they commit themselves, and they consequently level their aim at those who encourage them in vice, and who, in reality, are little better than themselves in morals, as knowing that, in many instances, they will not dare to bring them to punishment.

There are five principal roads leading from Adelaide; three into the interior, and two to the coast. Of the three first, one leads to the north, through Gawler Town, one as the Great Eastern Road leads to Mount Barker and the Murray, and the third

running southwards, crosses the range to Encounter
Bay. Of the roads leading to the coast, the one
goes to the Port, the other to Glenelg. In endeavouring to give a description of the country, and
enabling the reader to judge of it, I would propose
to take him along each of these roads, and to point
out the character and changes of the country on
either side, for the one is peculiar and the others
are diversified. My desire is to present such a
view of the colony to the minds of my readers, as
shall enable them to estimate its advantages and
disadvantages. I would speak of both with equal
impartiality and decision. The grounds of attachment I entertain for this colony rest not on any
private stake I have in its pastoral or mineral
interests, and I hope the reader will believe that my
feelings towards it are such as would only lead me
to speak as it really and truly should be spoken of.
There is no country, however fair, that has not some
drawback or other. There are no hopes, however
promising, that may not be blighted ; no prospects,
however encouraging, that may not wither. Unfit-
ness for the new field of enterprise on which a man
may enter —unpropitious seasons, the designs of
others, or unforeseen misfortunes ; one or more of
these may combine to bring about results very opposite from those we had anticipated. I would not
therefore take upon myself the responsibility of
giving advice, but enter upon a general description
of the province of South Australia as a tourist, whose

curiosity had led him to make inquiries into the
capabilities of the country through which he had
travelled, and who could therefore speak to other
matters, besides the description of landscape or the
smoothness of a road.

If we take our departure from Adelaide by the
great Northern Road, we shall have to travel 25
miles over the plains, keeping the Mount Lofty Range
at greater and less distances on our right, the plains
extending in varying breadth to the westward, ere
we can pull up at Calton's Hotel in Gawler Town,
where, nevertheless, we should find every necessary
both for ourselves and our horses.

That township, the first and most promising on
the Northern Road, is, as I have stated, 25 miles
from Adelaide; and occupies the angle formed by the
junction of the Little Para and the Gawler Rivers; the
one coming from south-east, and the other from north-
north-east; the traveller approaching from the south
therefore, would have to cross the first of these little
streams before he can enter the town.

Still, in its infancy, Gawler Town will eventually
be a place of considerable importance. Through it
all the traffic of the north must necessarily pass, and
here, it appears to me, will be the great markets for
the sale or purchase of stock. From its junction
with the Little Para, the Gawler flows to the westward to the shores of St. Vincent's Gulf. It has
extensive and well wooded flats of deep alluvial soil
along its banks, flanked by the plains of Adelaide—

the river line of trees running across them, only
with a broader belt of wood, just as the line of trees
near Adelaide indicates the course of that river.   If
I except these features, and two or three open box-
tree forests at no great distance from Albert Town, the
plains are almost destitute of timber, and being very
level, give an idea of extent they do not really possess, being succeeded by pine forests and low scrub
to the north from Gawler Town.

The Gawler discharges itself into a deep channel
or inlet, which, like the creek at Port Adelaide,
has mangrove swamps on either side ; still the
inlet is capable of great improvement, and the anchorage at its mouth, so high up the gulf is safe,
and if it were only for the shipment of goods, for
tran-shipment at Port Adelaide, Port Gawler as it is
called, would be of no mean utility, but it is probable that ships might take in cargo at once, in
which case it would be to the interest of the northern
settlers to establish a port there.   Captain Allen
and Mr. Ellis, two of the most independent settlers
in the province, are the possessors of the land on
both sides the Gawler, and I feel confident it is
a property that will greatly increase in value.   The
alluvial flats along this little stream, are richer and
more extensive than those of the Torrens, and they
seem to me to be calculated for the production of
many things that would be less successfully cultivated in any other part of the province.   Apart,
however, from any advantages Gawler Town may

derive from the facilities of water communication, it will necessarily be in direct communication with Port Adelaide, as soon as a road is made between them. At present the drays conveying the ore and other exports are obliged to keep the great northern line to within a few miles of the city, before they turn off almost at a right angle to the Port; but there can be no doubt as to the formation of a direct line of communication with the Port from Gawler Town, if not of the establishment of a railway, ere many years shall elapse, for not only are the principal stock stations of the province, but the more valuable mines to the north of this town.

Up to this point the traveller does not quit the plains of Adelaide, the Mount Lofty Range being to the eastward of him and the plains, bounded by the mangrove swamps extending towards St. Vincent's Gulf. Generally speaking, for their extent the soil is not good, but there are patches of alluvial soil, the deposits of creeks falling from the hills, that are rich and fertile. Yet, notwithstanding the quality of the soil, a great portion of the Adelaide plains have been purchased and are under cultivation. There is a great deficiency of surface water upon them, but it is procurable by digging wells; and Mr. Ellis I believe has rendered those parts of them contiguous to the Gawler available as sheep stations, by sinking wells for the convenience of his men and stock; neither can there be a doubt but that many other apparently unavailable parts of the

province might be rendered available by the adoption
of similar means, or by the construction of tanks in
favourable situations.

This is a point it is impossible to urge too much
on the attention of the Australian stock holder.
There is generally speaking a deficiency of water in
those Colonies, and large tracts of country favourable
to stock are unoccupied in consequence, but the present liberal conditions on which leases of Crown lands
are granted will make it worth the sheep farmer's
while to make those improvements which shall so
conduce to his prosperity and comfort.

In proof of this, I would observe that I had
several capacious tanks on my property at Varroville, near Sydney, for which I was indebted to Mr.
Wells the former proprietor, and not only did they
enable me to retain a large quantity of stock on my
farm, when during a season of unmitigated drought
my neighbours were obliged to drive their cattle to
distant parts of the Colony—but I allowed several
poor families to draw their supplies from, and to water
some of their cattle at my reservoirs.

Beyond Gawler Town the country changes in
character and appearance, whether you continue the
northern road across the river, or turn more to the
eastward, you leave the monotonous plain on which
you have journeyed behind, and speedily advance
into an undulating hilly country, lightly wooded
withal, and containing many very rich, if not beautiful
valleys. The Barossa Range and the districts round

it are exceedingly pretty. Here, at Bethany, the
Germans who have fled from the religious persecution to which they were exposed in their own country have settled, and given the names of several places
in their Fatherland to the features around them.
The Keizerstuhl rises the highest point in the Barossa Range, the outline of which is really beautiful,
and the Rhine that issues from its deep and secluded
valleys flows northwards through their lands.

In this neighbourhood Mr. Angas has a valuable
property, as also the South Australian Company.
Angas Park is a place of great picturesque beauty,
and is capable of being made as ornamental as any
nobleman's estate in England. The direct road to
the Murray River passes through Angas Park, but
a more northerly course leads the traveller past the
first of those valuable properties to which South
Australia is mainly indebted for her present prosperous state. I mean the copper mines of Kapunda,
the property of Captain Bagot, who, with Mr.
Francis Dutton, became the discoverer and purchaser
of the ground on which the principal lode has been
ascertained to exist. There has been a large quantity of mineral land sold round this valuable locality,
but although indications of copper are everywhere
to be seen, no quantity sufficiently great to justify
working had I believe been found up to the time I
left the Colony. As however I shall have to give
a more detailed account of the mines of South Aus-

tralia, it may not be necessary for me to speak of them at length in this place.

Captain Bagot is anxious to establish a township in the vicinity of Kapunda, and he will no doubt succeed, the very concourse of people round such a place being favourable to his views.

Beyond this point to the north the coast range of Mount Lofty, which thus far preserves a northerly direction, throws off a chain to the westward of that point, but the main range still continues to run up into the interior on its original bearing, rather increasing than decreasing in height. Upon it, the Razor Back Mount Brian, to the south of which is the great Burra Burra mine, and the Black Rock Hill, rise to the height of 2922, 3012 and 2750 respectively. On the more western branch of the chain, Mount Remarkable, Mount Brown, and Mount Arden, so named by Captain Flinders, form the principal features. This chain has been traced by Mr. Eyre to Mount Hopeless, in lat. $29\frac{1}{2}$, and has been found by him to terminate in the basin of Lake Torrens. The main range on the contrary has only been followed up to lat. 32° 10′, beyond which point it cannot extend to any great distance, as if it did, I should necessarily have seen something of it during my recent expedition. It is a remarkable fact that the further the northern ranges have been followed up, the more denuded of trees they have become. Immense tracts of land, through

Cap.ⁿ Frome. R.E delt

MOUNT BRYAN.

portions of which the Wakefield flows, rich in soil and abundant in pasture, have scarcely a tree upon them. The scenery round Mount Remarkable on the contrary is bold and picturesque, and much diversified by woodland.

Here again the indications of copper were so abundant, that 20,000 acres were taken as a special survey a short time before I left the Colony. The occupation of this land will necessarily extend the boundaries of location, but up to the period when the survey was taken, Mr. White, formerly a resident at Port Lincoln, was the most distant stockholder to the north.

Proceeding eastward from Angas Park, the road to the Murray river leads through a hilly country of an inferior description, portions only of it being occupied as sheep stations. From the brow of the last of these hills, the eye wanders over the dark and gloomy sea of scrub, known as the Murray belt, through which the traveller has to pass before he gains the bank of the river or the station at Moorundi. He descends direct upon the level plain over which he has to go, and after passing some pretty scenery on the banks of a creek close to which the road runs, and crossing an open interval, he enters the belt, through which it will take him four hours to penetrate. This singular feature is a broad line of wood, composed in the lower part of Eucalyptus dumosa, a straggling tree, growing to an inconsiderable height, rising at once from the ground with many slender stems, and affording but an imperfect shade. About the latitude of 34° the character of the Murray belt changes—it becomes denser and more diversified. Pine trees on sandy ridges, Acacia, Hakea, Exocarpi, and many other shrubs form a thick wood, through which it is difficult to keep a correct course. Occasionally a low brush extends to the cliffs overlooking the valley of the Murray, but it may be said, that there is an open space varying in breadth from half a-mile to three miles between the Murray belt and the river. It is a flat table land about 250 or 300 feet above the level of the sea, the substratum being of the tertiary fossil formation. The surface is a mixture of red sand and clay, mixed with calcareous limestone in small rounded nodules. The very nature of this soil is heating, and the consequence is that it has little herbage at any one time. There is however a succession of vegetation, especially during the spring months, which, from the fact of the cattle being particularly fond of it, must I should imagine be both sweet and nutritious.

Any one who has ever been on the banks of the Murray will admit that it is a noble river. The description I have already given supersedes the necessity of my dwelling on it here. In another place I shall have to speak of it, not in a commercial point of view, but as a line of communication between two distant colonies, and the important part it has acted in the advancement of the province of

South Australia. As a commercial river, I fear it will not be of practical utility. To prove this, it may be necessary for me to observe that the Murray runs for more than five degrees of latitude through a desert. That it is tortuous in its course, and is in many places encumbered with timber, and its depth entirely depends on the seasons. The difficulties, therefore, that present themselves to the navigation of the central Murray are such as to preclude the hope of its ever being made available for such a purpose, even admitting that its banks were located at every available point. Moorundi, the property of Mr. Eyre, the present Lieutenant-Governor of New Zealand, is ninety miles from Adelaide, and twenty-six from the N.W. bend of the Murray. It is part of a special survey of four thousand acres taken by Mr. Eyre and Mr. Gilles on the banks of the river, and in consequence of its appropriate position, was selected by Captain Grey, the then Governor of South Australia, as a station for a Resident Magistrate and Protector of the Aborigines, to fill both which appointments he nominated Mr. Eyre. There can be no doubt, either as to the foresight which dictated the establishment of this post on the banks of the Murray, or the selection of Mr. Eyre as the Resident. At the time this measure was decided on, the feelings of the natives on the river were hostile to the settlers. The repeated collisions between them and the Overlanders had kindled a deep spirit of revenge in their breasts, and although they suffered

severely in every contest, they would not allow any
party with stock to pass along the line of the river
without attempting to stop their progress; and there
can be no doubt but that, in this frame of mind,
they would have attacked the station next the river
if they had been left to themselves, and with their
stealthy habits and daring, would have been no
mean enemy on the boundaries of location. The
character and spirit of these people is entirely misunderstood and undervalued by the learned in England, and the degraded position in the scale of
the human species into which they have been put,
has, I feel assured, been in consequence of the little
intercourse that had taken place between the first
navigators and the aborigines of the Australian
Continent. I have seen them under every variety
of circumstances—have come suddenly upon them
in a state of uncontrolled freedom — have passed
tribe after tribe under the protection of envoys—
have visited them in their huts—have mixed with
them in their camps, and have seen them in their
intercourse with Europeans, and I am, in candour,
obliged to confess that the most unfavourable light
in which I have seen them, has been when mixed
up with Europeans.

That the natives of the interior have made frequent attacks on the stations of the settlers I have
no doubt; very likely, in some instances, they have
done so without any direct provocation, but we must
not forget their position or the consequences of the

extension of boundaries of location to the aborigines themselves. The more ground our flocks and herds occupy, the more circumscribed become the haunts of the savage. Not only is this the inevitable consequence, but he sees the intruder running down his game with dogs of unequalled strength and swiftness, and deplores the destruction of his means of subsistence. The cattle tread down the herbs which at one season of the year constituted his food. The gun, with its sharp report, drives the wild fowl from the creeks, and the unhappy aborigine is driven to despair. He has no country on which to fall back. The next tribe will not permit him to occupy their territory. In such a state what is he to do? Is it a matter of surprise that in the confidence of numbers he should seek to drive those who have intruded on him back again, and endeavour to recover possession of his lost domain? It might be that the parties concerned were not conscious of the injury they were inflicting, but even that fact would not lessen the fancied right of the native to repossess himself of his lost territory. Yet on the other hand we cannot condemn resistance on the part of the white man; for it would be unjust to overlook the fearful position in which they are placed, and the terrible appearance of a party of savages working themselves up to the perpetration of indiscriminate slaughter. No doubt many parties have gone to take up stations in the interior, with the honest intention of keeping on good terms with the natives, and who in accordance with such resolution have treated them with hospitality and consideration; but, it unfortunately happens that a prolonged intercourse with the Europeans weakens and at length destroys those feelings of awe and uncertainty with which they were at first regarded. The natives find that they are men like themselves, and that their intrusion is an injury, and they perhaps become the aggressors in provoking hostilities. In such a case resistance becomes a matter of personal defence, and however much such collisions may be regretted, the parties concerned can hardly be brought to account; but, it more frequently happens, that the men who are sent to form out-stations beyond the boundaries of location, are men of bold and unscrupulous dispositions, used to crime, accustomed to danger, and reckless as to whether they quarrel, or keep on terms with the natives who visit them. Thrown to such a distance in the wild, in some measure out of the pale of the law, without any of the opposite sex to restrain their passions, the encouragement these men give to their sable friends, is only for the gratification of their passions. The seizure of some of their women, and the refusal to give them up, provokes hostility and rouses resentment, but those who scruple not at the commission of one act of violence, most assuredly will not hesitate at another. Such cases are generally marked by some circumstances that betray its character, and naturally rouse the indignation of the Government. If the only consequence was the punishment of the guilty, we should rejoice in such retributive justice; but, unfortunately and too fre-quently, it happens, that the station belongs to a stockholder, who, both from feelings of interest and humanity, has treated the natives with every consi-deration, and discountenanced any ill-treatment of them on the part of his servants, but whose property is nevertheless sacrificed by their misconduct.

I have been unintentionally led into this subject, in the course of my remarks on the policy of Captain Grey, in establishing the post at Moorundi. The consequences have been equally beneficial to the settlers and aborigines. The eastern out-sta-tions of the province have been unmolested, and parties with stock have passed down the Murray in perfect safety. If any act of violence or robbery has been committed by the natives, the perpetrators have been delivered up by the natives themselves, who have learnt that it is their interest to refrain from such acts; and instead of the Murray being the scene of conflict and slaughter, its whole line is now occupied by stock-stations, and tranquillity everywhere prevails.

About fifteen miles below Moorundi is Welling-ton, where a ferry has been established across the Murray, that township being on the direct road from Adelaide to Mount Gambier, and Rivoli Bay.

A little below Wellington, Lake Victoria receives the waters of the Murray, which eventually mingle with those of the ocean, through the sea mouth.

The country immediately to the eastward of the Murray affords, in some places, a scanty supply of grass for sheep, but, generally speaking, it is similar in its soil and rock formation, and consequently in its productions to the scrubby country to the westward. The line of granite I have mentioned, in the former part of my work, as traversing or crossing the Murray below Wellington, continues through the scrub, large blocks being frequent amongst the brushes on a somewhat lower level than the tertiary fossil limestone in its neighbourhood. Round these blocks of granite the soil is considerably better, and there is a coating of grass upon it, as far as the ground consists of the decomposed rock.

About sixty miles to the E.S.E. of Wellington is the Tatiara country, once celebrated for the ferocity and cannibalism of its inhabitants, but now occupied by the settlers, who have of late crossed the Murray in considerable numbers to form stations there. The distance from Wellington to the district of Mount Gambier, said to be the fairest portion of South Australia, whether as regards its climate or its soil, is more than 200 miles. The first portion of the road, to almost the above distance, is through a perfect desert, in which, excepting during the rainy season, water is scarcely to be found, so that the journey is not performed without its privation. After passing Lake Albert the traveller has to journey at no great distance from the Coorong over a low country, once covered by the waters of the ocean, the noise of whose billows he hears through the silence of the night. The first elevation he reaches is a continuation of the great fossil bed, through which the volcanic hills, where he will ultimately arrive, have been forced up. Mount Gambier, the principal of these, is about 40 miles from the Glenelg, and 50 from Rivoli Bay. The country from either of these points is low for many miles, but well grassed, of the richest soil, and in many places abundantly timbered. Mount Gambier is scarcely visible until you almost reach its base— nor even then is its outward appearance different from other hills. On reaching its summit, how-ever, you find youself on the brink of a crater, standing indeed on a precipice, with a small sheet of water of about half-a-mile in circumference, two hundred feet below you; the water of which is as blue as indigo, and seems to be very deep; no bot-tom indeed has been found at 50 fathoms. The ground round the base of Mount Gambier is very open, and you may ride your horse along it un-checked for many miles. At the lower parts, and at some distance from it, the ground is moist, and many caverns have been found in which water of the very purest kind exists, no doubt deposited in the natural reservoirs by percolation from the higher

ground.   The whole formation of the district, these
capacious caverns, and the numerous and extensive
tea-tree swamps along the coast, plainly demonstrate
that they are supplied by gradual filtration, or find
their way through the interstices, or cells of the lava
to the lower levels.

It is generally admitted that the greater part of
the land in the neighbourhood of Mount Gambier is
equal to the richest soil, whether of Van Diemen's
Land or of Port Phillip, the general character
indeed of this district, and the fact of its being so
much farther to the south than Adelaide, its perpetual verdure and moister climate would lead to
the supposition that it is capable of producing grain
of the very finest quality, and there can, I think, be
but little doubt that it will rival the sister colonies
in its agricultural productions, and considering the
nature of the soil is similar to that round the volcanic peaks in the Mediterranean, it will also produce wine of a superior description.   Settlers both
from the province of South Australia and neighbouring colonies have vied with each other in secur-
ing stations in this fertile, but remote district, and
it would appear from the number of allotments that
have been purchased in the townships which have
been established on the coast that settlers are fast
flocking to it.

From what has been stated it would seem that
the district of Mount Gambier is adapted rather for
agricultural than pastoral pursuits, and that it is

consequently favourable for occupation by a rural population. Tea-tree swamps (melaleuca) are a feature, I believe, peculiar to South Australia, and generally indicate the presence of springs, and always of moisture. The soil is of the very richest quality, and there is, perhaps, no ground in the world that is more suitable for gardens, and as these swamps are both numerous and extensive in the lower country, behind Rivoli and Guichen Bays, this portion of the province promises equally fair for the growth of those European fruits which are less advantageously cultivated in the more northern parts of the province.

Returning to Adelaide, and proceeding from thence to the eastward, along the great eastern or Mount Barker line, we cross, in the first instance, the remaining portion of the plains lying between the city and the hills, to the base of which the distance is about three miles, the whole is laid out in farms, and is extensively and carefully cultivated. As you approach the hills, the country becomes lightly wooded and undulating, affording numerous sites for villas, on which many have already been erected, both by settlers and the more opulent tradesmen. Individuals indeed, residing in England, can form but a faint idea of the comforts and conveniences they enjoy, at such a distance from their native country. Being at sufficient elevation to catch the sea breeze, which passes over the plains of Adelaide, without being felt, they have almost the

advantage of living near the sea coast, and the cool
winds that sweep down the valleys behind them, and
constitute the land breeze, ensure to them cool and
refreshing evenings, when those dwelling at a lower
elevation are oppressed by heat.   On the first rise
of the mountains is the Glen Osmond Lead Mine,
which will be noticed hereafter.   The Mount Barker
district being more numerously settled than most
other parts of the province, and being one of its
most important and fertile districts, more labour has
been expended on the road leading into it, than on
any other in the colony.   From the level of the
Glen Osmond Mine, it winds up a romantic valley,
with steep hills of rounded form, generally covered
with grass, and studded lightly with trees on either
side, nor is it, until you attain the summit of the
Mount Lofty range, that any change takes place in
the character of the hills or the vegetation, you
then find yourself travelling through a dense forest
of stringy barks, the finest of which have been levelled to the ground, with the axe, for the purpose
of being sawn into planks for building, or split into
rails for fencing.   From Crafer's Inn, situated under
the peak of Mount Lofty, the road to Mount Barker
passes through a barren country for some miles,
and crosses several steep valleys, in the centre of
which there are rippling streams; the summit of the
ranges still continues to be thickly wooded, the
ground underneath being covered with shrubs and
flowers of numberless kinds and varied beauty.   In

illustration of this, I may observe, that the first time I crossed the Mount Lofty range, I amused myself pulling the different kinds of flowers as I rode along, and on counting them when I reached Adelaide for the purpose of arranging them in a book, found that I had no less than ninety-three varieties. The majority of these, however, consisted of papilionaceous plants, and several beautiful varieties of Orchideæ. On descending to a lower level, after crossing the Onkaparinga, the scenery and the country at once change, you find yourself upon rich alluvial flats, flanked by barren rocky hills, the air during the spring being perfumed by the scent of the Tetratheca, a beautiful hill flower, at that time in splendid blossom, and growing in profusion on the tops of the hills, mingled with the Chyranthera, with its light blue blossoms; both these plants it has always appeared, are well adapted for the edges of borders, but there are not many plants in Australia that would be fit for such a purpose.

It does not appear necessary, in a work like this, to trouble the reader with an account of every village or of every valley in the districts through which I lead him; my object is to give a general and faithful description of the country only, reserving the power of drawing attention to any thing I may deem worthy of notice. Taking the district of Mount Barker therefore in its full range, I would observe, that it is one of the finest agricultural districts in the province. It abounds in very many beautiful alluvial valleys, which, when I first crossed, had grass that rose above the horses middles as they walked through it, and looked luxuriant beyond description. These valleys are limited both in length and breadth, but are level and clear; their soil is a rich alluvial deposit, and the plough can be driven from one end to the other without meeting a single obstacle to check its progress. Independently of these valleys, there are other portions of good grazing land in the Mount Barker district, but there are, nevertheless, very many stony ranges that are entirely useless even to stock. The Mount Barker district may be said to extend from the village of Nairne to Strathalbyn, on the River Angas, the latter place being 15 miles from the shores of Lake Victoria. Within the range of this district, there are also the villages of Hahansdorf and Macclesfield, the former being a German village, at no great distance from Mount Barker. Immediately to the north of the village of Nairne is Mount Torrens, the river of that name has several branches to the north-east of it as high up as Mount Gould. The first of the Company's special surveys, and perhaps some of the finest soil in the province is in this locality. The surveys on the sources and tributaries of the Torrens are splendid properties, and the Company may well consider them as amongst the most valuable of its acquisitions; beyond the heads of the Torrens the country is more hilly and less available. There are, nevertheless, isolated spots sufficiently large for the most comfortable homesteads. From this point, a west-south-west course will soon lead the traveller into the plains of Adelaide, and at less than 10 miles after entering upon them, he will again find himself in the metro-polis. Again departing from it for the southern parts of the province, he will keep the Mount Lofty range upon his left, and will really find some diffi-culty in passing the numberless fences which now enclose the plains. The land indeed in this line of road is more fenced than in any other direction, a reason for this may be that the road runs nearer the base of the hills, and the land is consequently better than that on the lower ground. Many very excel-lent farms are to be found on the banks of the Sturt and the Onkaparinga, on the latter of which the village of Noorlunga has been established, at the point where the road crosses it. The Sturt has a tortuous course, somewhat to the northward of west, and falls into the gulf at Glenelg, after spreading over the flats behind the sand-hills at that place. The direction of the road is parallel to that of the ranges, or nearly south-south-west as far as the vil-lage of Noorlunga, when it turns more to the east-ward of south, for Willunga, which is 28 miles distant from Adelaide. The banks of the Onkapa-ringa, above the crossing place, are extremely inaccessible, insomuch that stock can hardly be driven down to water for many miles above that point. The hills however are rounded in form, grassy, and clear of trees, consequently well adapted for grazing purposes. It was at Noorlunga, which is not more than two miles from the gulf, and can be approached in boats, as high as the bridge there, that Captain Barker first landed on the South Australian shore. The country between it and Willunga is generally good, portions of it are sandy and scrubby, but Morphett's Vale is a rich and extensive piece of land, and I can well remember before it was settled seeing several large stacks of hay that had been cut, as it then lay in a state of nature. Willunga is close under the foot of the hills, which here, trending to the south-south-west, meet the coast line extremity of the Southern Aldinga plains. Close to this point is a hill, called Mount Terrible, almost of a conical shape, over the very summit of this, in the early stages of the colony, the road led to Encounter Bay; and I shall not forget the surprise I experienced, when going to that place, on finding I could not by any possibility avoid this formidable obstacle. On the other side of Mount Terrible the country is very scrubby for some miles, until, all at once, you burst upon the narrow, but beautiful valley of Mypunga. This beautiful valley, which had scarcely been trodden by the European when I first encamped upon it, was then covered with Orchideous plants of every colour, amidst a profusion of the richest vegetation. A sweet rippling stream passed within five yards of my tent-door, and found its

way to the Gulf about a mile below me to the west.
It was on the occasion of my going to the sea
mouth of the Murray, that I first stopped at this
spot.   Amongst the boat's crew I had brought with
me from Adelaide a young lad, of not more than
twenty-one, who had, for some weeks before, been
leading a very hard life. At Mypunga he was seized
with delirium tremens, and became so exceedingly
outrageous, that I was obliged to have his feet and
hands tied. In the morning he was still as frantic as
ever, but the policeman, under whose charge I had
placed him, having imprudently loosened the cord
from his ankles, he suddenly started upon his feet,
and gaining the scrub, through which we had
descended into the valley, with incredible swiftness,
secreted himself amongst it.   Nor could we, by the
utmost efforts during that and the succeeding day,
discover his hiding place.   I was accompanied by a
man of the name of Foley, a bushranger of great
notoriety, who had been captured by the Adelaide
police, and was sent with my party in the hope that
his knowledge of the coast would be of use to me,
but neither could he discover the unfortunate run-
away, who, there is no doubt, subsequently perished.
Beyond Mypunga, to the south, are the valleys of
Yankalilla and Rapid Bay, but very little, if in any
respect inferior to the first mentioned place.   The
country between them is, however, extremely hilly,
and contains some beautifully romantic spots of
ground.   The rock formation of this part of the

ranges is very diversified ; the upper part of Rapid
valley is a fine grey limestone ; a little to the southward veins both of copper and lead have been discovered, and I have good reason for supposing that
quicksilver will one day or other be found in this
part of the province.   At Willunga there is a small
stream, which issues from a valley close behind the
township, and appears in former times to have laid
many hundred acres of the flats below under water.
Their soil is composed of the very richest alluvial
deposit, and has produced some of the finest crops of
wheat in the province. Aldinga plains lie to the south-
west of Willunga, and are sufficiently extensive to feed
numerous sheep, but unavailable in consequence of
the deficiency of water upon them, and are an instance
of a large tract of land lying in an unprofitable
state, which might, with little trouble and expense,
by sinking wells in different parts, be rendered extremely valuable.   On ascending the hills above
Willunga, in following up the southern line of road
to Encounter Bay, it leads for several miles through
a stringy-bark forest, and brings the traveller upon
the great sandy basin, between Willunga and Currency Creek.   This gloomy and sterile feature bears
a strong contrast to the rich and fertile valleys I
have described, and is really a most remarkable
formation in the geology of the province.   At an
elevation of between 600 and 700 feet this basin is
surrounded on all sides by rugged stony hills, excepting to the south and south-east, in which direc-

tion it falls into the valley of the Hindmarsh and
Currency Creek respectively. Mount Magnificent,
Mount Compass, and Mount Jagged, rise in isolated
groups in different parts of the basin, the soil of
which is pure sand, its surface is undulating, and in
many parts covered with stunted banksias, through
which it is difficult to force one's way in riding along.
The Finniss rises behind Mount Magnificent, and
is joined by a smaller branch from Mount Compass,
as it flows from the eastward. At about 25 miles
from Willunga the traveller descends into the valley
of Currency Creek, and finds the change from the
barren tract over which he has been riding as sudden
as when he entered upon it from the rich flats of Willunga. The valley of Currency Creek is not, however, the same as those I have already described in
other parts of the colony ; it is prettily wooded and
grassy, but continues narrow for some distance after
you have entered it ; a small running stream, with a
rocky bed, occupying the centre of the valley, which
ultimately escapes from the hills by a kind of gorge,
and discharges itself into an arm of the Goolwa. The
extent of good land in Currency Creek is not very
great, and is bounded both to the north and south by
barren scrub. Due south, at the distance from 15 to
18 miles, is Encounter Bay, the country intervening
between the two points to the shores of the Goolwa is
very level, the soil is light but rich, and there appeared
to me to be many thousand acres that were adapted
for agricultural purposes, better adapted indeed than

the richer soils. Whether that view be correct or not, the valleys of the Inman and Hindmarsh immediately behind Encounter Bay would fully make up for the want of agricultural land in this part of the province. Hindmarsh valley is not of any great extent, but the soil is good, and its scenery in my humble opinion surpasses any other I remember in South Australia. I shall never, indeed, forget the beautiful effect of sunset, on a fine bold mountain at the head of it, called the Black Hill. The glowing orb was fast descending behind it to the west, and the Black Hill was cast into deep shade, whilst the sun's rays shooting down two valleys on either side gave the grass the appearance of young wheat. The extent of arable land in the valley of the Inman is very considerable, but in point of scenery bears no comparison with the first. I do not know whether I have made it sufficiently clear that there is a high range at the back of the coast hereabouts. If not, I would observe that it runs uninterruptedly from Mount Lofty to Cape Jarvis. Opposite to Encounter Bay it occupies nearly the centre of the promontory, and consequently forms a division of the eastern and western waters, there being a considerable breadth of barren stringy-bark forest between the heads of the opposite valleys, here as on the higher parts of the ranges near Mount Lofty, from the ascent of the great eastern road to the valley of the Onkerparinga.

It is a remarkable fact, but one that I believe I

THE MURRAY RIVER.

H.Melville

have already adverted to, that the farther north, towards the valley of the Wakefield, the more denuded of timber the country becomes, until at last not a tree of any kind can be seen. These extensive and open downs are, nevertheless, well grassed, and covered with a profusion of orchideous plants. Whether, however, there is any salt present in the soil, to check the growth of the trees, it is impossible to say. Undoubtedly many of the ponds in the Wakefield, as well as other parts of the pro vince are brackish, but the same denuded state of the country exists not any where else. These districts are far too valuable to be overlooked, and are therefore extensively occupied by cattle and sheep. My most worthy friend, Mr. Charles Campbell, and my companion Mr. John Browne, and his brother, both occupy the most distant stations to the north. Mr. Campbell has one of the finest cattle runs in the province, and my comrade, I believe, is perfectly satisfied with his run. The condition of their cattle and sheep would at all events lead to the conclusion, that neither suffer from the nature of the water they drink or the pasture on which they feed.

As regards the general appearance of the wooded portion of the province, I would remark, that excepting on the tops of the ranges where the stringy-bark grows; in the pine forests, and where there are belts of scrub on barren or sandy ground, its character is that of open forest without the slightest undergrowth save grass. The trees are more or less numerous according to the locality, as well as more or less umbrageous, a character they generally have on river flats, but the habit of the eucalyptus is, generally speaking, straggling in its branches. In many places the trees are so sparingly, and I had almost said judiciously distributed as to resemble the park lands attached to a gentleman's residence in England, and it only wants the edifice to complete the comparison.

The proportion of good to bad land in the province has generally been considered as divisible into three parts; that is to say, land entirely unavailable —land adapted for pastoral purposes only, and land of a superior quality. On due consideration, I am afraid this is not a correct estimate, but that unavailable country greatly preponderates over the other two. If, in truth, keeping the distant interior entirely out of view, and confining our observations to those portions of the colony into which the settlers have pushed in search for runs, we look to the great extent of unavailable country between the Murray and the Mount Gambier district, along the line of the Murray belt, and the extensive tracts at the head of the Gulfs, we shall find that South Australia, from the very nature of its formation, has an undue proportion of waste land. Those parts, however, which I have mentioned as being unavailable, were once covered by the sea, and could hardly be expected to be other than we now see them, and it may, therefore, be questioned how far they ought to be put into the scale. In this view of the matter, and taking the hilly country only into account, the proportion of unavailable and of pastoral land may be nearly equal; but that of the better description will still, I think, fall short of the other two. Taking South Australia in its length and breadth, the quantity of available land is, beyond doubt, very limited, but I regard it as exceedingly good, and believe that its capabilities have by no means been ascertained. I feel satisfied, indeed, that necessity will prove, not only, that the present pastoral districts are capable of maintaining a much greater number of stock upon them than they have hitherto borne, but that the province is also capable of bearing a very great amount of population; that it is peculiarly fitted for a rural peasantry, and that its agricultural products will be sufficient to support masses of the population employed either in its mining or manufactures. In this view of the subject it would appear that Providence has adapted the land to meet its new destinies, and that nothing we can say, either in praise or censure of its natural capabilities, will have the effect of concealing either the one or the other, as time shall glide on.

On the better soils the average crop of wheat is rather over than under twenty-five bushels to the acre. In many localities, and more especially when the ground is first cropped, it exceeds forty; and on some lands, once my own, in the Reed Beds, at the termination of the Torrens' river, five acres, which I sold to Mr. Sparshott, averaged fifty-two bushels to the acre. The Reed Beds may be said to be on the plains of Adelaide, and their very nature will account to the reader for the richness of their soil ; but the soil of the plains is not generally good, excepting in such places where torrents descending from the hills have spread over portions, and covered them with an alluvial deposit to a greater or less depth. The average crop of wheat on the plains does not exceed twelve or fifteen bushels to the acre, and depends on the time when the hot winds may set in. Barley on the light sandy soil of the plains is much heavier than wheat.

In the description I have thus endeavoured to give of South Australia, I have omitted any mention of the district of Port Lincoln, chiefly because sufficient was not known of it when I sailed for England to justify my hazarding any remark. Recent advices from the colony state that a practicable line of route from Adelaide has been discovered along the western shore of Spencer's Gulf, and therefore, the disasters that overtook early explorers in that quarter, are not likely again to occur. It is farther said, that the number of sheep now depastured on the lands behind Port Lincoln, amounts to 70,000—a proof of the utility, if not the richness of the country—as far, however, as I am aware, the soil must be considered of an inferior description—in other respects, the Port has advantages that will always render it an agreeable, if not altogether a desirable residence. It appears to be gradually improving, but the amount of its population is still low, not more than sixty. It is frequented by American and other whalers, but the duties collected add little to the revenues of the province. Port Lincoln, however, could hardly now be abandoned, since there are considerable interests at stake there. It has been stated that copper has been found in the interior, and I see no reason why it should not exist in the mountain formation of the Gawler Range, in such case an impulse will be given to the whole district, that would even change its prospects, and increase the mercantile operations of the province.

It does not appear to be the disposition of the English settlers to try experiments on the growth of intertropical productions. It must be admitted, however, that there are not many places in South Australia where they could be cultivated with advantage; for although both the plains of Adelaide and the valley of the Murray are warm in summer, the frosts, which are sufficient to blight potatoes, would necessarily injure, if they did not destroy, perennials, whilst in the hills the cold is adverse to any plants the growth of a tropical climate, if we except those which, as annuals, come to maturity in the course of a summer; but the true reason why the growth of extraneous productions is neglected in South Australia, is the expense consequent on the state of the labour market—for no doubt many pursuits might be followed there that would be remunerative. It is exceedingly difficult, however, to lead the pursuits of a community out of their ordinary course, and it is only where direct advantages are to be gained, that the spirit of enterprise and speculation breaks forth.

The climate of South Australia is admirably adapted for the growth of fruit trees of the hardier tropical kinds, for although the tenderer kinds grow there also, they do not arrive at perfection. The loquat, the guava, the orange, and the banana, are of slow growth, but the vine, the fig, the pomegranate, and others, flourish beyond description, as do English fruit trees of every kind. It is to be observed, that the climate of the plains of Adelaide and that of the hills are distinct. I have been in considerable heat in the former at noon, and on the hills have been in frost in the evening. The forest trees of Europe will grow in the ranges, but on the plains they languish; in the ranges also the gooseberry and the currant bear well, but in the gardens on the plains they are admitted only to say you have such fruits; the pomegranate will not mature in the open air, but melons of all kinds are weeds. Yet, such trees as are congenial to the climate arrive at maturity with incredible rapidity, and bear in the greatest abundance. The show of grapes in Mr. Stephenson's garden in North Adelaide, and the show of apples and plums in Mr. Anstey's garden on the hills are fine beyond description, and could not be surpassed

in any part of the world—it may readily be imagined, therefore, that the intermediate fruit trees,
such as the peach, the nectarine, the pear, the cherry,
the greengage, and others, are of the most vigorous
habits. All of them, indeed, are standards, and the
wood they make during one season, is the best proof
that can be given of their congeniality to the soil
and climate of the province.

There are in South Australia two periods of the
year which are equally deceptive to the stranger.
The one is when the country is burnt up and suffering under the effects of summer heat—when the
earth is almost herbless, and the ground swarms
with grasshoppers— when a dry heat prevails in a
calm still air. The other when vegetation is spring-
ing up under the early rains and every thing is
green. Arriving at Adelaide during the first period,
the stranger would hardly believe that the country,
at any other season of the year, would be so
clothed with herbage and look so fresh ; arriving at
the other, he would equally doubt the possibility of
the vegetable kingdom being laid so completely
prostrate, or that the country could assume so
withered and parched an appearance ; but these
changes are common to every country under a similar
latitude, and it would be unjust to set them down
to its prejudice, or advantage.

The following mean of heat at 2 P.M. throughout
the year, will give the reader a correct idea of the
range of the thermometer.   I have taken 2 P.M. as

being the hottest period of the day, and, therefore, nearest the truth.

January	85	—	106½	—	70
February	⁓9	—	94	—	71
March	77	—	103½	—	68½
April	67½	—	85	—	55½
May	62	—	76	—	53
June	58	—	67	—	49
July	55	—	60	—	49
August	59	—	68	—	52
September	61	—	72½	—	55½
October	68½	—	94½	—	55
November	74	—	94	—	59
December	83	—	100	—	68

The west and south-west winds are the most prevalent, blowing for 130 or 140 days in the year. During the summer months the land and sea breezes prevail along the coast, but in the interior the wind generally commences at E. N. E., and going round with the sun settles at west in the afternoon.

I need not point out to the reader, that the above table only shews the mean of the thermometer during a certain hour of the day; the temperature during the night must necessarily be much lower; the coolness of the night, indeed, generally speaking, makes up for the mid-day heat. There are some days of the year when hot winds prevails, which are certainly very disagreeable, if not trying. Their occurrence, however, is not frequent, and will be easily accounted for from natural causes. They sometimes continue for three or more days, during

which time clouds of dust fill the air, and whirlwinds
cross the plains, but the dryness of the Australian
atmosphere considerably influences the feelings on
such occasions, and certainly produces a different
effect upon the system from that which would be
produced at a much lower temperature in a more
humid climate; for, no doubt, it is to the united
effects of heat and moisture, where they more or less
exist, that the healthiness or unhealthiness of a
country may be ascribed. In such countries, generally speaking, either teaming vapours, or malaria
from dense woods or swamps naturally tries the
constitution, but to its extreme dryness, and the absence of all vegetable decay, it appears to me that the
general salubrity of South-east Australia is to be
attributed. So rarified, indeed, is the atmosphere,
that it causes an elasticity of spirits unknown in a
heavier temperature. So the hot winds, of which I
have been speaking, are not felt in the degree we
should be led to suppose. Like the air the spirits
are buoyant and light, and it is for its dis-
agreeableness at the time, not any after effects that
a hot wind is to be dreaded. It is hot, and
that is all you can say ; you have a reluctance
to move, and may not rest so well as usual; but
the spirits are in no way affected ; nor indeed, in
the ordinary transactions of business does a hot wind
make the slightest difference. If there are three
or four months of warm weather, there are eight or
nine months of the year, during which the weather

is splendid. Nothing can exceed the autumn, winter, and spring of that transparent region, where the firmament is as bright as it would appear from the summit of Mount Blanc. In the middle of winter you enjoy a fire, the evenings are cold, and occasionally the nights are frosty. It is then necessary to put on warmer clothing, and a good surtout, buttoned across the breast, is neither an uncomfortable nor unimportant addition. Having said thus much of the general salubrity of the climate of South Australia, I would observe, in reference to what may be said against it, that the changes of temperature are sudden and unexpected, the thermometer rising or falling 50° in an hour or two. Whether it is owing to the properties I have ascribed, that the climate of this place as also of Sydney should be fatal to consumptive habits, I do not know, but in both places I have understood that such is the case, and in both I have had reason to regret instances. It has been said that influenza prevailed last year in Adelaide to a great extent, and that it carried off a great many children and elderly persons. An epidemic, similar in its symptoms, may have prevailed there, and been severe in its progress, but it hardly seems probable that the epidemic of this country should have been conveyed through constant change of air, the best cure for such a disease, to so distant a part of the world. With all its salubrity, indeed, I believe it may be said, that South Australia is subject to the more unimportant maladies like other countries, but that there are no indigenous disorders of a dangerous kind, and that it is a country which may strictly be called one of the healthiest in the world, and will, in all probability, continue so, as long as it shall be kept clear of European diseases.

Having thus endeavoured to give a description of the general character and climate of this limited but certainly beautiful portion of the Australian continent, without encumbering my description with any remark on the principal and particular sources of wealth it possesses, which not being usual, could not, or rather would not, have been considered applicable. I hope the object I have had in view will be sufficiently clear to the reader. I have endeavoured to point out with an impartial pen, the real capabilities of the province, and the nature of those productions which are most congenial to her soil. Without undue praise on the one hand, or unjust depreciation on the other, it has been my desire to present a faithful picture of her to my readers, and I hope it will appear from what I have said, as is really and truly the case, that both in climate and other respects it is a country peculiarly adapted to the pursuits and habits of my countrymen. That its climate so far approaches that of England, as to be subject to light and partial frosts, which render it unfit for the cultivation of tropical productions, but make it essentially an agricultural country, capable of yielding as fine cereal grain as any country in the world,

of whatever kind it may be—that at the same time
the greater mildness of the climate makes it favourable to the growth of a variety of fruits and vegetables, independently of European fruit trees and
culinary herbs, which put it in the power of the set-
tler to secure the enjoyment of greater luxuries and
comforts, than he could possibly expect to have done
in his own country, except at a great expense, and
that as far as the two great desiderata go, on
which I have been dwelling, it is a country to which
an Englishman may migrate with the most cheerful
anticipations.

CHAPTER III.

SEASONS—CAUSE WHY SOUTH AUSTRALIA HAS FINE GRAIN—
EXTENT OF CULTIVATION — AMOUNT OF STOCK — THE
BURRA-BURRA MINE—ITS MAGNITUDE—ABUNDANCE OF
MINERALS—ABSENCE OF COAL—SMELTING ORE—IMMENSE
PROFITS OF THE BURRA-BURRA—EFFECT OF THE MINES
ON THE LABOUR MARKET—RELUCTANCE OF THE LOWER
ORDERS TO EMIGRATE—DIFFERENCE BETWEEN CANADA
AND AUSTRALIA—THE AUSTRALIAN COLONIES—STATE OF
SOCIETY—THE MIDDLE CLASSES—THE SQUATTERS—THE
GERMANS—THE NATIVES—AUTHOR'S INTERVIEWS WITH
THEM—INSTANCES OF JUST FEELING—THEIR BAD QUALI-
TIES—PERSONAL APPEARANCE—YOUNG SETTLERS ON THE
MURRAY—CONCLUSION.

It was my object in the last chapter, to confine my observations strictly to the agricultural and pastoral capabilities of the province of South Australia, which I thought I could not better do than by describing the nature of its climate and soil, for on these depend the producing powers of every country. In speaking of the climate, however, I merely adverted to its temperature, leaving its seasons out of question for the time, intending to close my remarks on these heads, by a short review of the state of the agricultural and pastoral interests of the colony at the present date.

It will be borne in mind that the seasons of Australia are the reverse of our own ; that when in

England the ground is covered with snow, there the
sun is hottest, and that when summer heats are
ripening our fruits, in Australia it is the coldest
season of the year, December, January, February,
and March being the summer months; June,
July, August, and September the winter ones.
An experience of ten years has shewn that the seasons of South Australia are exceedingly regular, that
the rains set in within a few days of the same period
each successive year, and that during the winter the
ground gets abundantly saturated. This regularity
of season may be attributed to the almost insular
position of the promontory of Cape Jarvis, and may
be said to be almost local, in elucidation of which, I
may refer to what I have stated in the former part
of my work, of the state of the weather in the valley
of the Murray when the expedition was proceeding
up its banks in the month of August, 1844. For
some time before there had been heavy rains in the
hills, and it was with some difficulty the drays crossed
them. During our stay at Moorundi, the ranges
were covered with heavy clouds, and the mountain
streams were so swollen as to stop one of my mes-
sengers; but the sky over the valley of the Murray
was as clear as crystal, morning mists it is true
curled up at early dawn from the bosom of its waters,
but they were soon dissipated, and a sharp frosty
night was succeeded by a day of surpassing beauty.

The regularity, however, both in its commencement and in the quantity of moisture that falls

during the rainy season in the colony, enables the
agriculturist to calculate with certainty upon it,
and the only anxiety of the farmer is to get his
grain into the ground sufficiently early, if possible,
to escape the first hot winds.   In a region, portions
of which are subject, it must be confessed, to long
continued drought, this is no inconsiderable advantage, although South Australia is not singular
in this respect, for the rainy seasons in the Port
Phillip districts are, I believe, equally regular and
more abundant, whilst the climate of Van Diemen's
Land almost approaches to that of England; neither,
indeed, fairly speaking, is South Australia more favoured than those of her immediate neighbours in
the quality of her soil.   Van Diemen's Land is the
granary of the southern seas, and there is unquestionably a very great proportion of the very best
soil in the Port Phillip district.   Nevertheless that
of South Australia has yielded a finer and a heavier
grain than has ever been produced in those colonies,
but the reason of this is, that with a naturally rich
soil to work upon, the agriculturists of South Australia have spared no pains in cultivating their lands,
but there can be no doubt that with equal care and
attention both the Vandemonians and the settlers of
Port Phillip would produce an equally fine sample.
The farmers of South Australia have enhanced the
value of their colony by their energy and skill in
cultivating it, and can boast of having sent the finest
sample of wheat to England that has ever been
exhibited in her market.

South Australia, in its length and breadth, contains about 300,000 square miles, or in round numbers more than 190,000,000 acres. The limits of location, however, do not exceed 4000 miles, or 7,000,000 acres. In this area, however, a great portion of desert country is included, or such, at least, as at the present moment is considered so. Of the more available land, 470,000 acres have been purchased, but the extent of country occupied by sheep and cattle stations is not known.

It may be necessary here to observe, that the returns of the land under cultivation last year were published after I left the colony ; but the comparison between the two previous years will shew the increase and decrease of the different grains, sufficiently to establish the progress of agricultural pursuits in the colony. In the year 1845, the number of acres of wheat sown was 18,848. In 1846 it was 26,135. Of barley, there were in the former year 4,342 acres, in the latter only 3,490. Of oats, there were 1,485 in the first year, which, in 1846, increased to 1,963. It would thus appear, that the increase of cultivated land in the course of one year amounted to between 6000 and 7000 acres, and that more than 400 agriculturists were added to the list of landed proprietors. The necessary consequence of such extensive farming operations is that the produce far exceeds the wants of the settlers, and that there is a considerable surplus for exportation ; the price of the best flour being from £12. to £13. per ton, whereas for a short period in 1839 it was £120 !!!

Whilst the agriculturists have been so earnest in
the development of the productive powers of the
colony, another class of its inhabitants were paying
equal attention to its pastoral interests. The establishment of stock stations over its surface followed
its occupation, and a mild climate and nutritive herbage equally contributed to the increase of cattle
and sheep that had been introduced. In 1844
the number of sheep assessed was 355,700, in the
following year that number had increased to 480,669,
or an addition of 120,000. At the present moment
there cannot be far short of a million of sheep in the
province, with an increase of 200,000 annually, at a
moderate computation. The number of other kinds of
stock in the possession of the settlers, at the close of
last year, was as follows :— of cattle, 70,000; 30,000
having been imported during the two previous years
from New South Wales. The number of horses
was estimated at 5000, and of other smaller stock,
as pigs and goats, there were supposed to be more
than 20,000.

It is impossible to contemplate such a prosperous
state of things in a colony that has only just completed the eleventh year of its existence, without
feeling satisfied that some unusually favourable circumstances had brought it about. Had South Australia been as distant from the older colonies on the
continent as Swan River, the amount of stock she
would have possessed in an equal length of time,
could not have amounted to a tenth of what they

now number. It is to the discovery of the Darling and the Murray that South Australia owes the superabundance of her flocks and herds, and in that superabundance the full and complete establishment of her pastoral interests. I stated in the course of my preliminary observations on the progress of Australian discovery, that when I was toiling down those rivers, with wide spread deserts on either side of me, I had little idea for what purposes my footsteps had been directed into the interior of the Australian Continent. If I ever entertained even a distant hope that the hilly country from which I turned back at the termination of the Murray, after having floated on its broad waters for eighty-eight days, might ever be occupied, I certainly never hoped that the discoveries I was then making would one day or other prove of advantage to many a friend, and that I was marking the way for thousands of herds and flocks, the surplus stock of New South Wales, to pass into the province of South Australia.

If then such consequences have resulted from enterprises, apparently of almost as hopeless a character as the one from which I have so recently returned, why, I would ask, should I despair, as to its one day or other being instrumental in benefiting my countrymen. There may yet be that in the womb of time which shall repay me for all I suffered in the performance of that dreary task — when I shall have it in my power to say, that I so far led the way across the continent as to make the remainder of easy attainment, and under the guidance and blessing of Providence have been mainly instrumental in establishing a line of communication between its northern and southern coasts. I see no reason why I should despair that such may one day be the case. The road to the point which may be termed my farthest north is clear before the explorer. That point gained, less probably than 200 miles—a week's journey with horses less jaded than mine unfortunately were, and with strength less reduced—would place him beyond the limits of that fearful desert, and crown his labours with success. I believe that I could, on my old route, make the north coast of Australia, to the westward of the Gulf of Carpentaria, before any party from Moreton Bay. If it is asked what practical good I should expect to result from such an undertaking, I would observe, that nothing would sooner tend to establish an intercourse with the inhabitants of the Malay archipelago, than the barter of cattle and sheep, that in truth there is no knowing what the ultimate results would be. The Malays who visit the northern coasts of Australia to collect the sea slug, have little inducement to keep up an intercourse with our settlements in Torres Straits, but there can be no doubt of their readiness to enter into commercial intercourse with us, which, if Torres Straits are to be navigated by steamers, would be doubly important.

When the stock from New South Wales was first brought down the Murray, the journey occupied from three to four months. Latterly it did not take half that time. In less than fifty days, from the Murray, on his way to the north, the stock-holder would find that he had passed the centre, and an equal number of days from that point would, it appears to me, take him to his journey's end. This, however, would depend on the nature of the country beyond where it is at present known, and the nature of the season during which it was undertaken, but experience alone, as in the instance of the journey down the Murray, would be the best guide and the best instructor.

In the early part of the year 1840, I had occasion to address a number of the colonists at the conclusion of a public entertainment and availed myself of the opportunity to state that whatever prospects of success the pastoral capabilities of the province appeared to hold out, I felt assured it was to the mountains, the colonists would have to look for their future wealth, for that no one who pretended to the eye of a geologist could cross them as I had done, without the conviction that they abounded in mineral veins. There is something, in truth, in the outline and form of the Mount Lofty chain that betrays its character. Rounded spurs, of very peculiar form, having deep valleys on either side, come down from the main range, the general outline of which bears a strong resemblance to that of the Ural chain.

In the year 1843, the first discovery of copper was made, but even this was scarcely sufficient to rouse the colonists to a full sense of its importance, and it was only by degrees, as other mines were successively discovered, that the spirit of speculation burst forth, and the energies of the settlers were turned for a time from their legitimate channels. A short time before this, their circumstances had been reduced to the lowest ebb. There was no sale for agricultural produce, no demand for labour, the goods in the shops of the tradesmen remained unsold, and the most painful sacrifices of property were daily made at the auction mart. The amount of distress indeed was very great and severe, but such a state of things was naturally to be expected from the change that had taken place in the monetary affairs of the province. It was a change however which few anticipated, and for which few therefore were prepared.

It is a painful task to advert to past scenes of difficulty and distress, such at least I feel it to be, more especially where there is no immediate object to be gained by a reference to them ; let me therefore turn from any inquiry into the causes which plunged South Australia into difficulties that threatened to overwhelm her, to those which raised her from them.

Notwithstanding the spirit and firmness with which the colonists bore their reverses, there could not but be a gloom over the community where every

thing seemed to be on the brink of ruin. Men's
minds became depressed when they saw no relief
in the present, and no hope in the future. But
Time, with a rapid wing, brought about changes
that appear permanently to have altered the circumstances of the colony, and to have placed it at once
as one of the most flourishing of the British possessions. The first circumstance, I have understood,
which partially cheered the drooping spirits of the
settlers, was a slight rise in the price of wool, in the
year I have mentioned. The discovery of the mines
following soon upon this, the sun of prosperity burst
at once upon the province, and gladdened every
heart. From this period, mine after mine of copper
and lead continued to be discovered. Every valley
and hill-top was searched for hidden treasures, and
the whole energies of the colonists seemed to be
turned to this new source of wealth. I was absent
in the interior when the Burra Burra mine was secured, but the excitement it created had not sub-
sided when I reached Adelaide.

I do not know whether the presence of mineral
veins is indicated in other countries as in South
Australia by means of surface deposits. The opinion I formed that ores would be discovered in the
Mount Lofty ranges did not rest upon the discovery
of any such deposit myself, but on the peculiar form
of the hills, which appeared to me to have settled
into their present state from one of extreme fusion.
The direction of the ranges being from north to

south, these deposits lie also in the same direction. Those of iron are greater than those of copper, and it is impossible to describe the appearance of the huge clean masses of which they are composed. They look indeed like immense blocks, that had only just passed from the forge. The deposits at the Burra Burra amounted, I believe, to some thousand tons, and led to the impression that where so great a quantity of surface ore existed, but little would be found beneath. In working this gigantic mine, however, it has proved otherwise. I was informed by one of the shareholders just before I left the colony, that it took three hours and three-quarters to go through the shafts and galleries of the mine. Some of the latter are cut through solid blocks of ore, which glitter like gold where the hammer or chisel has struck the rock, as you pass with a candle along them.

It would be out of place in me, nor indeed would it interest my readers, were I to enter into a statistical account of the profits of the Burra Burra mine. A general notice will convey every necessary information on that head, and enable the public to judge as well of its value and importance as if I entered into minuter details. It will give the reader some idea of the scene of bustle and activity the Burra mine and road must present, and the very great amount of labour it requires.

The quantity of ore sent weekly from the mine to the port is from 430 to 450 tons, employing from

150 to 160 drays, and more than double that number of men. The total quantity of ore received at the port in December last was 10,000 tons, the average value of which at £20 per ton, amounts to £200,000, and the price of shares, originally of £5, had, by last advices, reached £160.

Considering the gigantic scale of the Burra Burra mine, it was supposed that few other mines would be found in the colony that would at all approach it, that indeed, it had been the principal deposit, and that whatever indications other mines might give, they would soon cease in working, or produce so little as to be valueless. I confess that such was my own opinion—surprised at the immense size of this magnificent mine, I hardly thought it possible that in mountains, after all of limited range, mines of great value would still be found, and that discoveries of new mines were frequently taking place, and that too in situations where no such feature would be supposed to exist. On York's Peninsula for instance, immediately across St. Vincent's Gulf, opposite to Port Adelaide, and directly on the sea shore, there are two sections, on which copper ore is abundant. The position of this mine can at once be determined by the reader, on a reference to the map. The land is very low, and the rock formation, tertiary fossil, but the various and anomalous positions in which copper is found in South Australia, baffles all ordinary calculations—as likely to exist in the valley, as on the hill—at the sea side as well as inland : there is not a locality in which it may not be looked for and found.

The whole of the mountain chain indeed, is a mass of ore from one end to the other, and it is impossible to say what quantity, or how many of the richer metals will ultimately be found in a country through which the baser metals are, without doubt, so abundantly diffused. The quantity of gold hitherto discovered has not been important, but it is reasonable to suppose, that where a small quantity has been found, large deposits must be at no great distance. This gold however, like the baser metals of South Australia, is very pure, there being few component parts mixed with it.

From the various examinations of the hills that have at different times been made, it would appear that precious stones, as well as metals, exist amongst them. Almost every stone, the diamond excepted, has already been discovered. The ruby, the amethyst, and the emerald, with beryl and others, so that the riches of this peculiar portion of the Australian continent may truly be said to be in their development only.

With such prospects before it, there can be but little doubt that the wealth of South Australia will, one day or other, be very great, neither can there be any doubt but that the discovery of the mines at the critical period, made a complete revolution in the affairs of that colony, and suddenly raised it from a state of extreme depression to one of independence, even as an individual is raised to affluence, from comparative poverty by the receipt of an unlooked-for legacy. The effect, however, which the discovery had on its present prospects, and the effect it must have on the future destinies of that colony, can hardly, it appears to me, be placed to the credit of any ordinary process of colonization. It has rather been in the shape of an unexpected auxiliary, that this immense and valuable supply of ore has been brought to bear upon its fortunes, for the condition to which the colony was reduced at one time, was such, that it would have taken many years to have acquired the appearance of returning prosperity, but the discovery of the mines was like the coming up of a rear-guard, to turn the tide of battle, when the main army had apparently been all but defeated. The assistance the colony received was complete and decisive, and has seemingly placed her beyond the hazard of failure or reverse: but, admitting the state of depression to which it was reduced, and the length of time it would have taken to bring about a healthy change, I yet believe, that the favourable position of the province as regards its connection with the other colonies, the character of its climate and soil, and the energies of its inhabitants, would have ensured its ultimate success. Before the depression in 1841, South Australia had become a pastoral country, in consequence of the number both of cattle and sheep that had been imported. In 1838, the city of Adelaide had scarcely been laid out, no portion of it had yet been sold, when flocks and herds were on their way to the new market, and from that period, even to the present, there has been no cessation to their ingress—first of all, as I have stated, the Murray, and then the Darling, became the high roads along which the superfluous stock of Port Phillip and New South Wales were driven to browse on South Australian pastures, and to increase the quantity and value of her exports.

However low therefore the price of wool might have kept, the natural increase of stock would still have gone on, and if we may judge from the unflinching energies of the agricultural portion of the community, their efforts to develop the productive powers of the soil, would rather have been stimulated than depressed by the misfortunes with which they were visited. I do them nothing more than justice when I assure the reader, that settlers in the province from the neighbouring colonies, could not help expressing their surprise at the state of cultivation, or their admiration of the unconquerable perseverance, that could have brought about so forward and creditable a state of things.

I have already stated that the general outline and form of the Mount Lofty chain, bears a strong resemblance to the outline and form of the Ural mountains. But it is of trifling elevation, running longitudinally from north to south, with a breadth of from 15 to 20 miles. The metalliferous veins crop out on the surface of the ground, preserving the same longitudinal directions as the ranges themselves, and the

rock in which the ores are imbedded, generally
speaking, is a compact slate.   As the Mount Lofty
ranges extend northwards, so does the Barrier or
Stanley range, over which the recent expedition
crossed on leaving the Darling; no copper ores were
found amongst those hills, but an abundance of the
finest ore of iron, running, as the out-croppings of
the copper ores, from north to south, and occurring
in depressed as well as elevated situations, the rock
formation being very similar to that of the more
western ranges.

If we are to judge from these facts, it is very evident that strong igneous action has influenced the
whole, nor can I help thinking, from general appearances, that the continent of Australia has been
subjected to a long subterranean process, by which
it has been elevated to its present altitude, and it
appears to me that that action, though considerably
weakened, is still going on.   The occurrence of two
slight shocks of earthquake felt at Adelaide, since
the establishment of the colony, would further
strengthen this opinion.

The copper ores of South Australia fetch a higher
price at the Swansea sales than those from any other
part of the world, not only because they are intrin-
sically rich, but because they are generally composed
of carbonates, which are necessary to facilitate the
smelting of the ores of sulphuret of copper from
Cuba and other places.   The necessity for sending
the ores from Adelaide to some foreign port to

undergo the process of smelting, will probably exist
for a considerable length of time ; until such time,
indeed, as the electric process shall be found to
answer on a sufficiently large scale to be profitable,
or, until smelting works are established ; but, the
great difficulty to be apprehended in carrying on
such operations would be the want of fuel, which
scarce even at the present moment, would soon be
more so—for there is not sufficient wood in the
vicinity of any of the mines to keep up the supply
for such a consumption as that which would be
required ; besides which, the cartage of the wood,
and the expenses attending its preparation for the
furnace, would materially diminish any profits arising
from the smelting of the ores.   In such a view of
the case I cannot but think that the establishment
of works at the mines will be found to be as unprofitable to their proprietors as to the smelter, and
that such works will only be remunerative when
carried on under more favourable circumstances—
for it would appear that coal is the only mineral South
Australia does not possess, and I am apprehensive
that no bed of it will ever be found in the colony.
I have ever thought the geological formation of the
country unfavourable to the presence of coal, but,
still, it is said to exist as a submarine formation
close to Aldingi Bay.   The discovery of this mineral
in the province would immediately give to it, within
itself, the means of the most unbounded wealth,
and would undoubtedly fill up the measure of its
prosperity to the brim.

By a late report of the Directors of the Burra
Burra mine, it would appear, that they had made
several successful attempts to smelt the ore, but, that
the cost, having exceeded that of cartage to the port,
and freight, the process has been abandoned.   Parties, however, had offered to enter into an engage-
ment to smelt the whole of the ore from the mine
at about Swansea prices ; notwithstanding the unfavourable circumstances under which such smelting
would necessarily be carried on.

As I understand the nature of this arrangement,
the ore will be smelted at the mine, and the remuneration to the smelter will be between fifty and sixty
shillings per ton perhaps, by way of " return
charges," or we will say between sixty and seventy
shillings, which is a sum exactly equal to the cartage
of the ore to the port.   If then the Directors abandoned their intentions, because they found they
could not smelt at so low a sum as the price of
cartage and freight, how will the contractor make
it pay under more unfavourable circumstances ?   No
doubt, if he should find it remunerative, the shareholders of the Burra Burra would find it still more
so, and it would be the interest of the proprietors of
the larger mines to enter into similar engagements ;
but, on a due consideration of this important subject,
I am led to believe that to make smelting works
successful in South Australia, Companies must
purchase the ore, and carry it off to localities
suitable for the operation.   Such an arrangement
would still considerably increase the profits to the

proprietors of the mine, nor would there be any difficulty in determining the value of the ore, by processes similar to those adopted at Swansea, by which the interests of both parties are equally protected.

In the South Australian Register of the 27th of November of last year, it is stated that a Mr. Hunt, one of the auctioneers in Sydney, offered for sale thirteen tons of pure copper ore of colonial manufacture, from ore the produce of the Burra Burra, in ingots weighing 80 lbs. each; the ore having been smelted by Mr. James at Mr. Smith's foundry at Newtown. This copper was however bought in at £80, the limit being £85. per ton.

It will give the reader some idea of the character of this prodigious mine, and of the profits arising from it, to know, that during the four months preceding the 23rd October, 1847, the directors declared and paid three dividends, amounting to 200 per cent. on the subscribed capital, and that the credits of the Association on the 30th September were £104,694. 4s 8d. The Burra Burra mine however is not the only one of importance. Several others have of late been discovered, and South Australia may be said to be a thriving country in every sense of the word, and one in which those profitable interests will rapidly increase.

We have hitherto been speaking of the mines of South Australia as the sources of wealth, and as the sudden, if not the remote cause of the prosperity of

that province.   It now becomes our duty to consider
how far the discovery of the mines has benefited or
interfered with the other branches of industry and
sources of wealth ; and as regards both these, it must
be admitted that their discovery has had an injurious
effect.   The high rate of wages given by the proprietors of mines, not only to the miners, but to all
whom they employ, draws the labourers from every
other occupation to engage with them.   The consequence has been a general want of labourers
throughout the whole colony, still more severely felt
by reason of the previous want of labour in the
labour market.   Every man who could obtain
sufficient money to purchase a dray and team of
bullocks, hurried to the mines for a load of ore to
take to the port, and disdained any ordinary employment when by carting ore he could earn £6. or
£7. in a fortnight.   The labourer was quite right
in going where he received the best remuneration
for his services ; but the consequences were in
many instances fatal to their former employers.
Many farmers were unable to put in seed or to cultivate their land ; many, after having done so, were
unable to gather it, and had it not been for the
use of Mr. Ridley's machine, the loss in the crops
would have been severely felt.   Not only did the
farmers suffer, but the stock-holders, and the colonists generally.   The want of hands, indeed, was
felt by all classes of the community, since the
natural consequence of the high wages given by

the mining proprietors to the men they employed, tended still more to depress the labour market, and to increase the demand upon it by leading many of the more frugal labourers to purchase land with the money they were enabled to save. As landed proprietors they not only withdrew their labour from the market, but in their turn became employers ; but I feel called upon to say at the same time, that equal distress was felt in the neighbouring colonies for working hands, where no mines had been discovered, and where they could not therefore possibly have interfered.

From what has been said of the province of South Australia, and setting its mines entirely out of the question, the description that has been given of its pastoral and agricultural capabilities, of its climate, and of the prospects of success which present themselves to the intending emigrant, it will naturally be inferred that the impression I have intended to convey is, that, as a colony, it is most peculiarly adapted for a British population, whether rural or other. The state of the colony is now such, that the way of the emigrant in landing is straight before him, for with honesty, sobriety, and industry, he cannot lose it. When I stated, in a former part of my work, that I would not take upon myself to give advice, which if followed, and not successfully, might subject me to the reproach of any one, I referred to those who have similar means of acquiring information to myself, and whose stakes, being considerable, make the responsibility of giving advice the greater. With the lower orders—the working classes—the case is different. They have not the means of acquiring information on these matters, and it becomes the duty of those who can promote their welfare to do so. I am quite aware that there are many of my poor countrymen who would gladly seek a better home than they possess at this moment, but who, clinging to the spot where they were born, disheartened at the thought of abandoning their hearth, and bound by early recollections to their native country, cannot make up their minds to turn their backs on the companions of their youth, and the haunts of their childhood.

Such a feeling undoubtedly claims our sympathy and respect. It is that very feeling,—the love of Home,—the belief that they can no where be happier, which has been the strength of England, and has given her sons the heart to love, and the spirit to defend her. But the period however, when those feelings were so strong, has passed away,—more general ones have taken their place, and the circumstances of the times have so changed, that neither hearth nor home have the same attractions; a restlessness pervades the community, and a desire to escape from those scenes, and that spot which they or their forefathers once thought the most hallowed upon earth. But two circumstances have militated against the migration of the rural population in this country, to the Australian colonies, at all events.

The one has been an apprehension as to the length and nature of the voyage; the other the expense, more especially to a family man. Had it not been for these causes, the Australian colonies would not have had to complain of the want of labour. The truth is, that the ignorance which prevails in the inland counties as to any matters connected with foreign parts, and the little means the labouring classes possess of defraying their own expenses, has kept them, except in a few instances, from seeking to go to that distant part of the world, which assuredly holds out to them the brightest prospect, and is most like their own home. They may however rest satisfied that the voyage to Australia is as safe as that to New York, that it is far more pleasant as regards the weather, and that little or no sickness has ever thinned the number of those who have embarked for the Australian colonies. The expense of the voyage is certainly greater than that of a passage to the Canadas, or to the United States, but it is to be hoped that the means of transport will soon be at their command. I would only in this place offer the remarks I conscientiously think the case requires, as one who, having witnessed the happiness of thousands in the land of which he is speaking, would gladly be instrumental in opening the way for thousands more of his countrymen to the same happy destiny. Having been both to Canada and the Australian colonies, if I were asked which of the two I preferred, I should undoubtedly say the latter. I do not desire to disparage the Canadas by this assertion, for I know that they have advantages in their soil and in the magnificence of their rivers beyond comparison, but Australia, on the other hand, has advantages over our transatlantic possessions, such as her increased distance from England, cannot counterbalance. Her climate, in the first place, is surpassing fine. There the emigrant is spared the trouble of providing against the severities of a Canadian winter. That season passes over his head almost without his knowledge, and the ground, instead of being a broad sheet of snow, is covered with vegetation. Her lands, unencumbered by dense forests, are clear and open to the plough, or are so lightly wooded as to resemble a park, rather than a wild and untouched scene of nature. Instead of having to toil with the saw and the axe to clear his ground before he can cultivate it, and instead of consuming a year's provisions before he can expect any return, he can there run the plough from one end to the other of his enclosures, without meeting a stone or a root to turn its point, and at once reap the produce of the soil. These surely are advantages of no ordinary kind, and, if the expense of a voyage to the Australian colonies is greater than that to America, I cannot but think that the contingent expenses to which the Canadian or Union emigrant is put, before he can consider himself as finally settled down, must necessarily exceed those of the Australian.

As before observed, the aspect of South Australia, and indeed of many parts of the neighbouring colonies, is essentially English. There, as in England, you see the white-washed cottage, and its little garden stocked with fruit trees of every kind, its outward show of cleanliness telling that peace and comfort are within. To sever oneself from our kindred, and to abandon the dwelling of our fathers, is a sacrifice of no imaginary magnitude, whether we are rich or poor, and the prospects of reward should be bright indeed to compensate for it. I conclude that it has been to combat the reluctance in the lower orders to leave their homes, that inducements too highly coloured in many instances, have been held out to them, the consequence of which has been that many, whose expectations were excited, suffered proportionate disappointment at the outset of their career as emigrants. Convinced of the injurious tendency of such a practice, and regarding it as a culpable and cruel mockery of misfortunes, which, having been unavoidable, claim our best sympathies, I should not have said so much as I have done on this important subject, had I not felt justified in so doing. The reader may rest assured that to the sober, the honest, and the industrious, the certainty of success in South Australia is beyond all doubt. An individual with these qualities may experience disappointment on landing, but he must recollect that this is always a period of anxiety, and the circumstances in which he first finds himself placed, may not come up to his expectations ; his useful qualities and regular habits cannot be immediately known, and we seldom alter our condition, even for the better, without some trouble or vexation.

I have, in the course of my remarks, in my recommendation of the Australian colonies as being favourable to the views of emigrants, given a preference to South Australia.   I have done so because I am better acquainted with its condition than with that of either of the other settlements.   Of it I have spoken as to what I know ; but, of the others, to a great extent, from hearsay.   The character however of those colonies needs no recommendation from me. As far as its pastoral and agricultural capabilities go, I believe Port Phillip to be as fine a district as any in the world.   The advantages indeed of the Australian colonies must be nearly equal, from the fact that the pursuits of their respective inhabitants are so nearly the same.   Local circumstances may give some parts of the continent a preference over others, but, as points of emigration there is little choice. The southern portions are not subject to the withering droughts to which parts of the eastern coast are liable, and may be preferred on that account, but still there are districts in New South Wales as unexceptionable as any in Port Phillip or South Australia.

It now remains to make some observations on the present state of society in the last-mentioned colony ; for it appears to me, that in order to give a correct picture of it, some notice on that head is required. I think too, I am the more called upon to do so, because many very mistaken notions are held of it. As in most of Her Majesty's possessions, so in South Australia, the Government officers form a prominent, and I may say, distinct class. Colonel Robe, the late Governor of the province, made Government House the seat of the most unmeasured hospitality, which he exercised beyond the point to which there was any public call upon him. His table was covered with every delicacy the season could afford, his wines were of the very best, and there was a quiet but effective manner about him, which gained universal esteem. As a soldier, he was exceedingly particular in the order and appearance of his establishment, nor was there anything wanting to complete the comfort of it. The number of the colonists who assembled round him occasionally, was from 50 to 60; on more public festive occasions they exceeded 300, and I may add, that on both, the scene differed not in the slightest degree from that of similar parties in this country, save that there was less of formality in the interchange of friendly communications between the visitors. Except also in giving a tone to society, and setting an irreproachable example to the community, the officers of the Government are exceedingly retired, their salaries are too limited to enable them to follow the example of their chief.

They live quietly, and as gentlemen, are ever happy to see their friends, but public parties are seldom given by any of them. Prudence indeed calls upon them to refrain from those displays, which they cannot reasonably afford, and the consequence was, that a warmer intimacy existed in their quiet intercourse with each other, than could have sprung from more formal entertainments.

The truth is, the salaries of the Government officers, bear no proportion to the means of the majority of the settlers, who have risen into affluence from a combination of circumstances, that have been unprecedented in the history of colonization. There are few private individuals in the province, who have not, at one time or other, benefited by some speculation, but I am not aware that any one of the Government officers have any private interests in the colony, if I except the possession of a section or two of land, on which they have built and reside, nor do I know that any of them have allowed a spirit of speculation to interfere with public duties.

Amongst the leading or upper classes of society, there are many very estimable persons. I do not mention names, but my recollection will bear me back to the many happy days I have spent with them, and certainly any one not desiring an extended circle of acquaintance could no where, whether amongst gentlemen or the ladies, find individuals more worthy of his regard or friendship than in the still limited society of South Australia.

Many of the tradesmen having succeeded in business, or acquired an independence from their interests in the mines, have retired, and live in suburban residences, which they have built in well selected situations, and with considerable taste. Attached to the customs of Home, many of the citizens of Adelaide possess carriages of one kind or another, and are fond of devoting their Sunday evenings to visiting places in the neighbourhood. As regards the lower classes, I do not think there is in any of Her Majesty's possessions, a greater amount of mechanical genius and enterprise than amongst the mechanics of South Australia. I speak confidently on this head, since I have had very many points referred to me, which have long satisfied me of this fact.

There are many societies in South Australia, of which the lower orders are members, all of them tending to promote social interests. The order of Odd Fellows is prominent amongst these, and spreads a feeling throughout all classes which cannot fail of doing good, for the charities of this order are extensive, and it supports a well-attended school. Taking then the lower orders of the province in the aggregate, they may be said to be thoroughly English, both in their habits and principles.

In speaking of the upper classes I did not notice

a portion of them included under the denomination of the "Squatters." It is a name that grates harshly on the ear, but it conceals much that is good behind it; they in truth are the stockholders of the province, those in whom its greatest interests would have been vested if the mines had not been discovered. Generally speaking, the squatters are young men who, rather than be a burthen on their families, have sought their fortunes in distant lands, and carried out with them almost to the Antipodes the finest principles and feelings of their forefathers. With hearts as warm as the climate in which they live, with a spirit to meet any danger, and an energy to carry them through any reverse of fortune, frank, generous, and hospitable, the squatters of the Australian colonies are undoubtedly at the head of their respective communities, and will in after days form the landed, as they do now the pastoral interests, from whom every thing will be expected that is usually required of an English country gentleman. Circumstanced as they are at the present moment, most of them leading a solitary life in the bush, and separated by such distances from each other as almost to preclude the possibility of intercourse, they are thus cut off as it were from society, which tends to give them feelings that are certainly prejudicial to their future social happiness, but I would fain hope that the time is coming round when these gentlemen will see that they have it very much in their own power to shorten the duration of many of the sacrifices they are now called upon to make, and that they will look to higher and to more important duties than those which at present engage their attention.

The views taken by the late Sir George Gipps of the state of society in the distant interior of New South Wales is perfectly correct, nor can there be any doubt but that it entails evils on the stock-holders themselves which, on an abstract view of the question, I cannot help thinking they have it in their power to lessen, or entirely to remove, when an influx of population shall take place; but, however regular their establishments may be, they cannot, as single men, have the same influence over those whom they employ, or the settlers around them, as if they were married; for it is certainly true, that the presence of females puts a restraint on the most vicious, and that wherever they are, especially in a responsible character, they must do good. I do not know anything, indeed, that would more conduce to the moral improvement of the settlers, and people around them, than that squatters should permanently fix themselves, and embrace that state in which they can alone expect their homes to have real attractions. That they will ultimately settle down to this state there cannot, I think, be a doubt, and however repugnant it may be to them at the present moment to rent lands, on the occupation of which any conditions of purchase is imposed, I feel assured that many of the squatters will hereafter have cause to thank the Secretary of State for having anticipated their future wants, and enabled them to secure permanent and valuable interests on such easy terms. Nothing, it appears to me, can be more convincing in proof of the real anxiety of Earl Grey for the well being of the Australian provinces than the late regulations for the occupation of crown lands.

I believe I am right in stating that every word of those regulations was penned by Earl Grey himself, and certainly, apart from local prejudices, I am sure a disinterested person would admit the care and thought they evince, and how calculated they are to promote the best interests of the squatters, and the future social and moral improvement of the people under their influence. There seems to me to run throughout the whole of these regulations an earnest desire to place the stockholder on a sure footing, and to remove all causes of anxiety arising from the precarious tenure upon which they formerly held property.

There is another division of the population of South Australia I have hitherto omitted to mention, I mean the German emigrants. They now number more than 2000, and therefore form no inconsiderable portion of the population of the province. These people have spread over various districts, but still live in communities, having built five or six villages.

The Germans of South Australia are quiet and inoffensive, frugal and industrious. They mix very little with the settlers, and, regarded as a portion of the community, are perhaps too exclusive, as not taking a due share in the common labour, or rendering their assistance on occasions when the united strength of the working classes is required to secure a general good—as the gathering in of the harvest, or such similar occasions. Their religious observances are superintended by different pastors, all of them very respectable persons. The oldest of these is Mr. Kavel, to whom the Germans look with great confidence, and hold in deserved esteem. Many of the Germans have been naturalized, and have acquired considerable property in various parts of the province, but very few have taken to business, or reside in Adelaide as shopkeepers. The women bring their market or farm produce into the city on their backs, generally at an early hour of the morning, and the loads some of them carry are no trifle. Here, however, as in their native country, the women work hard, and certainly bear their fair proportion of labour. The houses of the Germans are on the models of those of their native country, and are so different in appearance from the general style, as to form really picturesque objects. There is nowhere about Adelaide a prettier ride than through the village of Klemzig, on the right bank of the Torrens, that having been the first of the German settlements. The easy and unmolested circumstances of these people should make them happy, and lead them to rejoice that in flying from persecution at home they were guided to such a country as that in which they now dwell, and I have no doubt that as a moral and religious people, they are thankful for their good fortune, and duly appreciate the blessings of Providence.

My anxiety to raise the character of the natives of Australia, in the eyes of the civilized world, and to exhibit them in a more favourable light than that in which they are at present regarded, induces me, before I close these volumes, to adduce a few instances of just and correct feeling evinced by them towards myself, which ought, I think, to have this effect and to satisfy the unprejudiced mind that their general ideas of right and wrong are far from being erroneous, and that, whatever their customs may be, they should not, as a people, occupy so low a place in the scale of human society, as that which has been assigned to them. I am quite aware that there have been individual instances of brutality amongst them, that can hardly be palliated even in savage life—that they have disgusting customs — that they are revengeful and addicted to theft. Still I would say they have redeeming qualities; for the first, I would fain believe that the horrors of which they have been guilty, are local; for the last, I do not see that they are worse than other

uncivilized races. Treachery and cunning are inhe-
rent in the breast of every savage. I question, indeed,
if they are not considered by them as cardinal virtues;
but, admitting the Australian native to have the most
unbridled passions, instances can be adduced of their
regard for truth and honesty, that ought to weigh
in any general estimate we may form of their character. No European living, not even Mr. Eyre, has
seen so many of the Aborigines of the Australian continent as myself; and that, too, under circumstances
when strife might have been expected; and no man
certainly has had less reason to complain of them.
If my party has ever been menaced by these people,
if we have ever had their spears raised in hundreds
against us, it has been because they have been
taken by surprise, and have acted under the influence
of fear. If I had rushed on these poor people, I
should have received their weapons, and have been
obliged to raise my arm against them, but, by
giving them time to recover from their surprise,
allowing them to go through their wonted ceremo-
nies, and, by pacific demonstrations, hostile collisions
have been avoided. If I had desired a conflict, the
inclination might have been indulged without the
fear of censure, but I saw no credit, no honour
to be gained by such a course, and I therefore
refrained. I can look back to my intercourse with
the Australian aborigines, under a consciousness that
I never injured one of them, and that the cause of

humanity has not suffered at my hands ;—but, I am travelling out of my proper course, and beg the reader to excuse me, it is for him, I allow, not for me, to draw such conclusions.

I have said, that I thought I could adduce instances of a regard for justice and honesty that would weigh in favour of the Australian native. As one instance, let me ask, if anything could have been more just, than the feeling which prompted the native to return the blanket one of his tribe had stolen from the camp on the banks of the Castlereagh, as detailed in my former work, vol. i. page 141. The man who restored the lost property was apprehensive of danger, from the fact of his having come armed, and from his guarded and menacing attitude when the soldier approached to ascertain what he wanted. Had he been the father of the thief, we could only have said that it was a singular proof of honest pride by a single individual, but such was not the case, the whole tribe participated in the same feeling, for we learnt from them, that the thief had been punished and expelled their camp. Could anything have been more noble than the conduct of the native, who remained neuter, and separated himself from them, when the tribes attempted to surprise my camp on the Murrumbidgee, because I had made him presents as I went down that river, vol. ii. page 212. On the other hand, could anything have been more just than the punishment inflicted on the boy who

stole my servant Davenport's blanket at Fort Grey?
as mentioned in the present work ; or the decision of
the two sons of the Boocolo of Williorara, as regarded
the conveyance of our letter-bag to Lake Victoria?
Here are broad instances of honesty that would do
credit to any civilized nation. Surely men, who
can so feel, should not be put lowest in the scale of
the human race ?   It is true that all attempts to
improve the social condition of the Australian native
has failed, but where is the savage nation with which
we have succeeded better ?   The natives of New
Zealand will perhaps be the only instance. in modern
times, of a barbarous race surviving the introduction
of civilization amongst them. Without venturing
to compare the natives of Australia, to a people so
much superior, I would only claim for them a due
share of consideration. All I can say is that they
have submitted to our occupation of their country
with a forbearance that commands our best sympathies.

It will be borne in mind, that I have not here
spoken of their personal appearance. That that
generally is against them, cannot be doubted. If
there is any truth in phrenology, they must have
their share of the brutal passions. The whole appearance of the cranium indeed, would lead to the
conclusion that they possess few of the intellectual
faculties ; but, in a savage state, these are seldom
called forth. They are, nevertheless, capable of
strong attachment, are indulgent parents, and cer-

tainly evince a kindly feeling towards their relations,
are improvident and generous, having no thought
for the morrow.   On the other hand, they are revengeful and crafty, and treat their wives with much
harshness, imposing on them the burthen of almost
everything : that man being considered the richest
who has the greatest number, because he can sit in
his hut, and send them out to procure food.

I think it is agreed on all hands that the natives
of Australia are sprung from the same parent stock.
Their personal appearance and customs, if not their
dialects, shew this.   From what race they originally
sprang it is more difficult to determine, for there is
not one of the great families into which the human
race has been divided, with which they may properly be classed.   With such features as they generally possess, in the flattened nose, thick lip, and
overhanging brow, one can hardly fancy that they
would be good looking, but I certainly have seen
very good looking men amongst them—I may say
tribes, indeed, on the Darling for instance, and
on the Murrumbidgee, (see page 53, vol. ii. of my
last work.)   The men on Cooper's Creek were fine
rather than handsome.   Generally speaking, the
natives have beautiful teeth, and their eye, though
deep sunk, is full of fire.   Although their muscular
development is bad, they must have a very remarkable strength of sinew, or they could not otherwise
raise themselves, as they do, on so slender a footing
in climbing up the trees, and in many other

occupations. I have read in several authors that the natives of Australia have woolly hair. This is a mistake ; their hair is as fine and as curly as that of an European, but its natural beauty is destroyed by filth and neglect. Nothing can prove its strength more than the growth of their beards, which project from their chins, and are exceedingly stiff.

In many places the natives have but a scanty and precarious subsistence, which may in some measure account for the paucity of their numbers in some localities. In many parts of the country in which I have been I feel satisfied they can seldom procure animal food, as they would not otherwise resort to the use of some things which no time could, I should imagine, make palateable. Their dexterity at the chase is very great, although in hunting the kangaroo they become so nervous that they frequently miss their mark. I have seen them sink under water and bring up a fish writhing on the short spear they use on such occasions, which they have struck either in the forehead, or under the lateral fin, with unerring precision. Still some of our people come pretty close to them in many of their exercises of the chase, and the young settlers on the Murray very often put them to the blush. At the head of them is Mr. Scott, Mr. Eyre's companion, who has now succeeded him in the post at Moorundi. There is not a native on the river so expert in throwing the spear, in taking kangaroo or fish, or in the canoe, as he is. His spear is thrown with deadly precision, and he has so mixed with the natives, that he may be said to be one of themselves, having the most unbounded influence over them, and speaking their language as fluently as themselves. Mr. Scott is at the same time very firm and decided, and is exceedingly respected by the settlers on the Murray. Under such circumstances it is to be hoped he will emulate Mr. Eyre and effect much good among his sable friends. Their devotion and attachment to him is very remarkable, and every native on the Murray knows " Merrili," as he is called.

One great cause of the deaths amongst the Aborigines is their liability to pulmonary diseases from being constantly in the water. They are much annoyed by rain, nor will any thing induce them to stir during wet weather, but they sit shivering in their huts even in the height of summer. There is no people in the world so unprovided against inclemency or extremes of weather as they are. They have literally nothing to cover them, to protect them from the summer heat or the winter's cold ; nor would any charity be greater than to supply these poor people with clothing. A few blankets, a few Guernsey shirts, and woollen trowsers, would be to them a boon of the first importance, and I would that my voice in their favour could induce the many who are humane and charitable here to devote a small portion of that which they bestow in works and purposes of charity to think of these children of the desert. It is only by accustoming them to comforts, and to implements which they cannot afterwards do without, to supersede as it were their former customs, that we can hope to draw them towards civilized man and civilization ; for what inducement has the savage with his wild freedom and uncontrolled will, to submit to restraint, unless he reap some advantage ?

The yearly and monthly distribution of blankets and of flour to the natives at Moorundi is duly appreciated. They now possess many things which they prefer to their own implements. The fish-hooks they procure from the Europeans are valued by them beyond measure, since they prevent the necessity of their being constantly in the water, and you now see the river, at the proper season, lined by black anglers, and the quantity of fish they take is really astonishing, and those too of the finest kinds. I once saw Mr. Scott secure a Murray cod, floating on the top of the water, that weighed 72 lbs. This beautiful and excellent fish is figured in Mitchell's first work. It is a species of perch, and is very abundant, as well as several others of its own genus, that are richer but smaller; the general size of the cod varying from 15 lbs. to 25 lbs.

The manners and customs of the natives have been so well and so faithfully recorded by Mr. Eyre that I need not dwell on them here. My views have been philanthropic, my object, to explain the manner in which I have succeeded in communicating with such of them as had never before seen Europeans, in order to ensure to the explorer, if possible, the peaceable results I myself have experienced. There are occasions when collisions with the natives are unavoidable, but I speak as to general intercourse. I feel assured no man can perform his duty as an explorer, who is under constant apprehension of hostility from the people through whose country he is passing.

The province of South Australia could never at any time have been thickly inhabited. There are some numerous tribes on the sea-coast at the head of the Gulfs and in Encounter Bay, as well as on the Murray River, but with the exception of a few scattered families on the northern hills, and in the scrub, the mountain ranges are, and it appears to me have been, almost uninhabited. There are no old or recent signs of natives having frequented the hills, no marks of tomahawks on the trees, or of digging on the flats. The Mount Lofty ranges, indeed, are singularly deficient of animal life, and seem to be incapable of affording much subsistence to the savage, however luxuriant and beneficial the harvest they now yield.

The Adelaide tribe is not numerous; they occupy a portion of the Park lands, called the native location, and every encouragement has been given them to establish themselves in comfort on it, but they prefer their wild roving habits to any fixed pursuit. Nevertheless, they are variously employed by the townspeople, in carrying burthens, in cutting up wood, in drawing water, and similar occupations; and, independently of any assistance they may receive from the Government, earn an immense quantity of food from the citizens. The natives properly belonging to the Adelaide tribe are all more or less clothed, nor are they permitted by the police to appear otherwise, and as far as their connection with the settlers goes, they are fast falling into habits of order, and understand that they cannot do any thing improper with impunity.

The Murray tribe, as well as the tribes from the south, frequently visit their friends near the capital, and on such occasions some scene of violence or dispute generally ensues. Frequently the abduction of a lubra, or of an unmarried female of another tribe, brings about a quarrel, and on such occasions some angry fighting is sure to follow; and so long as that custom remains, there is little hope of improvement amongst them. The subject of ameliorating their condition is, however, one of great difficulty, because it cannot be done without violating those principles of freedom and independence on which it is so objectionable to infringe; but when a great ultimate good is to be obtained, I cannot myself see any objection to those restraints, and that interference which should bring it about. There is nowhere, not even in Sydney, more attention paid to the native population than in South Australia, and if they stand a chance of improvement it is there. Whilst every kindness is shewn to the adult portion, the children are under the direct care of the Government. There is, as I have elsewhere stated, a school, at which from thirty to forty boys and girls attend. Nothing can be more regular or more comfortable than this institution. The children are kindly treated, and very much encouraged, and really to go into it as a visitor, one would be disposed to encourage the most sanguine expectations of success. As far as the elementary principles of education go, the native children are far from deficient. They read, write, and cypher as well as European children of their own age, and, generally speaking, are quiet and well behaved; but it is to be regretted that, as far as our experience goes, they can advance no farther; when their reason is taxed, they fail, and consequently appear to be destitute of those finer qualifications and principles on which both moral feeling and social order are based. It is however questionable with me whether this is not too severe a construction to put on their intellect, and whether, if the effect of ancient habits were counteracted, we should find the same mental defect.

At present, the native children have free intercourse with their parents, and with their tribe. The imaginations of the boys are inflamed by seeing all that passes in a native camp, and they long for that moment, when, like their countrymen, they will be free to go where they please, and to join in the hunt or the fray. The girls are told that they are betrothed, and that, at a certain age, they must join their tribe. The voice of Nature is stronger even than that of Reason. Why therefore should we be surprised at the desertion of the children from the native schools? But it will be asked—What is to be done? The question, as I have said, is involved in difficulty, because, in my humble opinion, the only remedy involves a violation, for a time at all events, of the natural affections, by obliging a complete separation of the child from its parents; but, I must confess, I do not think that any good will result from the utmost perseverance of philanthropy, until such is the case, that is, until the children are kept in such total ignorance of their forefathers, as to look upon them as Europeans do, with astonishment and sympathy. It may be argued that this experiment would require too great a sacrifice of feeling, but I doubt this. Besides which, it is a question whether it is not our duty to do that which shall conduce most to the benefit of posterity. The injury, admitting it to be so, can only be inflicted on the present generation, the benefit would be felt to all futurity. I have not, I hope, a disposition for the character of an inhuman man, and certainly have not written thus much without due consideration of the subject, but my own experience tells me we are often obliged to adopt a line of conduct we would willingly avoid to ensure a public good.

It will not then, I trust, be thought that I have ventured to intrude this opinion on the public, with

any other views than those which true philanthropy
dictates. I am really and sincerely interested in the
fate of the Australian Aborigine, and throw out these
suggestions, derived from long and deep practical
experience, in the ardent hope that they may help
to produce the permanent happiness of an inoffensive
and harmless race.